# British Columbia

# Columbia

# INTERIOR

## An Altitude SuperGuide

D0206484

# British Columbia

# INTERIOR

## An Altitude SuperGuide

## *by*
## Meredith Bain Woodward
## and Ron Woodward

### Altitude Publishing
#### Canadian Rockies & Vancouver

# Publication Information

## Altitude Publishing Ltd.

1500 Railway Ave.
Canmore, Alberta T1W 1P6
1-800-957-6888
www.altitudepublishing.com

Copyright © 2003
Meredith Bain Woodward and Ron Woodward

All rights reserved. No part of this book may be reproduced in any form or by any means, electronic or mechanical, without the permission in writing from the publisher. Copyright in the photographs remains with the photographers; they have granted permission for their reproduction herein and are thus identified.

Extreme care has been taken to ensure that all information in this book is accurate and up to date, but neither the authors nor the publisher can be held legally responsible for any errors that may appear.

## Canadian Cataloguing in Publication Data

Woodward, Meredith Bain, 1944—

British Columbia Interior
(SuperGuide)
ISBN 1-55153-634-X
British Columbia—Guidebooks.

I. Woodward, Ron, 1944—II. Title. III. Series
FC3807.W66 1993  917.1104'4
C93-091031-1  F1087.W66 1993

## Acknowledgments

Thanks to the following people for their help and advice on the first edition:
Garry Anderson, Alex Berland, Paul Dampier, Gerry Frederick, Joyce Johnson, Ken Mather, Margaret Panderin, Robert Pinsent, John Pinn, Donna Pletz, Al Smith, and Frances Surtees.

## Made in Western Canada

Printed and bound in Western Canada by Friesen Printers, Altona, Manitoba, using Canadian-made paper and vegetable-based inks.

We acknowledge the financial support of the Government of Canada through the Book Publishing Industry Development Program (BPIDP) for our publishing activities.

## Altitude Green Tree Program

Altitude will plant twice as many trees as were used in the manufacturing of this product.

## Project Development

| Project Manager: | Scott Manktelow |
|---|---|
| Editor: | Andrea Murphy |
| Layout: | Linda Petras |
| Maps: | Hermien Schuttenbeld |
| | Mark Higenbottam |

## Photographs

*Front cover:* Orchards above Naramata, Okanagan Lake
*Frontispiece:* A dramatic chainsaw sculpture greets visitors at Hell's Gate in the Fraser Canyon
*Back cover:* Rugged peaks of the Bugaboos in Bugaboo Glacier Provincial Park

# Contents

# Maps

**British Columbia Interior is organized according to this colour scheme:**

Introduction

Trans-Canada Highway

Crowsnest Highway

Coquihalla-Nicola

Okanagan

West Kootenay

East Kootenay

Central Interior

Reference & Index

British Columbia

# How to Use the SuperGuide

*Mt. Sir Donald, Glacier National Park*

T he SuperGuide is designed to help you create a unique travel experience from among the Interior's many possibilities. In the SuperGuide, the "Interior" includes the lower half of BC's mainland from Prince George south, excluding Vancouver, the Lower Mainland, and the coast.

The introductory sections will provide you with background information about the nature of the landscape, flora and fauna, history, economy, and outdoor recreation.

The main section offers seven descriptive highway guides with maps and points of interest, emphasizing natural and historic attractions. Because most tourists to the Interior visit the southern quarter of the province, the emphasis is on that area. Guides for the Trans-Canada Highway (Highway 1) and the Crowsnest Highway (Highway 3), the two major east-west routes, begin this section. Then the north-south routes are listed: the Coquihalla-Nicola, the Okanagan, the West Kootenay, and the East Kootenay.

The Central Interior circle tour completes the guide. Beginning at Cache Creek, this tour highlights the Cariboo-Chilcotin region north to Prince George, the Yellowhead Highway (Highway 16) east to Mt. Robson Provincial Park, and the Yellowhead South (Highway 5) to Kamloops.

Throughout the text, boxes highlight selected subjects such as contemporary and historical figures, flora and fauna, historical events, and recreational activities. We also highlight our favourite sightseeing and recreational spots.

A final reference section contains useful information for vacationers.

*British Columbia Interior SuperGuide* does not include accommodations or restaurants except when they have historic or special significance. For accommodations and campgrounds, we refer you to the comprehensive *British Columbia Accommodation Guide*, published annually by the provincial government. The booklet is available free at tourist outlets and tourist information centres throughout the province.

**7**

# Introduction

*Spectacular wildflower displays occur throughout the interior in spring and summer*

B C's Interior is an ideal destination for vacationers who dream of losing themselves in the great outdoors. Part of Canada's westernmost and third largest province, the Interior covers about 900,000 of BC's 950,000 square km and includes 18,000 square km of inland water.

Larger than any US state except Alaska and twice the land mass of Japan, the entire province has only four million people—a population density of about four people per square km.

The Interior is famous for its variety—landscapes that include deserts, glaciers, lava beds, and rain forests. You can ride horses on the wide open spaces of Chilcotin cattle country, climb the spectacular and isolated peaks of the Rocky Mountains, boat on the warm waters of Shuswap Lake, water ski, snow ski, or pan for gold. In the last ten years, several communities have begun promoting their outdoor recreation and tourist offerings. Several have developed or redesigned championship golf courses and

four-season resorts.

You can also enjoy urban attractions. Kelowna, in the centre of the Okanagan, is the fastest growing city in the province and offers professional theatre, art galleries, fine dining, and winery tours. Nelson, in the West Kootenay, with its picturesque heritage buildings, boasts more artists and writers per capita than any place else in the country. Kimberley, in the East Kootenay, is a Bavarian-style alpine town with international-class skiing.

The history of human settlement in the BC Interior is as varied as the landscape. A number of Native cultures thrived for centuries before the fur traders arrived in the 18th century. If you are interested in First Nations history and

*Opposite: Wildflower display at Mt. Revelstoke Provinical Park*

culture, there are a number of museums, historic villages and other sites for you to explore. For further information, read Altitude's *Native Sites in Western Canada* by Pat Kramer.

In 1858, thousands of gold miners hurried to the Fraser River looking for fortunes and sometimes finding them. The construction of the Canadian Pacific Railway in the 1880s and subsequent mining booms in the 1890s drew more settlers. Museums and archives throughout the Interior tell stories of early pioneers, who include English orchardists, Chinese miners, Japanese fishermen, and Russian farmers—with an occasional marquis or mystic thrown in for good measure.

This SuperGuide highlights some of the best that the Interior has to offer in outdoor recreation, sightseeing and special events. But the possibilities are endless. Explore!

*Voyageurs at the O'Keefe Ranch, north of Vernon*

## SuperGuide's Ten Favourite...

### Popular Attractions
(In alphbetical order)
1. Barkerville Historic Site
2. Columbia Wetlands
3. Creston Valley Wildlife Centre
4. Emerald Lake, Yoho National Park
5. Hell's Gate, Fraser Canyon
6. LeRoi Underground Mine Tour, Rossland
7. Old Grist Mill, Keremeos
8. Fort Steele Historic Town
9. R.H. Atkinson Museum, Penticton
10. Rogers Pass

### Off-the-Beaten-Path Attractions
(In alphabetical order)
1. Canadian Museum of Rail Travel, Cranbrook
2. Cottonwood House
3. Hat Creek Ranch, Clinton
4. Lotzkar Park, Greenwood
5. Nakusp Hot Springs
6. Painted Chasm Provincial Park, Clinton
7. Sandon
8. Summit Drive, Revelstoke National Park
9. Wedgewood Manor, Crawford Bay
10. Zukerberg Island, Castlegar

### Events
(In alphabetical order)
1. Adams River Salmon Run, October
2. Caravan Theatre, Armstrong, Summer
3. Kamloops Cattle Drive and Trail Ride, July
4. Kelowna Regatta, July
5. May Ball, Clinton
6. Merritt Mountain Country Music Festival, July
7. O'Keefe Ranch Cowboy Festival, August
8. Okanagan Fall Wine Festival, October
9. Oktoberfest, Kimberley
10. Williams Lake Stampede, July

*Pictographs at Slocan Lake*

## BC Facts

**Provincial capital:** Victoria

Provincial motto: *splendor sine occasu–* splendor without diminishment

Provincial flower: Pacific dogwood

Provincial bird: Steller's jay

Provincial tree: Western red cedar

Provincial stone: BC jade

Population: 3.9 million

Top ten languages spoken: English, Chinese (Cantonese/Mandarin), Punjabi, German, French, Dutch, Italian, Tagalog, Spanish, Japanese.

Entered Confederation: July 20, 1871

Area: 948,596 km²; 9.5% of Canada's land surface; 0.64% of the world's land surface

Highest point: Mt. Fairweather, 4663 m

Highest mountain (highway) pass: Kootenay Pass, 1774 m

Provincial sales tax: 7%

Legal drinking age: 19

Area codes: 604 & 778 (Lower Mainland), 250 (rest of province)

Total length of paved roads: 23,710 km

Largest Interior cities: Kelowna, Prince George, Kamloops, Vernon, Penticton

## First Nations

### Attractions and Resources
(In alphabetical order)
En'owkin Centre, Penticton
Prince George Native Art Gallery
Quaaout Lodge, Chase
Secwepemec Museum, Kamloops
Sen Klip Native Theatre, Vernon
Siska Gallery, Lytton
Xats'ull Heritage Village, Soda Creek

### Events
(In alphabetical order)
Bonaparte Pow Wow
First Nations Cultural Exposition, Lillooet
Fish drying, Farwell Canyon & Lillooet
Pow Wow Days, Kamloops
Remembrance Day Pow Wow, Lytton
Squilax Pow Wow
St'át'imc Nation Gathering, Lillooet
Valentine's Pow Wow, Lillooet

### Pictograph Sites
(In alphabetical order)
Herald Provincial Park
Mabel Lake Provincial Park
Mahood Lake
Marble Canyon Provincial Park
Monck Lake Provincial Park
Old Hedley Road
Roderick Haig Brown Provincial Park
Scotch Creek Provincial Park
Slocan Lake
Texas Creek Provincial Park
Upper Hat Creek

# Lay of the Land

*It has taken the milky waters of Tokumm Creek 8000 years to carve its path through the limestone walls of Marble Canyon in Kootenay National Park.*

To many people, British Columbia is synonymous with mountains. And while three-quarters of the land is over 1000 metres above sea level, and less than three percent of the land is considered suitable for agriculture, the landscape of the Interior is one of great variety.

Part of both the Cordillera and Great Plains regions of North America, the Interior has three major geographical components: the Western system, dominated by the Coast and Cascade mountains; the Interior Plateau, which includes the relatively subdued contours of the Okanagan Valley and the Chilcotin; and the Rocky Mountain system.

Throughout the Interior, the area's geological development is dramatically evident. Earth was formed about 4.5 billion years ago. Over the next two billion years it cooled, forming land masses on the planet's surface. For millions of years since, the land masses have been shifting in a process known as continental drift, caused by the very slow and complex movements of

tectonic plates beneath the earth's surface. When these plates move they can collide, pushing material through the earth's crust, or they can pull apart, weakening the crust and creating opportunities for volcanic eruptions.

Throughout the Interior of BC, it is possible to see evidence of both these processes. Volcanic rocks are abundant through the Cariboo and Chilcotin area. And a drive through any of the Interior's mountain ranges reveals layers of sedimentary and metamorphic rock jutting and pushing into the air.

The third major element, glaciation, probably had the most far-reaching effects in BC. The Wisconsin Glaciation ended as recently as 10,000 years ago. Glacier National Park, with its

*Hoodoo formations at Dutch Creek in the East Kootenay*

exciting views of the Illecille-waet and Asulkan glaciers, offers accessible examples of the erosive powers of ice. Indications of the tremendous power of the ice-age glaciers and resulting meltwater can also be found in the terraced banks of rivers such as the Fraser. The presence of huge boulders (known as erratics) in the otherwise rock-free fields of the Columbia Valley can also be traced to the effects of the last ice age.

Finally, the erosive force of weather since the last ice age has also shaped the landscape. The hoodoo formations that occur throughout the Interior provide strikingly beautiful examples of this ongoing process.

Whether imperceptibly slow or cataclysmic, the transformation of the landscape is relentless. The Juan de Fuca Plate, for example, which lies off BC's coast, moves four to five centimetres a year in relation to the North American Plate. On the other hand, Mt. St. Helens in Washington state erupted violently as recently as 1980. BC experiences an earthquake every day, according to the Ministry of Energy and Mines. Although most tremors are not noticeable, residents are only too aware of expert predictions of a major event within the next two hundred years. In the meantime, enjoy the view!

## Mountains

BC's many peaks are part of the Cordilleran mountain system of western North America.

The Coast Mountains contain both Mt. Fairweather (4663 metres) in the northwest corner (partly in Alaska), and the Chilcotin's Mt. Waddington (4019 metres), BC's highest peak lying entirely within the province. However, the Rocky Mountains are undeniably more famous. In the southern half of the province, the BC-Alberta border lies on the ridge of this range. But in the north, the Rockies are entirely in BC. The tallest peak, at 3954 metres, is Mt. Robson, just west of Jasper, Alberta.

To the west of the Rockies and in the south, lie the Columbia Mountains, separated by the wide Rocky Mountain Trench. This straight, flat-bottomed valley runs the 1300-km length of the province and stretches from Montana into Alaska. The Columbia Mountains are made up of three parallel ranges: the Purcells, the Selkirks, and the Monashees, with the Cariboo Range to the north.

Many of BC's mountain ranges contain ore bodies. The deposits of gold, lead, zinc, silver, molybdenum, copper, coal, and iron have led to human settlement of many areas, and mining continues to be an important part of BC's economy.

## Rivers

Cutting through the mountain ranges are the waterways that were a lifeline for early inhabitants as recently as a hundred years ago. There are 843 rivers in the province, and over 10,000 named creeks and brooks. The Fraser River, which begins in the Rocky Mountains, travels 1370 km through the province to empty into the Pacific Ocean at Vancouver. It is the only major river in BC that begins and ends within the province's borders, and is a major spawning ground for Pacific salmon and steelhead trout.

The 2000-km Columbia River, which also has its headwaters in the Rockies, is a major source of hydroelectric power for BC and the north-western US. It leaves the province just south of the West Kootenay community of Trail, emptying into the Pacific at Astoria, Oregon.

The Thompson and Kootenay rivers are important tributaries of the Fraser and Columbia systems, respectively.

## Weather

The mountains have a major effect on the weather in British Columbia.

Moisture-laden winds from the ocean make a roller-coaster journey east across the province until they reach the Rockies. Generally speaking, the western slopes of the higher mountains receive more precipitation, so the amount of snow and rain varies between areas. On the western slopes of the Columbia Mountain ranges, average rainfall is about 250 centime-

*Lichen is the first form of plant life to find a niche on inhospitable rock surfaces. It catches dust and other organic matter, providing a rooting place for simple plants that eventually build soil.*

tres per year. By contrast, in the arid areas of the Interior Plateau, average annual moisture is a mere 20 centimetres.

Weather-wise, come prepared for anything. In winter, snow and low temperatures are possible anywhere. In the summer months, most areas offer warm to hot days and cool nights. BC's warmest

weather was recorded July 16, 1941, at both Lytton and Lillooet, with a temperature of 44.4° C. The province's coldest temperature was -58.9° C at Smith River on January 31, 1947.

### What the Weather Warnings Mean in the Interior

**Heavy Snow:** Expect at least 10 centimetres of snow in the next 24 hours.

**Heavy Rain:** Expect 25 millimetres of rain in the next 24 hours.

**High Winds:** Expect speeds of over 65 km/h or gusts up to 90 km/h.

**For current weather reports log on to:**
http://www.weatheroffice.ec.gc.ca/forecast/Maps/BC_e.html

**The federal government offers a more up-to-date weather service.** Call 1-900-565-5555 or 0-900-565-4455 if using a calling card from one of Canada's major telephone service providers. There is a fee of $2.99 per minute.

### Weather at a Glance

#### Average Temperatures (°C)

|  | Jan | April | July | Nov |
|---|---|---|---|---|
| Castlegar | -4 | 8 | 20 | 2 |
| Cranbrook | -3 | 6 | 18 | -2 |
| Creston | -4 | 8 | 20 | 1 |
| Kamloops | -5 | 9 | 21 | 2 |
| Kelowna | -3 | 8 | 20 | 3 |
| Osoyoos | -3 | 10 | 22 | 3 |
| Prince George | -12 | 4 | 15 | -3 |

#### Average Precipitation (mm)

|  | Jan | April | July | Nov |
|---|---|---|---|---|
| Castlegar | 85 | 44 | 36 | 81 |
| Cranbrook | 49 | 26 | 22 | 33 |
| Creston | 73 | 35 | 25 | 66 |
| Kamloops | 36 | 9 | 24 | 20 |
| Kelowna | 37 | 15 | 24 | 29 |
| Osoyoos | 41 | 20 | 19 | 30 |
| Prince George | 57 | 27 | 60 | 51 |

# Ecosystems

*The dappled colouring and instinct for stillness of this three-day-old fawn provides a natural camouflage. Abandoned, it was rescued by hunters near Lillooet, but government wildlife management officials discourage human interference with the natural course of events.*

T ravelling through the Interior, you will have the opportunity to view a number of ecological systems. The landscape ranges from sea level to Mt. Robson's 3954 metres, and includes everything from lush rain forests to deserts.

Since the glaciers began retreating twelve to fifteen thousand years ago, the regrowth of plant and animal life that we see today has been controlled by a number of factors. Climate and topography are perhaps the most important, but animal migration patterns, soil conditions, and erosion rates also affect which species grow where and how well.

The provincial government has designated nine ecoprovinces that group plant and animal life into geographic areas. The five zones included in this SuperGuide are:

**Coast and Mountains**—includes the lush rainforests and sparse alpine reaches of the eastern slopes of the Coast Mountains. The climate is determined by moist air masses from the Pacific Ocean. Western hemlock, western red cedar, and mountain hemlock are common tree species. Undergrowth is lush, typically containing mosses, ferns, devil's club, and thimbleberry. Animal species include deer, black and grizzly bear, and mountain goat.

**Southern Interior Ecoprovince**—one of the warmest and driest areas of the province. Population centres include Lytton, Lillooet, Kamloops, Vernon, Osoyoos, and Princeton. Its vegetation is made up of dry grassland, ponderosa pine and Douglas fir forests, and many lakes,

**15**

*Larch is the only coniferous tree that drops its needles, providing a spectacular golden colour in the fall. All three varieties that grow in Canada occur in the Interior, with the western larch being the most important to the lumber industry.*

wetlands, and rivers—habitats that attract the greatest variety of bird species in the Interior. Other wildlife include reptiles, deer, grouse, bighorn sheep, and large runs of salmon.

**Central Interior**—contains the Chilcotin and Cariboo plateaus. Vegetation ranges from dry grasslands to forests of ponderosa pine and Douglas fir, and includes lakes, rivers, and wetlands. Williams Lake is the major Interior town. Wildlife includes moose, cougar, black bear, coyote, wolf, California bighorn sheep, Barrow's goldeneye, and white pelican.

**Southern Interior Mountain**—encompasses portions of the Columbia and Rocky mountains and the Rocky Mountain Trench. Population centres include Castlegar,

Trail, Nelson, Cranbrook, Fernie, Golden, Revelstoke, Clearwater, and Valemount. Dense conifer forests are common, although the Rocky Mountain Trench has dry grassland, and the high peaks of the mountains feature alpine tundra.

The marshland of the Columbia and Kootenay rivers provides important habitat for wildlife. Species found in this zone include tundra swan, Canada goose, mountain goat, grizzly and black bear, deer, elk, caribou, bighorn sheep, and

## British Columbia Wildlife Facts

- British Columbia has the greatest variety of wildlife habitat of any province in Canada.
- Over 2000 species of flowering plants
- Over a million birds per year migrate along the Pacific Flyway
- 75 percent of the world's stone sheep
- 65 percent of the California bighorn sheep
- 60 percent of the Barrow's goldeneye population
- 50 percent of the trumpeter swans, blue grouse, and mountain goats
- 25 percent of the world's bald eagles and grizzly bears
- North America's largest wildlife-viewing spectacle occurs in the autumn every four years at the Adams River salmon run near Kamloops.

*Mountain asters are a common roadside wildflower throughout the Interior. There are 4000 species of flowering plants in Canada; 2000 of them are found in BC.*

the highest breeding concentration of osprey in Canada.

**Sub-boreal Interior**—includes Quesnel and Prince George, at the northern reach of the BC Interior SuperGuide. Summers are warm, but winter temperatures are affected by cold Arctic fronts. Forests are spruce, fir, pine, and deciduous trees, with some wetlands at the lower levels and alpine tundra at the higher elevations. Grizzly bear, moose, black bear, wolf, beaver, muskrat, boreal owl, trout, and salmon are included in the wildlife population.

## Ecological Reserves

The provincial government has established 131 ecological reserves for scientific study and recreation, about half of which are in the Interior. Although most are open to the public for wildlife viewing, bird-watching, and photography, access to some particularly sensitive areas is restricted. Motorized vehicles are not allowed, and hunting, tree-cutting, and camping are prohibited.

### SuperGuide's Top Ten Wildlife Viewing Areas

(In alphabetical order)
1. Adams River
2. Chilanko Marsh
3. Columbia Wetlands
4. Creston Valley Wildlife Centre
5. Hedley-Keremeos
6. Manning Park
7. Osoyoos Oxbows
8. Syringa Creek Provincial Park
9. Tranquille Marsh
10. Vaseux Lake

### Protect Ecosystems

**Although the Interior** seems vast, carelessness or ignorance can be irreparably destructive to ecosystems.
- Don't disturb fragile habitats, protected areas, or native animals.
- Don't introduce new species of plants or animals into an area. In the Okanagan, be aware of milfoil. In the Cariboo, the spread of knapweed is a major concern.
- Remove your garbage. Don't dump plastic or non-biodegradable items overboard or leave them in the woods.
- Don't collect or buy specimens or products that threaten wildlife or fragile plant species.

**17**

*The Kootenay River, part of the Southern Interior Mountain Ecoprovince, joins the Columbia River at Castlegar.*

## Herb Hammond, Forester, Slocan Park

**My career is living,** and I prefer most to live in a forest. Beyond that, you could call me a holistic forester.

One of the reasons I like BC is that it's a sea of lands and forests with islands of people in it. Our options are disappearing rapidly, but in BC, we still have a chance to show what it's like to be part of a forest in an ecologically and socially responsible way.

All organisms, whether they're human beings or bacteria or fungi or grizzly bears, are entitled to a fair and balanced part of the environment. Keeping all the parts in balanced use means zoning, making sure you have a plan that protects corridors.

You can zone a balance of human uses—timber, tourism, recreation, cultural and spiritual areas, wilderness areas. When people look at the forest landscapes of BC, they need to recognize that the conventional way we clearcut is not sustaining the forest, it's destroying it. Our forests have been living and dying for millennia. There's a biological legacy of dead tree bodies in the soil and above the soil that prop up the system.

The cutting and removal—with an underscore on removal—of even one tree is not a natural phenomenon. Mother Nature never cut down all the trees, loaded them on a truck and hauled them to the mill. When she burned up a forest or blew them all down, the bodies always stayed behind.

The fundamental principle is that the forest sustains us, we don't sustain the forest.

Herb Hammond is the author of *Seeing the Forest Among the Trees* (Vancouver: Polestar, 1991).

# Significant Dates in Interior History

*Entrepreneurs imported camels into the Interior in 1862, reasoning that the animals' ability to travel great distances without food or water would be useful. However, other packers objected to the foul-smelling, ill-tempered beasts. They were released into the desert near Cache Creek. The last one died in 1905.*

**ca. 9000-7000 BC** First Nations people establish communities throughout the Interior.

**1793** Fur trader Alexander Mackenzie of the North West Company travels through the Rocky Mountains to the Bella Coola area on the Pacific Ocean. He is the first known European to cross the continent north of Mexico.

**1805** The North West Company's Simon Fraser establishes the first fur-trading post west of the Rockies on McLeod Lake. He calls the area New Caledonia.

**1807** David Thompson, also of the North West Company, explores the Columbia River, establishing Kootenae House near present-day Invermere.

**1833** Scottish botanist David Douglas travels in the Okanagan, identifying the species known as the Douglas fir.

**1846** The Oregon Treaty defines the US-Canada border as the 49th parallel of latitude. A new Brigade Trail heads south from Kamloops to newly- established forts at Yale and Hope.

**1858** Prospectors discover placer gold along the lower Fraser River. In just a few months, between 20,000 and 30,000 people swarm into the area. New Caledonia becomes the colony of British Columbia as the British government takes over its administration from the Hudson's Bay Company.

**1860** Roman Catholic priests, under the leadership of Father Charles Pandosy, establish the first mission in the Okanagan and plant fruit trees.

**1862** A severe smallpox epidemic decimates BC's aboriginal population. Some estimates indicate 20,000 died.

**1865** The Cariboo Wagon Road is completed.

**1866** Vancouver Island and the mainland unite as the crown colony of British Columbia. Edgar Dewdney completes the Hope-Rock Creek Trail to Wild Horse Creek in the East Kootenay.

**1871** After several false starts, British Columbia enters Confederation. The federal government promises to build a national railway that will link BC with the rest of the country. Surveying begins.

**1885** The Canadian Pacific Railway is finally completed through the Rockies via the Kicking Horse, Rogers, and Eagle passes.

**1886** Regular steamer service is inaugurated on Okanagan Lake.

**1890-92** Mining booms begin in the West Kootenay.

**1900-20** British settlers, attracted by land developers' advertisements, and encouraged by the CPR and the federal government's National Policy, settle in the Kootenays and the Okanagan and Thompson valleys.

**1908** Peter the Lordly leads his Doukhobor followers to the West Kootenay in search of "toil and peaceful life...".

**1909** Charles Walcott discovers the fossils of the Burgess Shale near Field, which many claim are the most important paleontological find in human history.

**1913** Mt. Robson becomes the first provincial park in the Interior.

**1914-18** World War I. Many British settlers return to their motherland to fight. BC's pre-war population is 450,000.

**1916** The Kettle Valley

*University of BC archeology students excavated the Milliken site near Yale between 1959 and 1961. Charred cherry pits and other evidence suggests First Nations people used the site 7000 to 9000 years ago.*

Railway is completed from Midway to Hope.

**1938** Tweedsmuir Provincial Park, BC's largest, is created in the Chilcotin.

**1944** Japanese Canadians are interned in "relocation camps" in several Interior communities during WW II.

**1949** The Hope-Princeton Highway opens.

**1952** Hardware merchant W.A.C. Bennett becomes premier of the province and will remain so for the next

20 years—the longest tenure of any premier in the province's history.

**1957** Copper Mountain, once one of the largest mines in the British Empire, closes.

**1961** The Kettle Valley Railway is abandoned.

**1962** Rogers Pass is opened on the Trans-Canada Highway.

**1964** The Columbia River Treaty becomes effective between the US and Canada. Under the terms of the

*Guards watch over a gold shipment at the Bullion Mine in the Cariboo, probably in the early 1900s. Some say the mine produced 30 to 40 million dollars in gold during its lifetime.*

*Ktunaxa women, photographed near Windermere in 1922, are pulling a travois. The sled-like device was used extensively by nomadic tribes.*

## SuperGuide's Top Ten Historic Sites

(In alphabetical order)

1. 108 Mile Heritage Site
2. Barkerville
3. Cottonwood House
4. Fort Steele Historic Town
5. Fort St. James National Historic Site
6. Hat Creek Ranch, Clinton
7. Huble Homestead, Prince George
8. O'Keefe Ranch, Vernon
9. Sandon
10. The Old Grist Mill, Keremeos

controversial treaty, Canada builds three dams on the Columbia: the Duncan (1967), the Keenleyside (1968), and the Mica (1973). The Arrow Lakes are flooded, submerging farmland and entire towns.

**1984** Construction of Revelstoke Dam is completed on Columbia River. It is one of North America's largest hydroelectric developments.

**1991** Federal and provincial governments make an historic agreement to address Native land claims in BC.

**1994** The North American Free Trade Agreement, signed in 1992, becomes effective. It has major implications for the resource-based economy of the Interior.

## The Construction of the Canadian Pacific Railway

*Donald A. Smith drives the "Last Spike" of the CPR at Craigellachie*

**One of the** most important events in the development of BC's Interior was the construction of the CPR. Not only did it provide much-needed jobs, but it linked BC with the rest of the country.

Sir John A. Macdonald's Conservative government in Ottawa had agreed to the construction of a national railway within 10 years as part of confederation with BC in 1871. However, realization of this agreement faced many difficulties.

The route in BC had to cross four mountain ranges before reaching the Pacific Coast. Surveying was difficult. Planners such as Walter Moberly and Sanford Fleming couldn't agree where the line should cross the mountains. Rocked by the "Pacific Scandal," Macdonald's government was forced to resign in 1873 when it was revealed some cabinet members had taken bribes in return

for construction contracts.

Donald A. Smith, J.J. Hill, and George Stephen of the Canadian Pacific Railway Company eventually won the contract. In BC, construction began at Yale in 1880.

Thirty-year-old New York engineer Andrew Onderdonk obtained the contracts to build most of the railway through BC. Unable to find enough workers, he subcontracted for labourers from southern China. Estimates of their actual numbers range from 9000 to 17,000. Onderdonk later noted that likely three Chinese died for every mile of track laid.

As the railway pushed west from the Rockies and east from the coast, towns like Revelstoke and Golden were born. Others, like Kamloops and Yale, enjoyed rejuvenation as railway divisional points and supply centres. The coal-mining community of Merritt flourished. Enterprising entrepreneurs set up lumber mills to

supply railway ties and other building materials.

The "Last Spike" of the CPR was driven by Donald Smith at Craigellachie on November 7, 1885 (pictured above). The first passenger train reached Port Moody on the coast the following July.

The CPR appointed William Van Horne president in 1888. Under his guidance the company encouraged land settlement, developed a telegraph service, launched an international steamship line, and built tourist hotels. The introduction of elegant CPR paddlewheelers on Kootenay, Arrow and Okanagan lakes in the 1890s encouraged settlement and tourism. Van Horne negotiated the Crowsnest Agreement in 1897, which initiated the CPR's entry into the mining industry.

# Economy

*BC's Interior waterways provide an ideal system of transportation and storage of logs. This boom is on Slocan Lake in the West Kootenay region.*

Resource extraction has always been a strong component of BC's economy, particularly in the Interior. Prehistoric Native cultures used natural resources such as trees, animals, fish, and minerals for trade and sustenance. In the 18th and 19th centuries European fur traders explored BC's Interior then called New Caledonia looking for better trade routes and new territory. Commercial logging began with the gold rush in 1858 as towns were constructed, and it continued with the building of the CPR. Today, although resource extraction no longer dominates the provincial economy, most of the people who live in the Interior continue to rely on the province's natural resources for their livelihoods.

## Mining
Although logging is the number-one resource industry throughout the province, mining has played a more dramatic role in the development of the Interior. A gold rush on the lower Fraser River in 1858 began a stampede of men and women into the Cariboo, the Big Bend of the Columbia River, and the Kootenays, opening up the province for development. Logging, ranching, and road and railway building quickly followed.

Always a "boom or bust" industry, mining shutdowns are a major occupational hazard, and BC's Interior is full of ghost towns that were once thriving communities. Some, like Barkerville, have become major tourist attractions. Other communities that have always depended on mining are today being challenged to find alternatives to their long-standing economic

*Similco Mines closed its Princeton operation in 1999.*

bases. Many Interior towns are now looking to adventure tourism and outdoor recreation to create new jobs and economic stimulation.

## Forestry

Although the coastal logging industry dominated for most of the last 150 years, logging began in the Interior in the 1860s as mining developed and towns sprung up. With the construction of the CPR, enterprising mill operators supplied lumber for railway ties, trestles, and avalanche sheds. Once the rail lines were completed, mill owners exported timber to the developing towns of the Canadian prairies. Pulp mills did not appear in the Interior until the mid-1960s. It wasn't until the mid-1970s that Interior operations began providing half the province's forest products. At this writing, the province's softwood lumber industry is

| Mining Facts (1999) | |
| --- | --- |
| Total provincial mining sales (excluding oil and natural gas) | $4.9 billion |
| Coal | 34 % |
| Copper | 24 % |
| Gold, zinc, lead, silver and molybdenum | 35 % |
| Oil and gas production | $2.1 billion |
| Percentage of the total workforce in the province | 2 % |

| Forestry Facts (1999) | |
| --- | --- |
| Percentage of BC's land mass that is forested | 64 % (60 million hectares) |
| Softwood species: fir, hemlock, spruce, cedar | |
| Softwood products: lumber, plywood, shakes, shingles, newsprint, pulp and paper. | |
| Percentage of Canada's softwood lumber produced in BC | 50 % |
| Percentage of province's total gross domestic product | 6.1 % |
| Percentage of workers | 6.1 % |
| Percentage of total provincial exports | 52 % |
| Number of pulp and paper mills in the Interior | 7 % |

being seriously threatened by American interpretations of the North American Free Trade Agreement signed in 1992.

In the 1960s most of the Interior's small independent mills disappeared, bought out by larger, often multinational, interests—a practice of concern to many residents, who fear the longevity of the forests is not a priority of out-of-province corporations. Although some compromises have been reached (the preservation of the Stein Valley watershed near Lytton and the establishment of Valhalla Wilderness Provincial Park, for example) the decades-long debate about forest management continues between industry and environmentalists.

## Fishing

Most of BC's commercial fishing takes place on the coast, although the major spawning grounds are located in the Interior. Five Pacific salmon and two salmonoid trout species breed in the Fraser and Skeena river systems. The Interior also plays an important role in the province's freshwater sport-fishing industry, which contributed about $500 million (directly and indirectly) to BC's economy in 1999.

## Agriculture

Not surprisingly, since most of its land is mountainous and unsuitable for agriculture, BC only supplies five percent of Canada's total agricultural products. However,

## Treeplanting

*Recently burned forest*

**In BC, all** logged public land must be reforested. BC spends about $320 million a year on silviculture (the care and cultivation of forest trees), overseeing the planting of over 200 million trees per year. By 2000, nearly 4.5 billion trees had been planted since the provincial government began its program in the 1950s. Although the first concentrated effort at treeplanting in BC occurred in 1936 on Vancouver Island, extensive planting in the Interior didn't begin until the early 1970s.

According to government statistics, in the year 2000, workers planted over 203 million seedlings to replace trees that had been harvested or destroyed by fire, insects or disease. In the last ten years, two trees have been planted for every one tree that has been logged. Only native species are used for reforestation.

The provincial government contracts with private companies for its replanting programs, with as many as 150 outfits competing for contracts. Province-wide, the season can stretch from January to November, but the most concentrated planting occurs in May and June, making it ideal employment for students. In the Interior, experienced highballers can earn $300 to $400 per day, with average planters earning half that.

Most planting in the Interior begins in the spring at the lower elevations when the land is moist, and moves to the higher elevations as the snow melts. Equipped with digging tools called "dibbles" and bags of seedlings, planters work across a site, planting a tree every two to four metres. Planters may carry three or four species in their bags, making a planting decision based on factors such as soil, location, and amount of light. Depending on the terrain, a worker could plant as many as 1000 or more trees a day.

agriculture is still vital to the economy in the Interior. The Okanagan area, well-known for its orchards and vineyards, is one of Canada's three main fruit-growing areas and one of the country's two major wine-producing areas. The Creston Valley in the West Kootenay is also valued for its orchards and farm produce, and the cattle ranches of the Cariboo and the Nicola Valley have been an important part of the economy since the gold rush.

In the last two or three decades a booming underground economy has emerged with the production of marijuana as a lucrative and so far untaxed cash crop. The American Drug Enforcement Agency suggests that cannabis cultivation in BC is a billion-dollar industry, with a pound of "BC Bud" that goes for US$1500 locally selling for up to US$8000 in New York City.

BC's legitimate net farm income in 1999 was $260 million.

## Energy

The geography and climate of the Interior create abundant opportunities for hydroelectric development. The Kootenay River was dammed early in the 20th century to provide power for mining products. Since the 1960s the Columbia River has been flooded and dammed to increase hydroelectric potential both for export and domestic use.

Like other forms of resource development, hydroelectric power takes an environmental toll, disturbing delicate aquatic habitats. A public increasingly concerned with environmental protection is constantly challenging BC Hydro's proposals to further develop the province's waterways for power exports.

## Tourism

With resource-based industries facing an uncertain future, tourism is becoming more and more important to the economy of the Interior. The beautiful scenery, clean air and water, and wide variety of outdoor recreation activities attract visitors from around the world. In 1998, tourism generated over $4 billion in BC.

### Ginseng

**In the arid areas** of the southern Interior, travellers may see evidence of one of BC's newer cash crops: ginseng. Farmers have been cultivating the plant in Asia for 7000 years and in the United States since the 18th century, but commercial cultivation in BC didn't begin until 1982, near Lytton. It now ranks number 16  on BC's list of the top 75 agricultural commodities, right behind turkeys and in front of hothouse sweet peppers.

Identifiable by the large sheets of black plastic that protect the delicate plant from excessive moisture, ginseng fields bring about $25 million to BC's economy annually. There are about 135 large- and small-scale farms in the Interior, ranging anywhere from one-tenth of a hectare to 60 hectares. Although ginseng cultivation has not met economic expectations, about 700 hectares of land were under cultivation in 2001, up from 400 hectares ten years earlier.

Machinery, shading structures and other start-up costs are high. Seed alone can cost up to $5,000 per acre. It takes three to four years before the root can be harvested, but yields are anywhere from 2800 to 3400 pounds of root per acre at $50 to $60 per pound.

Ideal growing conditions exist around Kamloops, Merritt, Lytton, and Lillooet, and in the Okanagan Valley, with some farms in the Grand Forks and Creston areas.

Native to northern Manchuria, the northeastern United States, southern Ontario, and Quebec, ginseng is regarded as a "cure-all" by many. Although in BC farmers sell either dried root or seed, processed ginseng is sold as tea, capsules, soups, gum, and health drinks.

For more information about ginseng:
http://www.agf.gov.bc.ca/aboutind/products/plant/ginseng.htm

# Outdoor Recreation

*Children enjoy Slocan Lake on a hot summer day.*
*BC has 843 rivers and over 10,000 named creeks and brooks.*

From the warm-water lakes of the Okanagan to the glaciers of the Selkirks, opportunities for outdoor recreation are plentiful in BC's Interior. Whether horseback riding on a Cariboo guest ranch, powder skiing in the Kootenays, or rafting on the Thompson River, many

activities are near major highway routes. Travellers with a desire to get off the beaten track can hike, drive, or fly to more remote destinations and enjoy activities such as alpine hiking, heli-skiing, wildlife viewing and fly-in fishing.

SuperGuide focuses on noncommercial outdoor recreation activities, but we occasionally provide information on recreation companies where appropriate. The Outdoor Recreation Council of British Columbia, an umbrella organization that provides information on outdoor recreation opportunities and safe use of the

outdoors, is a useful resource.

When planning your vacation, keep in mind that areas like the Okanagan and Shuswap lakes tend to be quite popular in the summer months, whereas areas like the Kootenays and the Cariboo provide a little more breathing room.

However you use BC's natural areas, remember they are for everyone. "Take only photographs, leave only footprints" and "Pack it in, pack it out" are good rules to follow.

At Champion Lakes Provincial Park you can fish, canoe, or view flora and fauna from a boardwalk around the lakes.

## Provincial Parks Facts

*Glacier National Park's rugged terrain includes 140 km of trails.*

Number of provincial parks, ecological reserves, and recreation areas: 800

Total hectares: 11.3 million

Total vehicle-accessible campsites: 13,800

Total number of campgrounds: 344 (in 214 parks)

Number of parks with facilities for disabled campers: 234, containing over 13,800 vehicle accessible campsites at 344 campgrounds in 214 parks. Over 234 parks have facilities for disabled visitors.

Number of ecological reserves: 131 (open on a limited basis)

## Government Park Info

**The BC Parks website** (www.elp.gov.bc.ca/bcparks/) provides detailed information about specific parks, regulations, etc.

PO Box 9398, Stn. Prov Govt, Victoria BC V8V 9M9.

Phone: 250-387-4550

Reservations: (not all parks take reservations)

Online: www.discovercamping.ca/

Phone: 1-800-689-9025. 604-689-9025 in Greater Vancouver

**Forest District Maps:**
www.for.gov.bc.ca/hfp/rec/rec.htm (downloadable; free).

Or contact Ministry of Forests,
Box 9520 Stn. Prov Govt, Victoria BC V8W 9C2
Phone: 250-387-1946.

**The national parks in the Interior** are Mt. Revelstoke, Glacier, Yoho, and Kootenay. All but Mt. Revelstoke National Park have campgrounds.

For maps and interpretive publications: Parks Canada, 25 Eddy Street, Hull, Quebec K1A 0M5; 1-888-773-8888; parkscanada.pch.gc.ca/

Many books offer descriptions of hiking trails, climbing, and wilderness camping in specific areas, including Altitude's *Walks and Easy Hikes in the Canadian Rockies* and *Classic Hikes of the Lower Left-Hand Corner of British Columbia.*

## Resources

**The Outdoor Recreation Council of British Columbia**
322 – 1367 W. Broadway
Vancouver BC  V6H 4A9
604-737-3058
www.orcbc.ca/

**BC Adventure**
www.bcadventure.com

**Ministry of Water, Land and Air Protection**
PO Box 9360 Stn. Prov Govt
Victoria BC  V8W 9M2
250-387-9422
www.env.gov.bc.ca/bcparks/
Campsite reservations:
1-800-689-9025

**Ministry of Forests**
Box 9520 Stn. Prov Govt
Victoria BC  V8W 9C2
250-387-1946
www.for.gov.bc.ca/hfp/rec/
rec.htm
(Forestry recreation sites)

## Summer Activities

The summertime is when BC's diverse landforms can be most appreciated. Landscapes ranging from ancient glaciers and dormant volcanoes to arid grasslands and sandy beaches translate into a wide variety of recreational choices. Here are a few possibilities.

## Camping, Hiking, and Mountaineering

Campgrounds in the Interior range from commercial ventures with swimming pools and laundromats to spartan sites in remote alpine locations. Designated provincial parks include day-use only picnic areas, wilderness parks, and marine parks. BC Forest Service Recreation areas offer more rustic, isolated camping and an alternative to the sometimes crowded provincial campgrounds. Local tourist offices will also have information on regional district and community parks that are maintained for public use, as well as on commercial campgrounds.

## Fishing

BC is famous around the world for its sport fishing, with thousands of Interior lakes to choose from. Almost every area claims superior fishing opportunities, so you just have to pick your spot.

The provincial government's freshwater stocking program places 10 million fish into approximately 1100 lakes and streams each year. Species stocked include rainbow, cutthroat and steelhead trout, brook char and kokanee. The program uses eggs collected from wild native stock, making it unique in North America. The two hatcheries in the Interior (at Summerland and Cranbrook) are open to the public and have interpretive services.

A number of angling options are available, from flying in to remote resorts and guided wilderness trips, to solitary fly-fishing or leisurely family outings. Local tourism

## Trail Resources

**Alexander Mackenzie Heritage Trail Association**
Box 425, Station A
Kelowna, V1Y 7P1
604-762-424
Historic route following the path of the early explorer through the Chilcotin to the Pacific Ocean near Bella Coola.

**The Trails Society of British Columbia**
425 - 1367 West Broadway
Vancouver V6H 4A9
604-737-3188
www.trailsbc.ca

**Rails to Trails Conservancy**
www.orcbc.ca/r-to-t.htm

**Cycling the Kettle Valley Railway**
www.planet.eon.net/%7Edan/vve.html

**TrailPaq**
www.trailpaq.com/index.htm
—an online searchable database of trails

## Trans Canada Trail

**Still a work in progress** at this writing, the Trans Canada Trail when completed will span approximately 17,250 km, making it the longest trail of its kind in the world. A community-based project run by volunteers, the TCT uses existing trails wherever possible, but also runs over abandoned railway lines and alongside railways lines, through federal and provincial parks, crown land, and private land.

In BC, the completed hiking and biking trail will run from Victoria in the west to the Rockies in the east and Fort Nelson in the north. At present, Interior portions are completed from Hope to Creston, with non-linked portions from there to Elkford and Alberta.

For detailed information with maps, consult the Trails BC website (www.bctrail.bc.ca/), the Trans Canada Trail website (www.tctrail.ca/), or ask your local bookstore for *Trans Canada Trail: the British Columbia Route* (Mussio Ventures / Trails BC: 2001).

## Forest Fires

**Firefighters deal with** an average of 3000 fires in BC's forests every year, half of them caused by people, the other half by lightning. Please make sure you are familiar with regulations and restrictions regarding the building of campfires. To report a wildfire, call 1-800-663-5555 or *5555 from a cellular phone. For forest use restrictions, campfire bans, and current information on wildfires, call 1-888-3FOR-EST or 1-888-336-7378. More information on wildfires is available on the Ministry of Forests Protection Branch website (http://www.for.gov.bc.ca/protect/index.htm).

*An angler tries his luck at Dutch Creek in the East Kootenay.*
*Twenty species of game fish are commonly caught in the Interior.*

associations can provide current information about guides and excursions as well as where the fish are currently biting.

Many anglers prefer the voluntary "catch and release" approach to fishing, which fisheries management staff endorse. The practice, enabling fish to spawn or be caught again, is mandatory in some waters because of stock depletion.

In order to protect and maintain the fishery, a number of freshwater fishing regulations and licensing fees are in effect, and they include ice fishing. These vary from area to area. All non-Native anglers 16 years of age and older must buy a licence. Provincial licences are not valid in national parks. Copies of the provincial government's *Freshwater Fishing Regulations Synopsis* and licences are available from government agents, sporting goods stores and other selected retailers. (www.bcfisheries.gov.bc.ca/rec/fresh/regulations/intro.html).

## Water Sports

Marinas at most resort areas rent power boats, canoes, and other water sport equipment. At remote locations, rental facilities vary. Enquiries should be made in advance.

The Arrow, Shuswap, Christina, and Kootenay lakes are among those that have marine parks. Part of the provincial park system, these areas are accessible only by water.

Windsurfers will find good conditions at Kootenay, Windermere, Skaha and Nicola lakes.

## Game Fish in the Interior

Trout
Bass
Whitefish
Kokanee
Burbot
Sturgeon
Crappie
Yellow perch
Walleye

## Angling Guidelines

**Familiarize yourself** with fishing regulations. Most areas have some restrictions.

- Respect catch limits.
- Do not introduce aquarium or foreign species.
- Leave the fishing site in the same, or better, condition than you found it. Fines of up to $1 million are in effect for destruction of fish habitat.
- A private landholder has the right to grant or refuse access. Make sure you get the necessary permission.
- Voluntary "catch and release" is being adopted by more and more anglers, and in some places is mandatory.

Canoeing and kayaking are popular activities on the Interior's thousands of lakes and rivers. Possibilities include a slow meander down the Columbia River between Golden and Radium, an exciting whitewater journey on the Chilcotin River, and a seven- to ten-day paddle on the Bowron Lake circuit. Moving water is rated on a scale of one to six, with six being the most treacherous. Make sure you match your ability with the challenge of the river. Paddlers should always check locally, as conditions vary seasonally. One source of information is the Recreational Canoeing Association of BC, 604-437-1140 (www.3telus.net/CanoeBC). One of their web pages lists dozens of canoe routes throughout the province keyed to provincial forest service maps.

River rafting is popular on a number of Interior rivers including the Fraser, Thompson, Chilcotin, Adams, Kicking Horse, and Kootenay. Several private rafting companies offer excursions lasting a few hours to several days. Strict licensing and operating regulations are in effect for rafting companies, with safety the number-one priority. On the website www.bcadventure.com/adventure/rafting/adventures.htm, you will find a list of river rafting companies. You can also contact regional tourist information offices.

Water lovers who prefer a slow boat to nowhere may want to rent a houseboat on

## SuperGuide's Top Five Excursion Train Trips

(in alphabetical order)
1. Bavarian Mining Railway—Kimberley. 250-427-3666
2. BC Rail—Vancouver to Prince George. 604-984-5246
3. Kettle Valley Steam Railway—Summerland. 250-494-8422; 1-877-494-8424
4. Okanagan Wine Train—Kelowna to Vernon. 250-712-9888; 1-888-674-8725
5. Rocky Mountaineer—Vancouver to Jasper. 1-800-665-7245

## SuperGuide's Top Ten Paddling Routes

(In alphabetical order)

1. Bowron Lake Circuit in the Cariboo near Barkerville. Seven- to ten-day circuit covers ten lakes, with some portaging, through a wilderness area.
2. Columbia River. Novice to intermediate paddling from Canal Flats to Golden, and from Revelstoke to Arrow Lakes.
3. Fraser River. Several portions have canyons and rapids of advanced difficulty.
4. Goldstream River, north of Revelstoke. An 18-km, one day novice trip, with potential for lots of wildlife viewing. Isolated.
5. Kootenay River in the East Kootenay region from Gibraltar to Wardner. 132 km. For beginners and experienced paddlers.
6. Moose Valley, west of 100 Mile House. 14-km, two day novice loop with some portaging, depending on time of year.
7. Slocan Lake and River in the West Kootenay. Forty km-long lake and 60-km river. For beginners and experienced paddlers.
8. Similkameen River from Princeton to Cawston. Described as "a classic whitewater experience," this two-day trip covers 100 km.

9. Thompson River, from Clearwater to Kamloops. Ideal for novice or intermediate. Savona to Goldpan Campground near Spences Bridge is more challenging. Dangerous waters south to Lytton.
10. Wells Gray Provincial Park in the Cariboo Mountains. Clearwater, Mahood, and Murtle lakes offer 170 km of wilderness paddling.

*The Bowron Lake chain is one of BC's most popular destinations for paddlers. Reservations are advised.*

*Among the choices for golfers in the Interior are the championship links at Fairmont Hot Springs in the East Kootenay.*

Shuswap, Okanagan, Mara and Kootenay lakes. Sailing is more popular on the coast, but the larger Interior lakes (such as Kootenay, Okanagan and Windermere) do provide some challenging winds.

## Golf

A great many Interior communities have golf courses, with new ones constantly being developed, and many older ones being upgraded. In areas with milder climates such as the Okanagan, the season can stretch from March to

## Tips for Wildlife Viewing

- Check the season.
- Check the time. Best wildlife viewing times are early morning and early evening.
- Hide behind natural or artificial screens.
- Keep silent.
- Be patient.
- Read wildlife clues such as nests, tracks, and droppings.
- Use aids such as field guides and binoculars.

*The smallest members of the squirrel family, chipmunks are commonly seen at campgrounds throughout the Interior. Seeds are their most important source of food; DON'T feed them bread and junk food!*

## Bird watching Events in BC's Interior

- Creston Valley Osprey Festival. April. Creston Valley. 250-428-3260; www.crestonwildlife.ca/visit/vosprey/ospreyfest.html
- Wings Over the Rockies Bird Festival. May. Invermere. 1-888-933-3311; www.adventurevalley.com/wings/
- Golden Bear and Birding Festival. May. Golden. 1-800-622-4653; www.redshift.bc.ca/birds%26bears/
- Meadowlark Festival. May. Penticton. 250-492-5275; www.meadowlarkfestival.bc.ca/
- Salmon Arm Grebe Festival. May. Salmon Arm. 250-832-1389; www.grebe.shuswap.net/
- Manning Provincial Park Birding Blitz. June. www.env.gov.bc.ca/bcparks/explore/parkpgs/ecmaning/spevents.htm

## Wildlife Species

Total species of vertebrates found in BC: 700

| | |
|---|---|
| Bird species: | 448 |
| Mammal species: | 143 |
| Reptile species: | 19 |
| Amphibian species: | 20 |
| Fish species: | 73 |

## Birding Areas

**BirdLife International's Designated Important Birding Areas in the Interior**
(In alphabetical order)
- Chopaka Customs (near Osoyoos)
- Creston Valley Wildlife Management Area
- Douglas Lake Plateau (Nicola Valley)
- Kilpoola Lake (near Osoyoos)
- Osoyoos Oxbows
- Sumallo River/Skagit Valley (near Hope)
- Vaseux Lake (near Okanagan Falls)
- White Lake (near Oliver)
- For more information: www.bsc-eoc.org/iba/

November, or sometimes even year-round. Even the experts haven't played all of the Interior's more than 120 courses, but from Lillooet's unique Sheep Pastures to Invermere's championship greens, the possibilities are varied. We have included most of the top courses in the highway guide section. For a comprehensive description of courses and facilities, consult the BC Golf Guide (www.bcgolfguide.com) or the BC Golf Association, (101 - 7382 Winston St., Burnaby BC V5A 2G9; 604-294-1818; www.bcga.org/).

*Trail rides and guest ranches are found in almost every part of the Interior*

## Wildlife Viewing

BC's wide variety of terrain and ecosystems means an equally wide variety of wildlife habitats. As a result, BC has the largest number of species in the country. You will see signs for good wildlife viewing opportunities posted on highways throughout the Interior, and several promising spots are listed in the highway guide section of this book. Although bird and wildlife viewing are good throughout the province, if you are travelling to the eastern part of the Interior, make a stop at the Creston Valley Wildlife Centre a priority on your itinerary.

## Guest Ranches and Horseback Riding

Guest ranches provide an authentic western experience, with the Cariboo-Chilcotin and Nicola Valley considered by many to be the heart of cowboy country. (An annual rodeo circuit travels around the province, but if you want to see how they do it back

home on the ranch, look for the "real" rodeos in places like Anahim Lake and Riske Creek in the Chilcotin). There are a number of guest ranches in the East Kootenay as well.

For an up-to-date list of members of the BC Guest Ranch Association, write them c/o BCFROA, Box 3301, Kamloops BC V2C 6B9, or consult their website at www.bcguestranches.com.

Horses are for hire at

stables throughout the Interior, with guided trail rides lasting from a few hours to several days. Some communities, such as Kamloops, sponsor an annual cattle drive that is open to the public.

## Rockhounding and Gold Panning

With BC's varied terrain and history of volcanoes and glaciers, rockhounds can spend

| SuperGuide's Top Ten Gold Panning Spots |
|---|
| (In alphabetical order) |
| 1. Barkerville |
| 2. Emory Creek |
| 3. Fraser Canyon |
| 4. Lumby |
| 5. Lytton |
| 6. Moyie River |
| 7. Princeton area |
| 8. Quesnel |
| 9. Revelstoke |
| 10. Rock Creek |

| SuperGuide's Best Bets for Rockhounds |
|---|
| (In alphabetical order) |
| 1. Cache Creek |
| 2. Cranbrook |
| 3. Fernie |
| 4. Fraser Canyon |
| 5. Keremeos |
| 6. Lillooet |
| 7. Okanagan Falls |
| 8. Penticton |
| 9. Princeton |
| 10. Shuswap Lake |
| 11. Skookumchuck Creek |
| 12. Vernon |

**Mt. Assiniboine by horseback**

many rewarding hours poking around canyons and mountainsides. The Fraser Canyon, the Similkameen Region, the Okanagan, and the East Kootenay are among the good places to look.

Gold panners work creek beds in former gold strike locales such as the Fraser Canyon, the East Kootenay, and the Barkerville area. But many of these areas still have active claims. Check with local government agents or tourist offices for regulations.

## Cycling

In response to the growing popularity of cycling, several communities have developed bike trails. At Vernon's Silver Star Provincial Park, aficionados can take the chairlift up and rent a bike at the top for the trip down. Rossland declares itself the "Mountain Biking Capital of BC." And cyclists are a common sight along BC highways. Golden promotes a "Golden Triangle" bike route that takes in Radium Hot Springs and Lake Louise. (See www.mtb.bc.ca/trails/ on the Web for a listing of over 300 mountain bike trails in the province.)

## Winter Activities

Skiing is probably the province's number one outdoor winter sport, from heli-skiing in deep powder to cross-country skiing on well-groomed trails. In the last decade several new and/or improved downhill resorts have appeared on the scene. Many have groomed cross-country trails, tube and snow-boarding parks, as well as alpine villages and four-season activities.

If you prefer cross-country skiing, head for provincial parks, forestry roads and designated trails throughout the province. The Cariboo community of 100 Mile House sponsors an annual cross-country ski marathon that attracts hundreds of participants from around the world. Lac Le Jeune and Larch Hills are two popular cross-country skiing spots. Many private companies have ski-touring packages that offer everything from half-day outings on local trails to longer expeditions in remote backcountry.

The Bugaboos in the Purcell Mountains and the Premier Range in the Cariboo are well-known for heli-skiing. Revelstoke, Nelson, Invermere, Golden, and Valemount are among the communities where heli-ski operators are located.

Logging roads are popular in the wintertime for snowmobiling. Because of their relatively flat terrain, the Nicola Valley, the East Kootenay, and the Cariboo are particularly popular. Some communities have specially designated areas for snowmobiling. In multi-use areas, snowmobilers should be on the lookout for cross-country skiers and others using the same trails.

Other winter activities include dog sledding, snowshoeing, ice -fishing, ice climbing, and winter mountaineering.

### SuperGuide's Top Ten Interior Ski Resorts

(In alphabetical order)
1.  Big White, Kelowna
2.  Fernie Resort
3.  Kicking Horse Resort, Golden
4.  Kimberley Resort
5.  Panorama Resort, Invermere
6.  Powder Springs, Revelstoke
7.  Red Mountain, Rossland
8.  Silver Star, Vernon
9.  Sun Peaks, Kamloops
10. Whitewater, Nelson

## Metric Conversion Tables

**British Columbia**, along with the rest of Canada, uses the metric system for measurement. Distance is measured in kilometres (km), speed signs are in km per hour (km/h), gas is sold by the litre (L), and temperature is measured on the Celsius scale (C).

### Distance

| | |
|---|---|
| 1 centimetre (cm) | 0.39 inches |
| 1 metre (m) | . . . . . . . . 3.28 feet |
| 1 km (km) | . . . . . . . . 0.62 miles |
| 1 hectare (ha) | . . . . . 2.47 acres |
| 1 square km | 0.36 square miles |
| 1 kilogram (kg) | . . . 2.2 pounds |
| 1 tonne (t) | . . . . . . 1.10 US tons |
| | . . . . . . . . . . . . . . . 0.98 UK tons |
| 1 litre (L) | . . . . . 0.26 US gallons |
| | . . . . . . . . . . . 0.22 Imp. gallons |

### Speed (approximate)

| | |
|---|---|
| 15 km/h | . . . . . . . . . . . 10 mph |
| 30 km/h | . . . . . . . . . . . .20 mph |
| 50 km/h | . . . . . . . . . . . .30 mph |
| 65 km/h | . . . . . . . . . . . .40 mph |
| 80 km/h | . . . . . . . . . . . .50 mph |
| 95 km/h | . . . . . . . . . . . .60 mph |
| 110 km/h | . . . . . . . . . . .70 mph |

### Temperature

| | | |
|---|---|---|
| 100°C | Boiling point | 212°F |
| 30°C | Hot summer day | 86°F |
| 20°C | Comfortable room | 68°F |
| 0°C | Freezing | 32°F |
| -18°C | Cold winter day | 0°F |

## Alcohol Consumption in BC

- The legal drinking age is 19.
- It is unlawful to drive with an open bottle of alcohol in a vehicle.
- It is unlawful to consume alcohol in a public place such as a beach or park.
- In BC, alcohol is only sold at government liquor stores or specially licensed beer and wine stores. Grocery stores are not normally permitted to sell alcoholic beverages, although some grocery stores in small rural communities may be licensed.

## Driving in BC

**Speed limits** are usually 50 or 60 km/h on two-lane highways going through populated areas, and 90 to 100 km/h on the open highway.

Canada uses the metric measurement system, so all highway signs give distances in km. To calculate the distance between many BC locations, try: www.th.gov.bc.ca/bchighways/distances/calculator.htm

For current road reports and ferry information: www.th.gov.bc.ca/bchighways/

A pre-recorded telephone information service provides updated road information. Phone one of the following numbers and enter code 7623 (ROAD) on a touch-tone phone:

| | |
|---|---|
| Kamloops: | 374-2929 Kamloops |
| Kelowna: | 861-2929 Kelowna |
| Penticton: | 492-2929 Penticton |
| Prince George: | 564-2929 |
| Vernon: | 545-2929 Vernon |

International and US drivers' licences are valid in BC. Motor vehicle registration forms must be carried. If the driver is not the registered owner, she or he must have a letter of authorization from the registered owner. If the vehicle is a rental, a copy of the rental contract should be with the vehicle.

Drinking and driving in Canada is a serious offence. If asked by a police officer, a driver must provide a breath or blood sample for testing. Operating a motor vehicle while under the influence of drugs is also a criminal offence.

Seat belts must be worn by all passengers in motor vehicles. Motorcycle riders must wear safety helmets. Car seats must be provided for infants up to nine kilograms.

In winter, carry tire chains and emergency supplies.

Motorists involved in motor vehicle accidents should contact the nearest Insurance Corporation of British Columbia office.

## Winter Alert

- No matter where or how you enjoy the snow, make sure you are aware of the danger of frostbite, hypothermia, and avalanche potential in the area you plan to visit.
- Regretfully, every year there are fatalities due to avalanches. Do not underestimate the risks involved; respect avalanche warning signs and learn avalanche safety techniques.
- In winter, carry tire chains and keep essentials for several days' survival stored in your vehicle.

## Legal Holidays in BC

| | |
|---|---|
| New Year's Day: | January 1 |
| Good Friday: | Friday before Easter Sunday |
| Easter Monday: | First Monday after Easter |
| Victoria Day: | Third Monday in May |
| Canada Day: | July 1 |
| BC Day: | First Monday in August |
| Labour Day: | First Monday in September |
| Thanksgiving Day: | Second Monday in October |
| Remembrance Day: | November 11 |
| Christmas Day: | December 25 |
| Boxing Day: | December 26 |

## Time Zones

**BC's Interior** has two time zones. The Pacific Time Zone covers most of the province. However, the Mountain Time Zone is in effect in the Columbia River Valley along a corridor west of the Rockies from Mt. Robson Provincial Park to the US border. This corridor includes Golden, Invermere, Kimberly, Moyie, Cranbrook, Fernie, and Sparwood. The zone is marked by a yellow line on the provincial government road map.

If you are going from west to east, move your watch ahead one hour when you enter the Mountain Time Zone. When coming from the east, and entering the Pacific Time Zone, move your watch back an hour.

In both time zones, daylight saving time is in effect between April and October. "Spring ahead, fall back" is the saying that helps people remember how to adjust their clocks. On the first Sunday of April, time pieces are turned ahead one hour. On the last Sunday in October, they are turned back an hour.

But not in Creston. When daylight savings time comes into effect in the spring, Creston stays on Pacific Standard Time.

To be sure, check locally.

## Currency and Banking

**Canada's money** system is based on the decimal system. Paper denominations are $5 (blue), $10 (purple), $20 (green), $50 (red), $100 (brown), and up. Dollar coins are known as "loonies" and two-dollar coins are "toonies."

American money is accepted in most businesses, but banks and currency exchange desks usually give the best exchange rates.

Major credit cards are widely used, and travellers will find bank machines in most towns.

## Tax Refunds for Travellers

**Under certain** circumstances, visitors are eligible for rebates on the 7 percent federal Goods and Services Tax (GST) paid on accommodation and goods purchased. Forms and information are available at Canada Customs, Infocentres, and duty-free shops. For more information call 1-800-66VISIT (668-4748) within Canada or 1-613-991-3346 outside Canada; or write Revenue Canada, Customs and Excise, Visitors Rebate Program, Ottawa ON K1A 1J5 Canada.

# Trans-Canada Highway

*Sagebrush and ponderosa pine are typical vegetation in the arid Thompson River area.*

The scenic Trans-Canada Highway (Highway 1) is the longest paved highway in the world. Although a disarmingly easy journey through spectacular terrain today, the route through the Interior was agonizing for early travellers.

In the first portion of this route, the highway passes through the historic Fraser Canyon, where early Native residents used a system of rope ladders to travel along the steep rock walls above the turbulent Fraser River. In the 1860s, an eastbound traveller would board a stagecoach at Yale and then transfer to a paddlewheeler at Savona for a journey to the north end of Shuswap Lake. From there, a narrow mountain trail continued to the goldfields on the Big Bend of the Columbia River. The Big Bend Highway (from Revelstoke to Golden) was the only road through to the central Rockies until 1962 (official opening in 1963). Today's modern two- to four-lane paved highway makes the journey pleasant and manageable. Highway 1 is the most travelled route in the province.

The semi-nomadic Nlaka' Pamux (Interior Salish) are indigenous to the region. Many Interior towns and attractions on the Trans-Canada lie close to ancient villages and fishing and hunting grounds. Cities such as Lytton and Kamloops were Native encampments for thousands of years before Europeans and Asians settled here.

The first non-Native settlements were established by fur traders who built forts and brigade trails in the early 1800s. Beginning in 1858, several gold rushes—notably on the lower Fraser River, in the Cariboo, and in the East Kootenay—brought an influx of people to the southern Interior. The construction and expansion of trails and wagon roads soon followed, with the Canadian Pacific Railway track laid in

*Opposite: At 380m, Takakkaw Falls in Yoho National Park is one of the highest waterfalls in Canada*

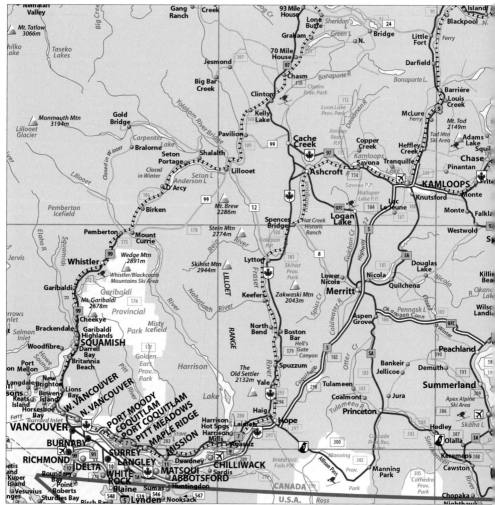

*Trans-Canada Highway*

## SuperGuide's Top Hiking Areas on the Trans-Canada Highway

1. Glacier National Park, east of Revelstoke. Several trails.

2. Mt. Revelstoke National Park. Summit accessible by vehicle. Over 64 km of improved trails.

3. Shuswap Lake Provincial Park.

4. Skihist Provincial Park, near Lytton.

5. Stein Valley, near Lillooet. Several trails through old-growth forest and sacred Native land.

6. Yoho National Park, east of Golden. Several trails.

*Illecillewaet, "the great glacier" is one of 400 glaciers in Glacier National Park.*

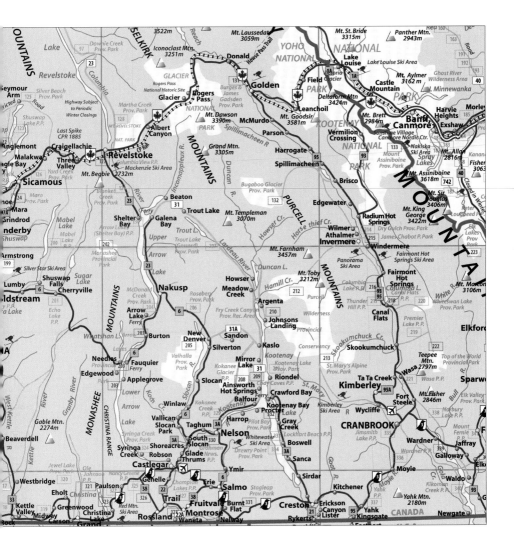

## Trans-Canada Highway: Ten SuperGuide Facts

1. Longest paved highway in the world.
2. Constructed during the 1950s and 1960s to connect Victoria, BC, with St. John's, Newfoundland.
3. Rogers Pass, in the Selkirk Range, opened in 1963. The visitor centre draws 160,000 visitors per year.
4. Total length: 7821 km
5. Cost: $1 billion
6. Cost of BC portion: $280 million
7. Distance from Hope to the Alberta border: 623 km
8/9. Highest passes: 1327-metre Rogers Pass in the Columbia Mountains and 1643-metre Kicking Horse Pass in the Rockies.
10. Campgrounds: on average, one every 160 km.

the 1880s. Farming, logging, and service communities quickly sprung up along the railway route. The Trans-Canada Highway parallels the rail line in many places.

## Hope

150 km (93 mi.) east of Vancouver
Population: 7032. Info Centre: 919 Water Avenue, Box 370, V0X 1L0. 250-869-2021; Fax: 250-869-2160. Email: info@hopechamber.bc.ca. Web: www.hopechamber.bc.ca.
Hope is the gateway to the Interior and the intersection of highways 1 (the Trans-Canada), 3 (the Crowsnest), 5 (the Coquihalla), and 7 (the Lougheed). (The signs can be confusing: watch carefully.) At Hope, the Fraser River leaves the Coast and Cascade mountains to begin the final portion of its journey west to the Pacific.

Simon Fraser passed this way on his 1808 expedition in search of the Columbia River. In 1846, the Hudson's Bay

*Hope's Christ Church was consecrated in 1861 and is one of BC's oldest churches.*

Company established a fur-trading fort here at the end of the Brigade Trail from Fort Kamloops. The town was an important centre during the 1858 gold rush on the lower Fraser River and again with the development of the railways. The Canadian Pacific Railway (1885), the Canadian National Railway (1915), and the Kettle Valley Railway (1916) all converged here.

## The Gold Bars

Between Hope and Yale there are many gravel bars on the Fraser River that yielded great riches during the 1858 gold rush. Emory Creek Provincial

## While You're In Hope ... Top Ten

1. Walk the "chainsaw carvings" tour (get the map from the Info Centre) to view over 30 large carvings by local artist Pete Ryan located throughout town.
2. Visit the Hope Museum (250-869-7322), located at the Info Centre on Highway 1 in the city centre, with its interesting collection of local history and restored gold-mining equipment.
3. Gaze at several mountain peaks, with elevations, from the signpost at Centennial Park by the Fraser River.
4. Join in the annual Brigade Days, held the second weekend after Labour Day.
5. Go fishing, canoeing, gold panning, river rafting, glider flying, or rockhounding. The Info Centre has details.
6. Birdwatch at Skagit Valley Recreation Area (3 km southwest of town).
7. Canoe or fly-fish on the Skagit River.
8. Pick up a map of the Rambo walking tour at the Info Centre. Several Hollywood films have used Hope as a location in recent years, among them *First Blood*.
9. Marvel at the Othello and Quintette tunnels, carved out of solid mountain rock for the Kettle Valley Railway. In the fall, spawning salmon make their way up Kawkawa Creek, and steelhead spawn in the Coquihalla River.
10. Go for a swim at the Lake of the Woods Rest Area, (5 km north of Hope on Highway 1).

*Alexandra Bridge was built in 1863 by Joseph Trutch as part of the Cariboo Wagon Road at a cost of $45,000.*

Park, 15 km north of Hope, marks one such site. Once the initial rush was over, most of the miners followed more promising rumors north. But many Chinese miners stayed behind here and at similar claims to dig a little deeper. Their patience and vigilance was often rewarded by less dramatic, but respectable finds. Today gold panners still try their luck at the river's edge.

Emory, hoping to become the terminus of the CPR in the 1880s, boasted 13 streets, 9 saloons, a newspaper, and a sawmill, but it became a ghost town when the railway bypassed it.

Hill's Bar, 4 km south of Yale, was one of the first and most lucrative finds in the lower Fraser gold rush. Less than one square km in area, it has been estimated that $20 million of placer gold was discovered here between 1856 and 1875.

Experts claim there are many varieties of rock on Fraser River banks, including nephrite, jasper, rhodonite, and garnet. The Coquihalla River, and Emory and Ruby creeks are also good places for rockhounding.

## Yale

32 km (20 mi.) north of Hope. Population: 200. Info Centre: 31187 Douglas St, Box 74, V0K 2S0. 604-863-2324 (museum). Fax: 604-863-2495. Seasonal. Email: info@historicyale.bc.ca

Yale is rich in history. Archeologists, excavating the Milliken Site near Yale in the 1950s and 1960s, found evidence of human settlement dating from 7000 to 9000 BC. When Simon Fraser made his historic journey through here in 1808, he recorded that he obtained canoes from the resident Natives.

Yale was established as a fort in 1848 by the Hudson's Bay Company, and a decade later it was a riotous gold town. Thirty thousand prospectors passed through its saloons and hotels.

Reverend William Crickmer petitioned his bishop for a new parish in Yale once it became clear that his current posting, the much-touted community of Derby near Fort Langley (in the Fraser Valley), did not have the future early administrators had envisioned. The Reverend's new church was completed in 1860, just one block from the saloons and hotels that formed the centre of Yale, which provided a source of serious competition to Reverend Crickmer's ministrations.

In 1861 Lady Franklin arrived in town, searching for her husband, the noted Arctic explorer Sir John Franklin, who disappeared in 1845 while looking for the Northwest Passage. Thirty-nine expeditions

## While You're In Yale ... Top Five

1. Catch a glimpse of Yale's rich history at the Yale Historical Museum (31179 Douglas Street, 250-863-2324).

2. Visit Reverend Crickmer's St. John the Divine Church, one of the oldest on the mainland.

3. Walk in the past at the Pioneer Cemetery, which has its own stories to tell of the gold rush and railway construction days.

4. Stop at Lady Franklin Rock, just north of town on Hwy 1.

5. Hike the Spirit Cave Trail (1 km south of town), a one-hour hike to spectacular views of the Cascade mountains.

searched for his party. According to one source, Lady Franklin's determination to sail up the Fraser River on her quest was blocked by the rock that now bears her name. While she remained in Yale, she was the centre of a social whirl, and organized the building of pews and choir stalls at the new church. The remains of Sir John's expedition were finally discovered in 1880 on King William Island in the Arctic.

Rivalling Fort Hope as the dominant settlement on the lower Fraser River, Yale gained the upper hand when it became a terminus for steamships on the Interior route to Fort Kamloops, and the starting point for the Cariboo Road in the 1860s. The treacherous waters of the Fraser Canyon were deemed unnavigable north of here, despite the *S.S. Skuzzy*. When the CPR was completed in the 1880s, the Cariboo Road was eradicated and Yale's importance diminished.

## Lower Fraser Canyon

Carved by centuries of glacial torrents, the Fraser Canyon was, and remains, a daunting sight. Originally, Natives used a series of ladders and paths along narrow ledges to travel this route. The Europeans first tried to bypass it by establishing the Harrison-Lillooet and Coquihalla trails. But at the urging of Governor James Douglas, in the 1860s the precarious trail was widened into the celebrated Cariboo Wagon Road. It was supported by log cribbing and stone retaining

walls.

The CPR destroyed much of the road when building its line through the Fraser Canyon in the 1880s, but some portions are still visible, such as the original bridge at Alexandra Bridge Provincial Park one km north of Spuzzum. A 15-minute walk from the parking area goes down the old road to the bridge for a walk across the Fraser River. With the advent of the automobile, a highway was re-established in the 1920s.

Access to the 13-km round-

trip Old Brigade Trail is 300 metres north of Alexandra Lodge. Built in 1848 by the Hudson's Bay Company, the Brigade Trail was the main transportation route into the Interior after the Oregon Treaty was signed and the border with the US established in 1846. Prior to that, the fur brigades had travelled up the Columbia River and through the Okanagan Valley.

## Hell's Gate

One of the most spectacular portions of the Fraser Canyon

### Simon Fraser's Journal

**June 26, 1808**
[Hells' Gate and the Black Canyon] *This morning all hands were employed the same as yesterday … the navigation was absolutely impracticable … as for the road by land we scarcely could make our way in some parts even with our guns. I have been for a long period among the Rocky Mountains, but never have seen anything to equal this country for I cannot find words to describe our situation at times. We had to pass where no human being should venture. Yet in those places there is a regular footpath impressed, or rather indented, by frequent travelling upon the very rocks. And besides this, steps which are formed like a ladder, or the shrouds of a ship, by poles hanging to one another and crossed at certain distances with twigs, suspended from the top to the foot of immense precipices and fastened at both extremities to stones and trees, furnished a safe and convenient passage to the Natives—and we, who had not the advantage of their experience, were often in imminent danger, when obliged to follow their example.*

*The tram at Hell's Gate carries visitors 500 metres from the highway to the Fraser River below.*

## Hell's Gate Rafting Companies

**Canadian Outback Adventure Co**. 1-800-555-8735. www.canadianoutback.com Rivers: Chilko/Chilcotin.

**Chilliwack River Rafting Adventures**. 1-800-410-7238. www.denoc.com/chilliwackrafting Rivers: Thompson.

**Fraser River Raft Expeditions**. 1-800-363-7238. www.fraserraft.com Rivers: Chilko/Chilcotin, Fraser, Nahatlatch, Thompson.

**Hell's Gate Rafting Adventures**. 1-888-434-2837. www.hellsgaterafting.com Rivers: Fraser, Thompson.

**Hyak Wilderness Adventures**. 1-800-663-7238. www.hyak.com Rivers: Chilko/Chilcotin, Fraser.

**Kumsheen Raft Adventures**. 1-800-663-6667. ww.kumsheen.com Rivers: Chilko/Chilcotin, Fraser, Nahatlatch, Thompson.

**Reo Rafting**. 1-800-736-7238. www.reorafting.com Rivers: Chilko/Chilcotin, Nahatlatch, Thompson.

**River Quest**. 604-898-4635. rafting@mountain-inter.net Rivers: Chilko/Chilcotin, Fraser.

is Hell's Gate, named—with indisputable logic and first-hand knowledge—by Simon Fraser. At peak flow (35 km per hour), 908 million litres of water per minute pass through the 34-metre-wide gorge—twice the volume of Niagara Falls. A 500-metre-high air tram gives visitors an only slightly terrifying ride over the chaos below. (Hell's Gate Air Tram, 31 km north of Yale, May to October. 604-867-9277, www.hellsgate.bc.ca/)

If you want to walk down to Hell's Gate you can take the path that begins in the parking lot 500 metres south of the tramway concession on the highway. A suspension footbridge crosses the river at the lower level.

In 1914, when the CNR was blasting bedrock for its track, a slide blocked the river, destroying the salmon run. Recorded catches of 31 million fish in 1913 were reduced to 1.8 million in 1921, and some say they have never recovered. Between 1944 and 1946, a Joint Canadian and US International Fisheries Commission built concrete fish ladders that have since restored the run, although the gorge is narrower than it was before the blasting. An interpretive display at river level explains how the fish ladders work. The concrete structures slow the water to about five km per hour, giving the fish a fighting chance to swim upstream.

Local rafting companies offer expeditions through Hell's Gate from Boston Bar to Yale. The Nahatlatch River, accessible via a secondary road across the Fraser at Boston Bar, is another popular

## The Fraser River: Ten SuperGuide Facts

Length: 1378 km

Headwaters: Near Mt. Robson in the Rocky Mountains at an elevation of 1109 metres.

Drainage area: 238,000 square km, about one-quarter of the province, an area larger than Great Britain.

Major tributaries: Nechako, Chilcotin, Quesnel, and Thompson rivers.

Annual average discharge: 3972 cubic metres per second. Over 80 percent of the flow occurs between May and mid-July. The greatest flow is 15,000 cubic metres per second in the spring. The smallest flow, 400 cubic metres per second, is in winter.

Biggest fish in the river: white sturgeon, which can range from 13 kilograms to 180 kilograms and can live to be 100 years old.

Besides water, the river moves about 17 billion kg of clay, silt, sand, and gravel per year, equal to 1.5 million killer whales.

Memorable description: "Too thick to drink, and too thin to plough." –Ray Mueller, riverboat man from Sinclair Mills, east of Prince George (*Vancouver Province*, Sept. 15, 1991).

First European to travel the river: Simon Fraser in 1808. The trip took him 35 days from Fort George (present-day Prince George) to the Pacific. He thought he was on the Columbia River.

Approximately 800 million juvenile salmon migrate to the Pacific via the Fraser River annually.

Number of dams: 0.

## S.S. *Skuzzy*

**In order that CPR** construction proceed as quickly as possible, contracts were let for sections of the line. Andrew Onderdonk, a thirty-year-old engineer from New York, won the contract for two of the sections in the difficult Fraser Canyon. Obviously he thrived on challenge, because he then bought out two other contractors, taking responsibility for the entire 200 treacherous kilometres between Emory's Bar and Savona.

Onderdonk was not one to let anything get in his way. Unable to find sufficient numbers of qualified workers, he imported thousands of laborers from China. One source claims he had 7000 men working for him and contracts worth $18 million at the height of his projects in BC.

Because the tolls on the Cariboo Road were costing Onderdonk dearly in freight costs, in 1881-82 he had a boat built that would meet the mighty Fraser head-on. The *Skuzzy* was 37 metres long and 7.5 metres wide, with a hull divided into 24 watertight bulkheads, a paddlewheel aft and a steam winch in the bow.

The reputation of the Fraser Canyon was well-known, and no one wanted the dubious honour of captaining the vessel. After two unsuccessful attempts, two daring brothers, captains S.R. and D.S. Smith, who had successfully challenged dangerous portions of the Columbia, Snake, and Willamette rivers, were hired for the job at a fee of $2250. In the spring of 1882, with a crew of 17, they began a two-week trip up

the canyon to Lytton from Spuzzum, battling the fury of Hell's Gate and a drop in the river of nine metres in five km on one stretch of river. Eventually 150 Chinese workers winched her through Hell's Gate by using a separate line from the shore.

The valiant *Skuzzy* made it through the Canyon, but it was a one-time-only trip.

*The dramatic confluence of the muddy Fraser and clear green Thompson rivers at Lytton.*

whitewater-rafting trip close by. The Nahatlatch Lakes chain is also a favourite with canoeists.

In a route filled with challenges to early travellers, Jackass Mountain, 25 km north of Boston Bar, must have been rated high on the list. Some say the name was a comment on the foolishness of the men and women who travelled the route in search of the elusive motherlode; others claim the namesake was a fully loaded mule who fell off the narrow roadway in the 1860s to its death in the canyon below.

## While You're In Lytton ... Top Ten

1. Go whitewater rafting.
2. Hike in the Stein Valley.
3. Examine the relief display of a "jelly roll" outside the Info Centre. It's a geological record of the swirling sediment created by melting glaciers. (Although a common occurrence, this sample is unusual because it measures in metres what normally occurs on a much smaller scale.)
4. Enjoy Lytton Days during the May long weekend.
5. Visit the Lions Club Heritage Park (8 km north on Hwy 12), where you'll find nature trails, a reconstructed Native pit house and archeological dig, and gold panning. You must get access information from the Info Centre.
6. Sit on a bench downtown and watch the river flow by.
7. Shop for soapstone carvings, jewellery and other Native arts and crafts at the Siska Art Gallery, run by the Siska First Nations Band (12 km south on Hwy 1; 250-455-2219).
8. Enjoy a fabulous view of the Thompson River Canyon via the 2- to 3-hour loop trail in Skihist Provincial Park (6 km east on Hwy 1).
9. Take a side trip over the new bridge to Lillooet via Highway 12. Botanie Road is a good place for viewing Rocky Mountain bighorn sheep and alpine meadows.
10. Take in the Remembrance Day Pow Wow in November.

## Lytton

108 km (67 mi.) north of Hope. Population: 366. Info Centre: 420 Fraser Street, Box 640, V0K 1Z0. 250-455-2523; Fax: 250-455-6669. Email: lyttoncc@goldtrail.com

Lytton, at the confluence of the Thompson and Fraser rivers, was called *camchin*, "the place that crosses over," by indigenous people. One of the oldest continuously inhabited spots in North America, Lytton was renamed by Governor James Douglas it after his friend Sir Edward Bulwer-Lytton, who secured his place in literary history by opening his novel *Paul Clifford* with the words "It was a dark and stormy night".

The town, an early fur-trading post and stop on the Cariboo Road, now bills itself as the "Whitewater Rafting Capital of Canada." There are 18 major rapids in the 37 km of the Thompson River between Lytton and Spences Bridge, with such encouraging names

*The Canadian National Railway, completed in 1915, parallels the CPR from Kamloops to Vancouver and transports only freight.*

as the Frog, Devil's Kitchen, and Jaws of Death. Other local attractions include gold panning and rockhounding. The museum next to the Info Centre houses local history displays and the archives. Across the street, the caboose offers displays of railway history.

Just down the street, the waters of the muddy Fraser and the clearer green Thompson rivers provide a stark contrast before blending together and continuing to the Pacific Ocean. A reaction ferry—a small vessel attached to a cable that uses the river's current for locomotion—crosses the Fraser here. The free ferry carries only two or three cars a trip and provides access to Stein Valley Nlaka'pamux Provincial Park, an old-growth forest whose preservation was

the focus of heated protests in recent years.

Regarded as a sacred site by the Lytton people, the 107,191-hectare area is one of the last untouched watersheds in this part of the province. Designated as a park in 1995, it is jointly managed by the Lytton First Nation and BC Parks. Containing three glaciers, four lakes, and 250 square km of alpine meadows, the valley's attractions also include giant trees, petroglyphs, and pictographs. It has over 150 km of trails ranging from easy to advanced.

Be prepared for hot summer temperatures. The second-highest temperature recorded in Canada was at Lytton and Lillooet on July 16, 1941, when the thermometer soared to 44.4°C.

## Thompson Canyon

The Fraser Canyon is impressive for its imperviousness, but the Thompson Canyon is breathtaking for its geological spectacle. Pinnacles, outcroppings, sheer cliffs, slides, shadowy canyons, and waterfalls in colours ranging from deep reds and oranges to cool greens and greys line the route, with the waters of the Thompson travelling swiftly below. The high river terraces and white silt bluffs visible along the highway are evidence of the mile-thick ice sheets that once covered the province, receding as recently as ten thousand years ago. As the glaciers melted, huge volumes of meltwater containing sand, gravel, and boulders carved new paths, shifting the river's course, and creating the terraces.

## Wild Grasses

**We regard many** of the grasses seen along the highways as useless weeds, at best providing interesting shades and textures to the landscape. But most were put to a variety of uses by First Nations people.

A number of species that are not true grasses, including sedges, tule, cattail, and bear grass, shared common uses with rye, sweet, pine, and reed grasses.

The Ktunaxa used the leaves of the bear grass plant for making their distinctive hats, whereas the Okanagan wove the highly prized material into their birchbark baskets. Only the Ktunaxa had direct access to bear grass, so other First Nations people had to trade for it.

Rye grass, a robust species commonly found in a wide variety of habitats in the Interior, was used in a number of ways. The Thompson people used the hollow stems to decorate cedar root baskets. Some Okanagan tribes made arrows from the stems and used the leaves as a lining material for floors or steaming pits in food preparation. The Prairie Blackfoot used the leaves for bedding.

Rye grass is found in such diverse conditions as moist river banks or dry gulleys, on slopes or plains from the Thompson to the Rocky Mountain Trench. Among its uses, Flathead Native boys put hawthorn points on the stems and used them to inflict pain when preparing for battle.

The Trans-Canada Highway veers away from the Fraser River at Lytton to follow the Thompson River, passing through several old communities. The Thompson River was named by Simon Fraser in honour of his contemporary David Thompson, who explored the eastern part of the Interior, but never saw this waterway.

In the Thompson Canyon, the transformation from wet coastal rainforest to arid desert vegetation is complete, as sagebrush and pine replace cedar and thimbleberry. Known today as "the Arizona of Canada" because of its desert ecology, this hot and dusty section must have tested the stamina of even the most intrepid stagecoach travellers in the 1860s. If you are hiking, be aware of small prickly pear cactus and rattlesnakes that hide in the sagebrush and rocks.

South of Spences Bridge, a marker tells of the Great Landslide, a 1905 event that dammed the Thompson River for several hours and killed 18 people.

## Spences Bridge

40 km (25 mi.) north of Lytton. Population: 138. Tourist info: Gold Country Communities Society, PO Box 1480, Ashcroft V0K 1A0. 250-453-9467.

Just off the highway, the restored Spences Bridge Hotel, surviving today as the Garuda Inn (886-849-3940; garudainn.myevisionlink.com/), claims to be the oldest existing hotel in BC. While lounging in the natural foods restaurant, it could do no harm to nonchalantly inquire about the

### While You're In Spences Bridge ... Top Five

1. On a hot day, go for a dip in the Nicola River—the Thompson's current is too swift.

2. In spring and fall, watch for bighorn sheep on the bluffs between Spences Bridge and Ashcroft.

3. Visit the grave of Jessie Ann Smith, a young widow who allegedly developed the famous Granny Smith apple here in the early 1900s.

4. Look for volcanic rock at Red Hill Rest Area, (28 km north), evidence of activity that occurred before the last glaciation.

5. In the fall, join savvy fisherman from everywhere who angle for world-famous steelhead.

*Overleaf: The Thompson Valley near Ashcroft*

treasure supposedly buried here. The story goes that a prospector, returning from the northern fields with a smile on his face and a bag of gold, was robbed and killed nearby. The thieves were caught and hanged, but not before they stashed the loot, which no one has ever found. If buried treasure is not your style, ask about good fishing spots for the prized steelhead trout that this area is famous for.

## Ashcroft

43 km (27 mi.) north of Spences Bridge. Population: 1995. Info Centre: Box 183, V0K 1A0. 453-2642. Seasonal.

In this sparse landscape the oasis of Ashcroft Manor on the Trans-Canada Highway is a welcome relief on a hot summer day. Built in 1862 as a roadhouse by the Cornwall brothers, it was considered one of the most reputable and hospitable hotels on the road. Englishmen to a T, Clement and Henry Cornwall imported foxhounds and instituted the coyote hunt, a Cariboo version of the traditional British foxhunt. Clement Francis Cornwall later became one of BC's first senators after Confederation and the province's lieutenant-governor in 1881.

The original manor was destroyed by fire in 1943, but travellers can still enjoy refreshments in the tearoom, and the several restored buildings on the site house interesting displays (250-453-9600). The original roadhouse served as the first courthouse in the area with the legendary Judge Begbie in attendance.

*Ashcroft Manor, a favourite roadhouse on the Cariboo Wagon Road, displays relics of the past.*

### While You're In Ashcroft ... Top Five

1. Stop at the Info Centre, which also houses the museum (250-453-9232) and local history displays.
2. View the tiny red building on Main Street that was the first firehall.
3. Take a side trip to the Highland Valley and Merritt via Highway 97C.
4. In June, mix with the locals at the Ashcroft Rodeo.
5. Buy fresh fruit from a roadside stand.

## Cache Creek

50 km (31 mi.) north of Spences Bridge. Population: 1136. Info Centre: 1340 Highway 97, Box 460, V0K 1H0. 250-457-9566. Seasonal. Cache Creek was a trading site for Native people long before the arrival of the Europeans. Fur traders used to stash their furs here, thus "Cache" Creek.

Later a fur-trading post was built, and then the settlement became an oasis on the hot and dusty Cariboo Wagon Road. Today it retains its Old West flavour without even trying—you'll see plenty of working ranches, cowboys, and tumbling tumbleweed.

The town is on the edge of a long-dormant line of ancient volcanoes stretching into the Cariboo. Rock formations millions of years old make interesting exploration for rockhounds.

## Kamloops

80 km (50 mi.) east of Cache Creek. Population: 79,566. Info Centre: 1290 Trans-Canada Highway West, V2C 6R3. 250-374-3377; 1-800-662-1994; Fax: 250-828-9500. Email: tourism@kamloopschamber.bc.ca. Alternate website: www.kamloopsguide.com People of the Secwepemc (Shuswap) nation have lived in this area for at least seven thousand years, naming the site *Cumloops* ("meeting of the waters"), due to its location at the confluence of the South and North Thompson

### Walhachin

**Between Cache Creek** and Kamloops, look for fragments of a wooden flume along the north side of the highway, the vestige of a dream that flowered and faded in the early 1900s.

American developer C.E. Barnes decided to transform the sagebrush and desert into lush orchards and genteel living. He bought land and called the site Walhachin, attracting upper class English families with his claims of "heaven on earth."

In 1907 Barnes oversaw the building of a dam on Deadman Lake near Cache Creek and the construction of a two-metre-wide wooden flume to carry water over the dry ravines and hillsides for 30 km to the settlement.

A hotel was built, the

wealthy Marquis of Anglesey created a luxurious estate and invested money, and the town and orchards thrived.

When World War I broke out in 1914, many of the men rallied to the call of the motherland. Of 107 men in the community, 97 eventually enlisted, the largest number per capita in the British Empire.

The lack of manpower and financing, combined with a devastating flood and an untenable original goal, led to the demise of the experiment. By the end of the war, Walhachin was finished.

Today, a small community remains on the site of the original townsite on the south side of the Thompson River. Watch for direction signs on the highway.

### While In Cache Creek Top Five

1. Shop for world-famous jade at the Cariboo Jade Shoppe downtown (250-457-9566). They also have jade cutting and polishing demonstrations.
2. Revel in the past at historic Hat Creek Ranch, 11 km north on Hwy 97. (See Cariboo-Chilcotin section).
3. Cheer for the hometown favourite at the Nl'ak'apxm Eagle Motorplex (6 km south on Hwy 1)—NHRA drag races are held from spring through fall.
4. Go trout fishing in Loon Lake (20 km north) or visit the Loon Creek Fish Hatchery.
5. Ask locally for good rockhounding spots.

## Wildlife Viewing in Kamloops

**Tranquille Marsh**, 10 km west of North Kamloops on Tranquille Road. Birds: snow geese, blue heron, pelicans, trumpeter and whistling swans. Mammals: mule deer, coyotes, and bighorn sheep.

On Highway 1 east of Kamloops watch for swans, Canada geese and osprey.

Take Highway 5A, the old route to Merritt, to see sandhill cranes in September and April, as well as birds of prey such as hawks, kestrels, and owls.

## Kamloops Trout Fishing Lakes

**With 1500 area lakes** to choose from, 200 within an hour's drive of Kamloops, the choices can be a little overwhelming. Here are some tried and true suggestions, accessible by car, good for families, novices, and experienced anglers.

Jacko Lake (11 km NW of Kamloops)

Lac Le Jeune (35 km S of Kamloops)

Paul Lake (23 km NE Kamloops)

Roche Lake (38 km SW Kamloops)

Stake Lake (25 km S of Kamloops)

Tunkwa Lake (14 km from Logan Lake)

*St. Joseph's Church was built on the Kamloops Band's land in the 1870s by Roman Catholic missionary Father LeJeune.*

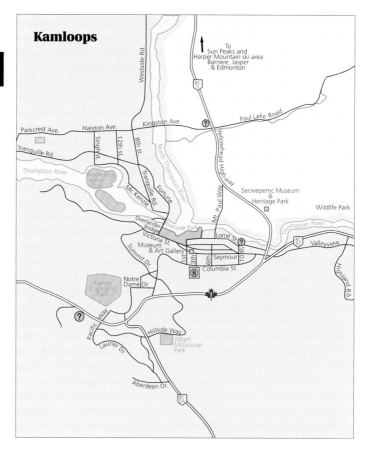

*Swimmers enjoy a late afternoon dip in the Thompson River at Riverside Park in Kamloops, where the North and South Thompson rivers join.*

rivers. The Kamloops Band was one of 20 groups that made up the powerful Secwepemc nation.

Fort Kamloops was established in 1812 by David Stuart of the American-based Pacific Fur Company. Both the Hudson's Bay Company and the North West Company also vied for supremacy, and fur traders fought at least one bloody battle for control of the area. In the 1820s Fort Kamloops was a way station on the early Fur Brigade Trail to the Columbia River, and over 600 horses pastured on the lush surrounding grasslands. In the 1850s and 1860s, as the fur trade waned, Kamloops became a stopover on the route to goldfields in the Cariboo and the Big Bend of the Columbia. The Overlander Bridge commemorates a particularly courageous group of gold seekers who made a perilous journey down the North Thompson River in 1862.

Access to markets was enhanced by the completion of the CPR in 1885, and ranching and farming became the

## Kamloops Annual Events–Best Bets

**February**–Wine Festival; Ice Fishing Tournament
**March**–Cowboy Festival
**April**–Kamloops Pro Rodeo
**July**–Alpine Blossom Festival at Sun Peaks; International Air Show (250-554-0700); Bluegrass Festival; Music concerts in Riverside Park
**August**–Pow Wow Days; Music concerts in Riverside Park
**September**–Winter Fair
**December**–Wildlights, light display & winter activities at Wildlife Park

## Kamloops Great Outdoors ... Top Five

1. Golf at one of Kamloops' seven championship 18-hole courses.
2. Hike and bike the 40 km of trails in 800-hectare Kenna Cartwright Park on Dufferin Mountain, the largest municipal park in the province. Great views and easy access (just off Hwy 1 on Hillside Drive).
3. Hike, bike, swim, fish and watch wildlife at Paul Lake and Lac Le Jeune provincial parks, within a half hour's drive of town.
4. Enjoy four-seasons recreation at Sun Peaks Resort (250-578-7842), 45 minutes north on Hwy 5. Canada's downhill sweetheart, Nancy Greene Raine, is director of skiing.
5. Paddle your heart out on the Thompson River. The one- to two-day trip between Chase and Kamloops is a favourite. Watch for hoodoos, unusual pillared rock formations formed by erosion of clay benches that once formed the bottom of a glacial lake.

economic mainstay of Kamloops. In the latter part of the 20th century, logging and mining were economically dominant.

## Chase

56 km (35 mi.) east of Kamloops. Population: 2466. Info Centre: 400 Shuswap Avenue, Box 592, V0E 1M0. 250-679-8432; Fax: 250-679-3120. Email: chccom@mail.ocis.net
Chase is located on Little Shuswap Lake and the South Thompson River, and is surrounded by a profusion of wildflowers in spring and summer. To the west lie dry range lands and sagebrush hills, and to the east lie the lusher forests of the Shuswap Lake area. It is within easy access of dozens of parks and lakes for both summer and winter recreation. Wildlife viewers can look for bighorn sheep on the surrounding hills, or take the short hike to Chase Creek Falls at the rest area just east of town. The 57-km gentle paddle down the South Thompson to Kamloops reveals hoodoos, kekulis (Native pit houses), and a variety of birds.

In 1992 the Little Shuswap Indian Band opened a $4.3 million resort, Quaaout Lodge, on Shuswap Lake. The resort features many native elements: the lobby is based on the kekuli dwelling design and the restaurant menu "honours Native traditions of the region." Teepees are available for rent on the grounds as well. (1-800-663-4303; www.quaaout.com).

In July, don't miss the Squilax Pow Wow, an annual intertribal gathering with traditional singing, dancing, and

*Many original log buildings from pioneer days remain throughout the Interior. This barn is near Shuswap Lake Provincial Park.*

## While You're In Kamloops ... Top Ten

1. Saddle up! Join the annual Cattle Drive (250-372-7075; www.cattledrive.bc.ca) and herd them little critters all the way from Nicola Ranch to Kamloops in a five-day ride.
2. Visit the Secwepemc Museum and Heritage Park (345 Yellowhead Highway, 250-828-9801). The museum is housed in the reserve's former residential school and features Secwepemc cultural traditions, an archeological site, and a gift shop.
3. Get cultured at the Kamloops Museum and Archives (207 Seymour, 250-828-3576), which emphasizes Native culture, the fur trade, and the railway; and at the Art Gallery (101-465 Victoria; 250-828-3543), where the displays change monthly.
4. Stroll through the city on the heritage walking tour, which includes buildings dating back to 1887. (Obtain maps at Info Centre and Museum.)
5. Watch the salmon spawning at the world-famous Adams River run in October.
6. Cruise the Thompson River on the locally built paddlewheeler *Wanda Sue.* (Departs from the old Kamloops Yacht Club, 1140 River Street, 250-374-7447, on varying schedules between May and October.)
7. Enjoy a show at the Western Canada Theatre Company (250-372-3216; www.westerncanadatheatre.bc.ca), one of the Interior's only professional companies.
8. Go fossil hunting. Several companies offer tours of this rockhounds' paradise. Ask at the Info Centre.
9. Visit the award-winning Kamloops Wildlife Park (12 km east on Hwy 1), the largest non-profit zoo in the province. Over 70 species of indigenous and exotic animals range nearly 50 hectares of land. There's also a railway museum and miniature train. Open year-round. (250-573-3242; www.kamloopswildlife.org/).
10. Walk the shores of the North and South Thompson rivers via the 16-km Rivers Trail. (Map available at Info Centre.)

*Shuswap Lake is one of the Interior's most popular summer destinations.*

## Roderick Haig-Brown Provincial Park

**66 km** (41 mi.) east of Kamloops, 5 km (3 mi.) north of Squilax. 250-851-3000, Fax 250-828-4633. Web: http://www.env.gov.bc.ca/bc-parks/explore/parkpgs/roderick.htm.

The annual Adams River salmon run in October is a major wildlife-viewing attraction in North America. When the run peaks every four years (2002, 2006, 2010, etc.), an estimated two million sockeye find their way home—one of the largest spawning phenomena in the world. Thousands of people come to witness this fascinating event as the river changes colour with the red bodies of the dying salmon. In off-years, lesser numbers of sockeye, spring, coho and pink salmon, and steelhead trout repeat the marathon upriver battle, 485 km from the Pacific Ocean via the Fraser and Thompson rivers.

The 1059-hectare park, named after well-known BC conservationist and writer Roderick Haig-Brown (1908-1976), runs along both sides of the 11-km Adams River between Shuswap and Adams lakes. Whitetail and mule deer, black bear, beaver, river otter, mink, osprey, bald eagles, harlequin ducks, and mergansers are among the other species found here.

In the fall, the entire river is utilized for spawning, although most people watch from platforms on the eastern bank on the lower part of the river. The area is also of archeological interest. You can still see evidence of *kekuli* and pictographs.

Hiking, boating, and fishing are all permitted in the park. Visitors are asked to remember that this is a conservation site, and any interference with artifacts or spawning fish is illegal. Beware of poison ivy along the dry exposed slopes: "Leaves in three, let them be."

drumming. Participants come from BC, Alberta, Washington, California and Mexico.

The Chase Museum (1042 Shuswap Ave., 250-679-8847) is in the former Blessed Sacrament Church, built in 1909. It houses photographs and artifacts of both European and First Nations people.

## Shuswap Lake

With over 1000 km of warm navigable waterways and 20 provincial parks, Shuswap Lake attracts large numbers of summer vacationers. You can rent a variety of aquatic devices for enjoying the lake; many people choose houseboats The fishing is excellent for rainbow trout, Dolly Varden and whitefish. Other good fishing lakes close by are Adams, Little Shuswap, White, and Mara.

At Scotch Creek and Herald provincial parks, watch for the shallow depressions that are

*Salmon Arm, the largest town in the Shuswap area, is a service centre for agriculture and forestry.*

remains of Native pit houses used for winter dwellings. A recreated replica of a pit house has also been built. On the cliffs of the lake itself are fading ochre pictographs over a hundred years old.

The odd H-shape of Shuswap Lake converges in

## Special Events in Salmon Arm—Best Bets

**January**—Reino Keski Salmi Loppet, Larch Hills (larchhills skiclub.bc.ca/loppet.htm)

**February**—Shuswap International Film Festival

**May**—Grebe Festival (www.grebe.shuswap.net/)

**June**—Father's Day Air Show; Salmon Arm Rodeo

**August**—Roots and Blues Festival

**September**—Fall Fair & Harvest Festival

## While You're In Salmon Arm ... Top Ten

1. Birdwatch at Waterfront Nature Enhancement Preserve (follow the signs on Lakeshore Drive), home to over 150 species of birds and waterfowl and one of four places in the province to view nesting western grebes.
2. Stroll through Haney Heritage Village (June to September, 250-832-5243), just south of town on 97A. This 16-hectare park features turn-of-the-century heritage buildings, a 2-km nature trail, and a forest featuring local flora. In summer, enjoy the Villains and Vittles Dinner Theatre.
3. Catch a concert on the wharf (summer).
4. Indulge your passion for golf at Salmon Arm's two semi-private 18-hole golf courses: the Salmon Arm Golf Club (250-832-4727) and Shuswap Lake Estates (1-800-661-3955).
5. Go wine tasting. Larch Hills, 110 Timms Road, 250-832-0155, www.LarchHillsWinery.bc.ca; Recline Ridge, 2640 Skimikin Road, Tappen, 250-835-2212; www.recline-ridge.bc.ca.
6. Walk to Margaret Falls in Herald Provincial Park just east of Tappen, or try the Rotary Trail (one hour) from downtown.
7. Cross-country ski at Larch Hills' 150 km of trails.
8. Go for a swim in the lake.
9. Buy local crafts and other delights at the Shuswap Craft and Farm Market every Tuesday and Friday morning at Piccadilly Place Mall parking lot (summer).
10. Rent a houseboat.

## Fore! SuperGuide's Best Bets along Highway 1

### Golden

**Golden Golf & Country Club**. Semi-private. 18 holes. Par 72. 6845 yards. Design: Bill Nevis. One of Score Magazine's top 100 Canadian courses, 2001. Box 1615, V0A 1H0. 250-344-2700 or 1-866-727-7222. Email: golfgolden@redshift.bc.ca. Web: www.golfgolden.com

### Hope

**Hope Golf & Country Club**. Semi-private. 18 holes. Par 72. 900 Golf Course Rd., V0X 1L0. 604-869-5881

### Kamloops

**Aberdeen Hills**. Semi-private. 18 holes. Par 71. 6147 yards. 1185 Links Way, V1S 1S8. 250-828-1143. Email: acordero@mail.ocis.net. Web: www.come.to/aberdeenhills

**The Dunes**. Semi-private. 18 holes. Par 72. 7120 yards. Design: Graham Cooke. One of Score Magazine's top 100 Canadian courses, 2001. Other awards. 652 Dunes Dr., V2B 8M8. 888-881-4653. Email: info@golfthedunes.com. Web: www.golfthedunes.com

**Eagle Point Golf & Country Club**. 18 holes. Par 72. 8888 Barnhartvale Road, V2C 6W1. 1-800-863-2453. Email: eaglepoint@telus.net. Web: www.golfeaglepoint.com

**Kamloops Golf and Country Club**. Semi-private. 18 holes. Par 72. 6762 yards. #16–2960 Tranquille Rd., V2B 8B6. 250-376-3231

**Rivershore**. Semi-private. 18 holes. Par 72. 7007 yards. Design: Robert Trent Jones. One of Score Magazine's top 100 Canadian courses, 2001. 330 Rivershore Drive, V2H1S1. 866-886-4653. Email: rivershore_golf@telus.net. Web: www.rivershoregolflinks.com

**Sun Peaks Resort**. 18 holes. Design: Graham Cooke. 1280 Alpine Rd., Sun Peaks, V0E 1Z1. 250-578-5431. Email: golf@sunpeaksresort.com. Web: www.sunpeaksresort.com

**Sun Rivers Golf Resort Community**. 18 holes. 7000 yards. Design: Graham Cooke. 866-571-7888. Email: golf@sunrivers.com. Web: www.sunrivers.com

### Revelstoke

**Revelstoke Golf Course**. Public. 18 holes. Par 72. 6521 yards. At Columbia Park. Box 1860, V0E 2S0. 250-837-4276

### Salmon Arm

**Salmon Arm Golf Club**. Semi-private. 18 holes plus a 9-hole executive course. Par 72. 6738 yards. Redesign: Less Furber, 1994. 3641 Highway 97B S.E., V1E 4P6. 250-832-4727. Email: info@salmonarmgolf.com. Web: www.salmonarmgolf.com

**Shuswap Lake Estates**. Semi-private. 18 holes. Par 72. 6467 yards. 2405 Centennial Dr., Blind Bay, V0E 1H0. 1-800-661-3955. Email: sleproshop@telus.net. Web: www.shuswaplakeestates.com

All courses are public, unless indicated. Play is seasonal. For information on all courses in this region: www.bcgolfguide.com

Cinnemousun Narrows, evidence of the glaciation that rounded mountain peaks and steepened valley walls in the last ice age. The rock is mostly metamorphic, altered extensively by heat and pressure. Rockhounds should look for blue-grey and banded agate, crystalline geodes, and amethyst, particularly on Squilax Mountain near Chase, the Enderby Cliffs, and Mount Ida near Salmon Arm.

## Salmon Arm

53 km (32 mi.) east of Chase. Population 15,034. Info Centre: 1-751 Marine Park Dr NE V1E 2W7. 250-832-2230. Toll free: 1-877-725-6667. Fax: 250-832-8382. Email: sacofc@shuswap.net. Web: www.visitsalmonarm.com. Tourism Shuswap, Box 1670, V1E 4P7. 250-832-5200. 1-800-661-4800. Salmon Arm's name dates back to the days when salmon were so abundant that settlers scooped them out of the lake and onto their fields for fertilizer. Today, Salmon Arm calls itself the "Gem of the Shuswap." Summer temperatures are pleasantly warm, making this a popular summer recreation headquarters.

## Sicamous

25 km (16 mi.) east of Salmon Arm. Population: 3082. Info Centre: 110 Finlayson St., (by government dock) Box 346, V0E 2V0. 250-836-3313; Fax: 250-836-4368. Email: chamber@sicamous.com. Web: www.sicamouschamber.bc.com Idyllically situated between Shuswap and Mara lakes, Sicamous calls itself the "houseboat capital of Canada," advertising over 350 vessels for rent. For those who don't have a week or two to lollygag about

*Once a CPR construction site, Sicamous is now "the houseboat capital of Canada."*

the lake, the modified stern-wheeler *Phoebe Anne* (250-836-2200) takes visitors on a historic trip up Seymour Arm and back on daily sailings during July and August. The same company runs tours and rents recreational equipment and boats.

In 1865, miners in search of gold on the Big Bend of the Columbia River made the same journey as the *Phoebe Anne*, disembarking at Ogdenville to make their way overland through the Monashee Mountains to the goldfields. Ogdenville was once a bustling town with six saloons, thirteen stores, five bakeries, and one bathhouse. It became a ghost town in two short years as the promise of gold dwindled.

## While You're In Sicamous ... Top Ten

1. Explore the 1000 km of shoreline on a houseboat.
2. See the work of local artists at the 1922 vintage Blue Manor Art Gallery (12 Bruhn Road, 250-836-2854) on CPR Hill.
3. Immerse yourself in the past at the Eagle Valley Museum in Finlayson Park (250-836-4635), open late June to late August.
4. Indulge your senses at the D Dutchmen Dairy (250-836-4304, 1 km east on Hwy 1), with its 50+ flavours of homemade ice cream and free zoo.
5. Try out exotic water recreation like the floating hot tub!
6. Stroll through Riverfront Nature Park (access at end of Silver Sands Road or from Sicamous Beach Park).
7. Cycle the 4-km old Sicamous Highway (access north of Hwy 1, about 500 metres west of bridge over Sicamous Narrows towards Salmon Arm).
8. Shop at the Farmers Market on Saturdays at the Red Barn, a designated heritage site.
9. Check out the view from the hang-gliding ramp (or jump if you've got wings). Access from Sicamous Solsqua Road and 1800 Forest Service Road. Ask locally.
10. Walk across the Eagle River on the Malakwa Suspension Bridge, built in 1919 (20 km east on Hwy 1).

*The Last Spike at Craigellachie marks a major event in Canadian history*

## Craigellachie

One of the most important moments in BC history occurred at Craigellachie, 30 km east of Sicamous in the Monashee Mountains. It was here on November 7, 1885, that Donald Smith drove the CPR's famous "last spike" into the rails to complete the transcontinental railway. In return for completing the project, the CPR was awarded generous land grants and began building a huge financial empire that grew to include hotels, airlines, shipping, and mining.

## Eagle Valley

About 20 km further east on the Trans-Canada Highway is Eagle Valley and the 1790-metre Eagle Pass. One of the great natural clefts in the mountains, the pass was

### Steller's Jay

*Cyanocitta stelleri*

Jays belong to the same family as crows and magpies. Of the 37 species of jay that exist, the three that occur in Canada also occur in the Interior: the blue jay, the gray jay, and the Steller's jay.

The bright blue Steller's jay, BC's official bird, was the only crested jay found west of the Rockies until recently when the blue jay has started to expand into this range. In Canada, it is only found in BC and southwestern Alberta. Common in coniferous forests, it is known for its gregarious and sometimes cheeky scolding. Fearless as well as curious, the Steller's jay will frequently demand handouts in campsites and picnic areas.

First noted in the mid-1700s in Alaska by Georg Wilhelm Steller, a naturalist on the Bering expedition, the Steller's jay is found from Alaska to Central America, and throughout BC's Interior.

Their natural food supply includes carrion, insects, eggs, nestlings, fruit, nuts, and berries. They have the capacity to carry nuts and other food in pouches to storage caches. Research indicates they can remember the location of hundreds of food caches.

Not a true migrator, the Steller's jay tends to disappear deeper into the woods when nesting, becoming more acquiescent and secretive.

### Ghost Towns along Highway 1

**Donald**, in the East Kootenay on the bank of the Columbia River near Golden. A construction centre and divisional point for the CPR, it was the chief town of the Kootenays in 1889. During its heyday, gold dust was accepted as payment for groceries.

**Three Valley Gap**, 19 km west of Revelstoke. Consists of more than 20 buildings restored and furnished with antiques.

Walhachin, south side of **Thompson River**, 18 km east of Cache Creek. English settlers came in 1907 to create an elegant society in the sagebrush desert. Ruins of flumes, buildings, and a few skeletons of apple trees remain.

revealed to surveyor Walter Moberly when he watched eagles fly through it in the summer of 1865. The CPR took advantage of the route to construct the railway in the 1880s.

## Three Valley Gap

The original town of Three Valley had its heyday in the 1880s. The present ghost town has been reconstructed from twenty buildings collected around the province. Along with a resort hotel (1-888-667-2109), there are displays of Native artifacts, live performances in the Walter Moberly Theatre, and a flower garden beside Three Valley Lake. (The attractions are open April to October.)

Although many people think they're entering the Rockies as the mountains

*Three Valley Gap resort complex in the Eagle Valley now stands where Walter Moberly found a route through the wilderness of the Monashee Mountains in 1865.*

emerge on this portion of Highway 1, these peaks are in fact the Columbia Mountains. The Rockies are on the other side of the Rocky Mountain Trench beyond Golden.

### While You're In Revelstoke ... Top Five

1. Pick up the heritage walking tour brochure from the Info Centre. The beautifully restored Revelstoke courthouse has original stained glass windows, marble panelling, fixtures, and furnishings.

2. Explore the past: Revelstoke Museum (315 First Street, 250-837-3067) has displays of railway, riverboating, and other early area history. The Revelstoke Railway Museum (719 Track Street West, 1-877-837-6060) houses a restored engine and cars. The Revelstoke Fireman's Museum has a fully restored 1923 International Bickle Fire Engine.

3. Stroll the pedestrian-only Grizzly Plaza with its powerful bronze sculptures by West Kootenay artist Tom Lynn. (Free entertainment most summer evenings; farmers' market on Saturday mornings.)

4. Tour the Revelstoke Dam (250-837-6211), one of North America's largest hydroelectric developments (4 km north on the old Big Bend Highway), or the Mica Dam (another 145 km north), the highest earthfill dam in North America, with a generating capacity of 1805 megawatts (250-834-7382; seasonal).

5. Hang out at the Mountain Arts Festival in September.

### The Great Outdoors Revelstoke–Best Bets

1. Take an aerial, heli-hiking or heli-skiing tour of the alpine areas.

2. Sign up for a river-rafting adventure.

3. Cast a line into man-made Lake Revelstoke, where a world-record Dolly Varden was caught in 1991.

4. Go rockhounding in Goldstream Provincial Park (garnet, soapstone, and serpentine) or try your hand at recreational gold panning. (Contact the government agent on First Street.)

5. Paddle down the Columbia River to Shelter Bay (2-3 days).

6. Ski Powder Springs on Mt. Mackenzie, home to the world's largest snowboard half-pipe, (17 runs, 1,100 vertical feet). Heli-ski/cat-ski, and snowmobile packages are available (1-800-991-4455).

*Tours of Revelstoke Dam, completed in 1984 under the terms of the Columbia Treaty, include an elevator trip to the top of the 175-metre high concrete structure.*

*Revelstoke's courthouse, built in 1912, is the centrepiece of a $2.3 million heritage revitalization project completed in 1987.*

# Revelstoke

70 km (43 mi.) east of Sicamous. Population: 8507. Info Centre: 204 Campbell Avenue, Box 490, V0E 2S0. 250-837-5345; Fax: 250-837-4223. 1-800-487-1493. Email: corev@revelstoke.net Once a sleepy railway town, Revelstoke, with its heritage buildings and four-season outdoor recreation, has become one of the Interior's hidden treasures. (It was recently rated as one of North America's top ten adventure destinations by Shape magazine.)

First settled in the mid-1800s, it was originally called Big Eddy and later Second Crossing, in reference to its location on the Columbia River. In 1880 a townsite called Farwell was laid out. But in 1886, when an English banker named Lord Revelstoke put some money into the CPR, the town got a new name and it soon became an important centre on the rail line.

In the days before the Rogers Pass route opened in 1962, Revelstoke was the western entrance to the infamous Big Bend Highway, a long, dusty route around the Selkirk Range that followed the Columbia River. The railway had a big role in the town's development, and more recently logging, hydroelectric projects, and outdoor recreation have helped keep the economy alive.

Highway 23 south of Revelstoke connects with Highway 6 at Nakusp and the West Kootenays. The schedule of the ferry across the Arrow Lakes from Shelter Bay to Galena Bay is posted on the highway in Revelstoke. It does *not* run 24 hours and there are no concessions at the ferry docks.

*Locals cut a trail to the top of Mt. Revelstoke in 1908. Today a 26-km drive over a paved road takes visitors to spectacular alpine wildflower displays and picturesque Balsam Lake.*

## Mt. Revelstoke National Park

P.O. Box 350, Revelstoke, V0E 2S0. 250-837-7500, Fax: 250-837-7536. Email: revglacier_reception@ pch.gc.ca. Web: parkscan.harbour. com/mtrev/reach.htm
Bordering the town of Revelstoke is 260-square-km Mt. Revelstoke National Park, created in 1914. Summit Drive, one km northeast of Revelstoke on the Trans-Canada Highway, is a 26-km drive up a paved road providing easy access to the 1938-metre summit of Mt. Revelstoke. Pull-outs allow spectacular views of the Columbia River, Eagle Pass, and surrounding mountains. In the summer, the alpine meadows are filled with brilliantly coloured wildflowers. Trails at the top lead to nearby lakes. Camping is not permitted in the park, but there are private campsites in

Revelstoke and several provincial parks nearby.

The Trans-Canada Highway follows the southern border of the park and the Illecillewaet River. There are many trails off the highway that lead to alpine meadows, passing near waterfalls and through forest land. Near the western entrance to the park, Skunk Cabbage and Giant Cedars trails are easy self-guided nature walks.

## National Parks

**Motorists planning to stop in national parks** must have valid permits on their vehicles. Permits can be obtained at highway booths at the park entrances.

- It is illegal to feed, touch, disturb, or hunt wildlife in a national park. Poachers can be fined up to $150,000 or imprisoned for six months.
- Pets must be leashed at all times in national parks. Dogs are not permitted overnight in the backcountry.
- Provincial fishing licences are not valid in national parks. Park information centres sell national park fishing licences and have information on regulations.
- For overnight stays in the backcountry, park-use permits must be purchased from information centres or warden offices.
- It is illegal to remove or destroy plants and other natural or historic objects in national parks.

*Rogers Pass eluded CPR surveyors looking for a route through the Selkirk Mountains in the 1870s. Highway construction through the rugged area began in 1956 and took six years to complete.*

One of the most photographed points along the Trans-Canada is the 1327-metre Rogers Pass. The Info Centre has a number of displays, and in the summer months the staff offer interpretive programs.

Major A.B. Rogers, chief engineer of the CPR, first found this pass through the Selkirk Range in 1881. Strong-backed men armed with picks and shovels created a track for the CPR, which linked BC with the rest of Canada in 1885. But it wasn't until 1962 that the Trans-Canada Highway was built.

You can see the Illecillewaet, Asulkan, and Swiss glaciers from the Info Centre. The Illecillewaet Campground affords a closer view of the glaciers and has trails to the alpine areas.

Hikers can pick up information on the park's 140 km of trails at the Info Centre. (Overnighters must register with the park staff.) Of the 21 routes in the park, one of the easiest, the 30-minute Abandoned Rails Trail, starts just behind the Info Centre. Two other gentle 30-minute walks are the Meeting of the Waters Trail, starting at the Illecillewaet Campground, and the Loop Trail at the Loop Brook Campground.

Much of the park is alpine tundra that includes many flowering plants. Incomparable photographic opportunities are available from May through August. The eastern boundary of the park marks the beginning of the Mountain Time Zone: eastbound travellers should set clocks ahead one hour.

## Albert Canyon

37 km (23 mi.) east of Revelstoke. 250-837-2420; winter 250-837-2629. www.canyonhotsprings.com/hotsprings.htm
At the end of a long hard day of sightseeing, Albert Canyon Hot Springs provides happy relief. Besides 26°C and 40°C pools, there is a commercial campsite with all the amenities plus trail rides, whitewater rafting, fishing, and hiking. Seasonal.

## Glacier National Park

P.O. Box 350, Revelstoke, V0E 2S0. 250-837-7500, Fax: 250-837-7536. Email: revglacier_reception@pch.gc.ca. Web: parkscan.harbour.com/mtrev/reach.htm

Not to be confused with the American park of the same name just south of the BC/Alberta border, the Canadian Glacier National Park covers 1349 square km. Over 400 glaciers sit on the lofty peaks of the Purcell and Selkirk ranges.

Glacier National Park lies in particularly rugged country, inhospitable to all but the most tenacious wildlife—mountain goats, mountain caribou and moose or hibernators like marmots or black and grizzly bears. Evidence of frequent avalanches is found in the treeless slides that line the highway. This constantly challenges those charged with keeping the road and rail line clear.

## Golden

150 km (93 mi.) east of Revelstoke. Population 4107. Info Centre: 500-10th Avenue North, Box 1320, V0A 1H0. 250-344-7125; 1-800-622-4653; Fax: 250-344-6688. Email: goldcham@rockies.net

The site where Golden now lies was visited by David Thompson as early as 1807. But the first building was not erected till 1882, when the settlement was known as "The Cache." It was then named "Golden City" to lure prospectors, rivalling "silver City" near Banff. Major Rogers used it as his headquarters while surveying his route through the mountains to the west. From the time the CPR was completed until the spur line south was finished, Golden also enjoyed a memorable era as the northern terminus for sternwheelers on the Columbia steaming north from Lake Windermere. The town has the distinction of having the oldest curling club in western Canada. Curlers first hurled their stones on the frozen Columbia River in 1892.

As soon as the railway was completed, the CPR began working at ways to keep the railway viable, and a strong interest in tourism was born. The company hired Swiss guides in the 1890s to ensure the safety of trekkers and mountaineers. Memorabilia can be found in the Golden and District Museum (1302-11th Avenue and 13th Street, 250-344-5169).

If you're an outdoor enthusiast you may never want to leave this little town. It's a centre for a variety of activities including river rafting, hut-to-hut high-country hiking, ski-ing, paragliding, heli-skiing, fishing and mountain biking. The new Kicking Horse Mountain Resort offers superb skiing, and the Golden Golf and Country Club has been rated one of the 100 best courses in the country.

### Jean Feuz Vaughan

**Edelweiss Village, Golden**

Jean Feuz Vaughan was born and raised in Golden. "I've never left the area," she says. "I never saw the need. It's warm in the summer; not too cold in the winter."

Possibly another reason she stays is the Edelweiss Village. Jean's grandfather, Edward Feuz, was one of the first Swiss guides employed by the CPR to guide tourists in the Rockies in the 1890s. His three sons, Walter, Ed Jr., and Ernest, followed as teenagers. In 1912 the CPR built houses for the guides so they wouldn't need to return to Switzerland each year, and the Feuz brothers moved to Canada permanently.

Jean, the youngest of Walter's eight children, says the brothers never had an accident. Walter eventually developed goitre, gave up guiding, and managed the boats at Lake Louise for several years. But Ed Jr. climbed until he was 84, leading first ascents of 78 mountains in the area. The last of the original Swiss guides, he died at Golden in 1981, at the age of 96.

Jean and Allen Vaughan now own the six restored gingerbread-trimmed chalets and rent out all but one. That's the one Jean was raised in.

### Golden River Rafting Companies

**Adams River Rafting**. 1-888-440-7238. Rivers: Adams and Thompson.

**Alpine Rafting**. 1-888-599-5299. www.kickinghorseriver.com. Rivers: Kicking Horse.

**Glacier Raft Co**. 250-344-6521. Rivers: Kicking Horse and White.

**Kinbasket Adventures Wilderness Tours**. 1-866-344-6012. www.bcrockiesadventures.com. Rivers: Columbia.

**Rocky Mountain Rafting**. 1-888-518-7238. www.rockymountain adventure.com. Rivers: Kicking Horse.

**Wet N Wild Adventures**. 1-800-668-9119. www.canadianrockies. net/wetnwild. Rivers: Blaeberry, Kicking Horse and Columbia.

Golden

## Golden Trout Fishing Lakes

Wilbur & Nine Bay lakes
Susan & Jeb lakes
Gorman Lake
Loon, Mitten & Nixon
    lakes (Parson area)
Cleland and Jade lakes
    (Brisco area)

## Special Events In Golden –Best Bets

**February**—Willy Forrest Snowfest

**May**—Golden Wildlife Festival of Birds and Bears

**June**—Mt. 7 Psychosis (Downhill Mountain Bike & Whitewater Festival)

**July & August**—Hangliding & Paragliding Championships; Sounds of Summer (free street performances)

**August**—Golden Rodeo; Parson Fall Fair

## While You're In Golden ... Top Ten

1. View wildlife at Burges and James Gadsden Provincial Park, a wildlife sanctuary and nature study area on the north side of the Columbia River west of Golden.
2. Golf at the award-wining Golden Golf and Country Club.
3. Paddle the Columbia wetlands south to Radium Hot Springs or up the thrill level and go for a whitewater rafting trip.
4. Birdwatch at Reflection Lake, part of the Rotary's trail network around Golden.
5. Bike "The Golden Triangle," a 316-km route through magnificent scenery, connecting Golden, Lake Louise, and Radium Hot Springs.
6. "Mush!" along on a dog-sled tour.
7. Dine at the Eagle's Eye, at 7700 feet above sea level the highest restaurant in Canada, and enjoy a 360-degree view of the Rocky, Purcell, and Selkirk mountains. Stick around for the skiing. (Kicking Horse Mountain Resort, 250-439-5400; 1-866-SKI-KICK.)
8. Saddle up for a horseback ride on the trails of Beaverfoot Valley, Blaeberry Valley or Canyon Creek.
9. Watch the hangliders and paragliders from right downtown as they revel in Golden's famed "thermals".
10. Walk the trails along the Kicking Horse River. Stroll over the Timber Frame Pedestrian Bridge.

*Emerald Lake was "discovered" in 1882 by CPR surveyor Tom Wilson. Today it is one of the most popular stops on the Trans-Canada Highway.*

## Yoho National Park

(West of Field)
P.O. Box 99, Field, V0A 1G0.
250-343-6783.
Email: yoho_info@pch .gc.ca
East of Golden, the highway finally enters the Rockies and Yoho National Park. With its lofty peaks, glaciers, spectacular waterfalls, and lakes, Canada's second oldest national park is often compared to the Himalayas and the Swiss Alps. Thirty of its peaks stand over 3000 metres. Yoho is one of several parks in the area (Banff, Jasper, and Kootenay are the others) which, along with the Burgess Shale, have been designated by UNESCO as world heritage sites, in recognition of their continuing natural, historic, and recreational value.

We have the CPR to thank for this national treasure. Once workers had pushed the track over the majestic Kicking Horse Pass, the company built their first hotel at Field to avoid hauling a dining car up The Big Hill to the east. At the encouragement of the CPR, tourists, climbers, and artists migrated to the town, and in 1886 Mt. Stephen Reserve was set aside. Yoho National Park was established in 1911.

The highway follows the Kicking Horse River through the 131,300-hectare park, within close range of several popular attractions. (The information centre at Field has maps and descriptions.)

The river was given its name when James Hector, a 24-yr-old doctor and geologist with the Palliser Expedition of

## Top Ski Areas along Highway 1

**Kicking Horse Mountain Resort**, Golden. 1260 m vertical. 38 runs, 3 lifts. Four seasons. Alpine village, dog sledding, rentals, snowboard park, restaurants, snowmobiling, cross-country, ice rink, shopping, daycare, night skiing, ski shop, tube park. 1-866-SKI-KICK. www.kickinghorseresort.com/

**Powder Springs Resort**, Revelstoke. 335 m vertical, 12 runs, 3 lifts. Longest run: 6.7 km. Accommodations, rentals, snowboard park, cat skiing, heli-skiing, restaurants, snowmobiling, cross-country, shopping, daycare, night skiing, ski shop. 1-250-837-5151. 1-800-991-4455, 1-877-4CATSKI.

**Sun Peaks** (near Kamloops). 881 m vertical, 8 lifts, 87 runs; longest run is 8 km. Four-season resort. Alpine village, dog sledding, rentals, snowboard park, restaurants, snowmobiling, cross-country, ice rink, shopping, daycare, night skiing, ski shop. 1-800-807-3257. www.sunpeaksresort.com/

1857-60, was searching for a route through the Rockies to the Columbia River. On August 29, 1858, stopping near Wapta Falls, young Hector was kicked in the chest by a pack horse and rendered unconscious. His colleagues presumed he was dead, and it was a momentous occasion when he revived—so momentous that they renamed the Wapta River to mark it.

## Field

55 km (34 mi.) east of Golden.
Population: 280.
The tiny town of Field exists because of the CPR. A railway camp was constructed here in 1884, and in 1886 Field House was built, drawing visitors from around the world.

Located in Yoho National Park, Field is the closest settlement to the Burgess Shale, a major paleontological

discovery. In 1909, Charles Walcott first came across the perfectly preserved fossils near a massive limestone reef that dates back over 500 million years. The sites are very delicate and access is extremely limited. Parks officials report that viewing is disappointing to ordinary mortals, who will find the displays at the information centre and the Takakkaw Falls turnoff much

## While You're In Yoho National Park ... Top Ten

*Formerly a waterfall, the Natural Bridge was created when the waters of the Kicking Horse River encountered a resistant limestone layer in the bedrock.*

1. Hike into 30 m-high Wapta Falls (an easy hour). Take the 2-km Wapta Falls Road south past the west entrance. Other falls in the park are higher, but the width of these carry a spectacular peak flow of 255 cubic metres per second. The marsh along the side of the road is home to beaver, muskrat, blue heron, and moose.

2. View the hoodoo formations. Some geologists feel these are the best examples in the world (access via Hoodoo Creek Campground Road). These sculpted pillars of glacial sediment have boulders balancing on their peaks—evidence of their relative youth.

3. Drive to the Natural Bridge, where the ceaseless action of the river over thousands of years has worn a hole in solid bedrock.

4. Keep going another 6 km to Emerald Lake, where you can hike around the lake, go for a horseback ride, rent a canoe, or wander through the world-famous chalet, built in 1902 (250-343-6321). This is one of the most photographed lakes in the Rockies.

5. Walk right up to Takakkaw Falls (via the road at Kicking Horse Campground through the Yoho Valley). At 380 metres, it's one of the highest waterfalls in Canada. Although the falls are visible from the parking lot, the 10-minute walk will bring you close enough to need a raincoat.

6. View mountain goats at Takakkaw Falls and the Lower Spiral Tunnels Viewpoint.

7. Marvel at the engineering masterpiece visible from the Upper Spiral Tunnels Viewpoint. The tunnels were built in 1909 to prevent trains from derailing on the steep downhill grade from Kicking Horse Pass known as The Big Hill.

8. Reserve a spot on the bus or hike into "the fairest of mountain lakelet tarns", which is how mountaineer James Outram described Lake O'Hara in 1900. The lodge is the starting point for over 30 trails. Reservations must be made far in advance to stay overnight or ride the bus (250-343-6418).

9. Stand astride the Continental Divide at Kicking Horse Pass (1625 m): on the west, steams and rivers flow into the Pacific Ocean via the Columbia River system, and on the east, they flow to Hudson Bay and the Atlantic Ocean via the Saskatchewan River system.

10. Find a quiet spot, shut your eyes, listen and breathe!

*The Upper Spiral Tunnels viewpoint, right beside the Trans-Canada Highway, offers a look at a unique solution to an engineering nightmare. Built in 1909, the track loops in a figure eight under Mt. Ogden and Cathedral Mountain— it is possible to watch one end of a train leaving the tunnel while the other end is entering.*

more informative. Parks staff are emphatic in discouraging all but the most serious visitors. However, there are hiking tours available for those with an unabiding passionate interest, through park headquarters or the Yoho Burgess Shale Foundation (1-800-343-3006; www.burgess-shale.bc.ca/).

Field is also a base for the slightly exotic sport of ice climbing, best attempted between December and March. Features not normally regarded as attractive, such as subfreezing temperatures, blue ice, and spindrift avalanches have made the area's many frozen waterfalls excellent training ground for some of Canada's top climbers.

For a more detailed description of this and other parks and attractions in the Rockies, refer to *Yoho: A History and Celebration of Yoho National Park*, the *Canadian Rockies SuperGuide* and *Walks and Easy Hikes in the Canadian Rockies*, published by Altitude.

## Bear Tips

- Always check locally for bear warnings and advice. Let someone know your backcountry route and schedule.
- Don't store food or garbage in tents or leave it unattended. In the backcountry, elevate food and garbage at least five metres between two trees.
- Don't hike alone. Singing or carrying a bell when hiking often warns the bears away; however, it sometimes attracts them.
- If you notice bear droppings, tracks, or dead animals, get out of the area. Avoid mothers with cubs.
- If you meet a bear, keep calm, slowly back away, or climb well up a tree. Some experts say that if you are attacked, drop to the ground and assume the fetal position, hands behind neck, but this is not necessarily effective.
- Dogs can attract and/or annoy bears. Keep them quiet and leashed. Better yet, leave them home.
- Never feed bears. They'll come to expect it and become a problem. Make sure you properly dispose of all uneaten food or garbage.
- It's easier for humans to adjust their behaviour and protect bears than it is for Nature to replace "problem" bears that must be destroyed.

## Fossils of the Burgess Shale

**In the summer of** 1909, Dr. Charles Doolittle Walcott, head of the Smithsonian Institution and an eminent paleontologist, was conducting field research at the higher elevations of Mt. Stephen, near Field. On the last trip down the mountain, as the first snow was falling, Mrs. Walcott's horse stopped at an obstruction. As Dr. Walcott stooped to lift the rock from the path, he discovered the fossilized remains of a 500-million-year-old creature embedded in the shale. It was one of the most important paleontological discoveries in human history.

The Walcotts had literally stumbled upon the vestige of a vast prehistoric sea that once lapped the shores of the Rocky Mountains. The Cambrian creatures had become embedded in the silt on the ocean floor, immune to predators and rapid decay. As time passed, more and more layers of material pressed down, hardening into rock, and the earth continued to shift and change. Miraculously, the fossils remained perfectly preserved, in some cases right down to the contents of their stomachs. An incredibly wide variety of species were represented.

Prevailing scientific biases resulted in a rather conservative original evaluation of the find. It wasn't until 1966, after chipping out ten thousand more specimens, that Cambridge paleontologist Harry Wittington and his colleagues discovered that there were at least 15, perhaps 20, creatures in the Burgess Shale fossils that defied classification in currently existing categories.

These fossils are not only objects of great beauty, says Harvard paleontologist Stephen Jay Gould, but they challenge the foundations of our ideas about life itself. For more information, read Gould's book *Wonderful Life: The Burgess Shale and the Nature of History* (New York: Norton, 1989) or visit the Yoho-Burgess Shale Foundation: http://www.burgess-shale.bc.ca/.

## Bears

**Bears are the largest** carnivores on land. They are not generally aggressive, but under certain circumstances they can be. Because of this unpredictability, all bears should be regarded as dangerous.

In the Interior there are two species: black bears and grizzlies. Grizzlies average 3 metres, weigh 150 to 300 kilograms, have a large hump on their shoulders, and range in colour from pale yellowish to dark brown with white tips on the hairs. Black bears average

2 metres, weigh 125 to 300 kilograms, and range in colour from white (not common in the Interior) to cinnamon brown and black. Since bears may require many kilometres of foraging territory, they rarely congregate, unless at rich feeding grounds such as spawning runs. Except for other bears and people, bears have few natural predators.

Bears sleep during the winter, so an encounter is unlikely between November and April. During the rest of the year, they range throughout the Interior. Disastrous encounters between people and bears are rare, but they do occur.

# Crowsnest Highway

*A stopover on the Dewdney Trail in the 1860s, Creston is now an important agricultural area in the Kootenays. Over 12,000 hectares of farmland have been reclaimed in the floodplain of the Kootenay River.*

I n 1859, Edgar Dewdney, a 24-year-old civil engineer from England, arrived at Governor James Douglas's door in Victoria looking for work. "I possessed a strong constitution and unbounded confidence, and arrived here with a light heart", Dewdney later wrote in his memoirs.

Almost immediately, Dewdney began helping Colonel Richard Clement Moody build a trail from Hope to Rock Creek, east of present-day Osoyoos. After working on other road-building projects in the Interior, Dewdney extended the route as far as the town of Wild Horse in the East Kootenay in 1865, and it became known as the Dewdney Trail.

Today Highway 3 (also known as the Crowsnest route) is the modern version of this early transportation corridor. Some sections of the original trail are still visible from Highway 3. Other parts are being preserved and reclaimed as recreation trails.

Highway 3 starts in Hope (see Trans-Canada Highway section), crossing the southern Interior by climbing up, around, through, and down the Cascade Mountains, the Thompson Plateau, the Okanagan Highland, the Columbia Mountains, and the Rockies, before it reaches the Alberta border near Sparwood. It is a modern, mostly two-lane paved highway that crosses varied terrain. The highest passes are Allison (1342 m) between Hope and Princeton, Bonanza (1535 m) between Grand Forks and Castlegar, Kootenay (1774 m) between Salmo and Creston, and Crowsnest (1382 m) in the Rockies.

*Opposite: The "Vest Pocket Desert" on Osoyoos Lake is home to several unique species of flora and fauna*

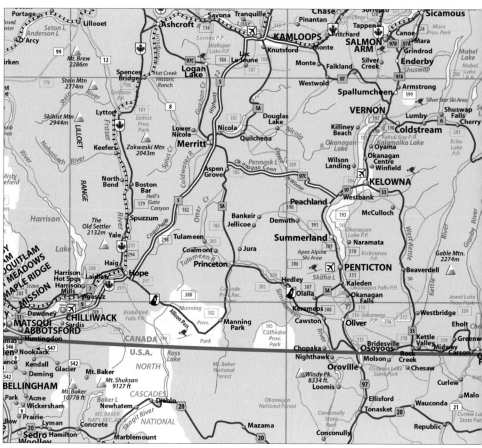

*Crowsnest Highway*

The Nlaka'Pamux (Interior Salish) and Ktunaxa (Kutenai) were the dominant First Nations cultures in the region, and in several places along this route faded images of pictographs still tell their stories.

Rockhounding, gold panning, river rafting, canoeing, kayaking, fishing, swimming, hiking, golfing, wildlife viewing, and biking are just a few of the fair-weather outdoor-recreation possibilities. In the winter, outdoor enthusiasts pursue skiing, ice fishing, skating, snowboarding, and snowmobiling.

Logging and mining are important to many communities along Highway 3, as is agriculture, particularly in the Similkameen, Okanagan, and Creston valleys. However, as the economics of resource extraction falters, many communities are developing their tourism and recreation potential.

## Hope-Princeton Highway

The infamous Hope-Princeton Highway, the first leg of the Crowsnest route, has always been a difficult stretch of road. Officially opened in November 1949 at a cost of $12 million,

for many years it was subject to slides, washouts, and white-knuckle twists and turns. However, work on the road is ongoing, and today the route is a pleasure to drive, with sections of four-lane highway, passing lanes, easy grades, and spectacular scenery.

Despite the improvements to the highway, the route can be dangerous. Motorists should drive with regard for weather conditions, and heed slide and avalanche warnings and no-passing signs. Speeders beware: this stretch of Highway 3 is meticulously patrolled by the RCMP.

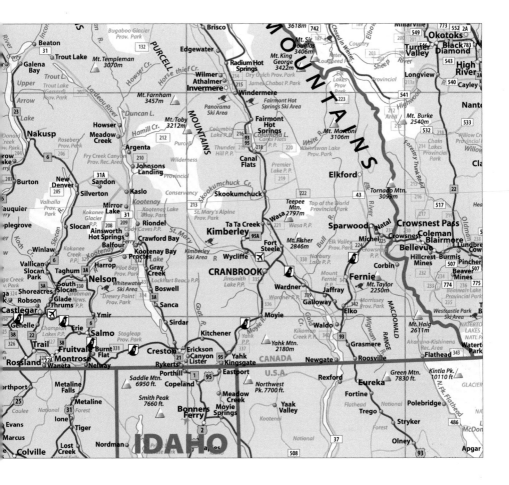

## The Hope Slide

**In January 1965**, an estimated 100 million tonnes of rock, earth, and trees slid off the face of Johnson's Peak about 16 km east of Hope. The rock and debris travelled across the highway, 150 metres up Mount Coulter on the other side, and back down again. Caused by minor earthquakes, the slide obliterated about 3 km of highway and a small lake. At least four people lost their lives. The road was rebuilt over the top of the rubble, and vegetation is slowly creeping back, but the bare face of the mountain remains.

*The peaks of the Three Brothers in the Cascade Mountains are popular with hikers in E.C. Manning Provincial Park.*

## E.C. Manning Provincial Park

26 km (16 mi.) east of Hope, 48 km (30 mi.) west of Princeton. Box 3, 69 km, Hope-Princeton Hwy, Manning Park, V0X 1R0. 250-840-8836.

It is the traveller's good fortune that Highway 3 passes through Manning Provincial Park, providing easy access to alpine meadows, sparkling lakes, and wilderness trails. Only three hours from Vancouver, Manning Park is popular year-round.

Along the highway's route through the 66,500-hectare park, the landscape transforms from lush coastal rain forest to the dry forest land of the Interior Plateau. Evidence of the shift can be dramatically demonstrated in abrupt weather changes near Allison Pass. Here, in minutes, moody grey rain clouds can give way to a bright blue Interior sky. This occurrence repeats across the province. Typically, eastbound clouds release their moisture on the western slopes of the mountain ranges. The eastern-facing slopes thus tend to be drier.

### While You're In E.C. Manning Provincial Park ... Top Ten

1. Watch for wildlife: deer, bear, coyote and over 190 species of birds.
2. Rent a canoe and paddle the Lighting Lakes (Lodge: 250-840-8822).
3. Go for a trail ride (Stables: 250-840-8844).
4. Drive up to Cascade Lookout (take the paved road just across the highway from the lodge) for a spectacular view and an opportunity to converse with blue jays and chipmunks. Another 9 km will take you to the Alpine Meadows.
5. Hike the old Dewdney Trail (36 km/2 days by horseback), built in 1860.
6. View the splashy shows of colour at the Rhododendron Flats in May and June. (20 minute walk, 33 km west of the Visitor Centre.)
7. Head off to Mexico on the Pacific Crest Trail, a 4000-kilometre, six-month backpacking route that extends all the way south (trailhead is 5 km east of the Visitor Centre).
8. Cross-country ski 100 km of trails in winter.
9. Check out the downhill runs at Gibson Pass Ski Area (250-840-8822).
10. Walk the Rein Orchid Trail (begins at Gibson Pass Road parking lot; 15 min.) for orchids and other bog flora in June and July.

*Beaver habitat is visible at several locations along Highway 3 in the park.*

## Beaver

### Castor canadensis

Canada's largest rodents, beavers weigh from 15 to 35 kilograms when mature, and are found across the country. Beavers are easiest to spot in the early morning or late evening.

Beavers live in lodges up to three metres high, constructed out of mud, twigs, and branches beside slow-moving water. The entranceways are under water, but the living quarters are raised above water level. Beavers don't hibernate; their winter food supply of leaves, bark, twigs, buds, and other plant material is stored in a large mound beside the lodge.

Canada's national symbol, the beaver is easily recognizable. Its coarse outer layer of red-brown fur covers the soft undercoat that inspired the early fur traders. Felted, this fur was a prestigious material for men's hats in 18–19th century Europe.

A beaver tail resembles a thick, scaly paddle. When frightened, the animals slap their tails on the water as a warning. They are excellent swimmers, and can stay under water for up to 15 minutes at a time.

Beavers will often live in colonies of lodges. One lodge will house one adult pair and their newborn and yearling offspring. They usually breed in January or February and give birth in April or May after a 14-week gestation.

The Beaver Pond in Manning Park provides one of many good viewing sites in the Interior.

## Copper Mountain

Thirty-five km past the East Gate of Manning Park, a viewpoint acknowledges the now defunct mine at Copper Mountain, which operated from 1905 to 1957. Although an elderly Similkameen Native discovered the copper mineral in 1884, a man named "Volcanic" Brown, who had grandiose plans for saving the world, filed the claim in 1895. Brown eventually sold his rights for $45,000, but his ideas for world harmony shifted inexplicably, and he ended up buying himself some solid gold teeth instead.

When the mine was operating, an average of 1.4 million tonnes of ore was produced per year—mostly copper, with some gold and silver. During its heyday, Copper Mountain was one of the largest mines in the British Empire.

### SuperGuide's Top Ten Hiking Areas on the Crowsnest

(in alphabetical order)
1. Akamina-Kishinena Provincial Park
2. Cathedral Lake Provincial Park
3. Dewdney Trail
4. Elk Lakes Provincial Park
5. Fernie Alpine Resort
6. Kikomum Creek Provincial Park
7. Kettle Valley Railway Line
8. Manning Provincial Park
9. Red Mountain and Old Glory near Rossland
10. Skagit Valley Recreation Area

*Towering above the Similkameen River, Bromley Rock marks a favourite swimming spot east of Princeton.*

## Princeton

134 km (83 mi.) east of Hope. Population: 2943. Info Centre: Old Train Caboose at west entrance to town on Highway 3. 57 Highway 3 East, Box 540, V0X 1W0. 250-295-3103; Fax: 250-295-3255. Email: chamber@nethop.net. Web: www.town.princeton.bc.ca

At the confluence of the Tulameen and Similkameen rivers, Princeton has an ancient relationship to mining. Long before the advent of Europeans, First Nations people used the site to trade the red ochre of nearby Vermilion Bluffs with distant tribes like the Ktunaxa and Prairie Blackfoot. Tulameen is a Native word meaning "red earth", and Princeton was at one time called Vermilion Forks.

Twelve km west of Princeton on Highway 3, Similco Mines' gigantic open-pit copper mine was a mainstay of Princeton's modern economy, processing 23,000 tonnes of ore per day until it suspended operations in 1999. In 1995, an experimental project from the Greater Vancouver Regional District saw the dumping of Nutrifor, a by-product of treated municipal sewage, on a company tailing pond. Proponents of the experiment, including the BC Lung Association, claim that a polluting eyesore was turned into a lush productive meadow in just one season.

### While You're In Princeton ... Top Ten

1. Explore the Princeton Museum (167 Vermilion Avenue, 295-7588) with its displays of fossils and Interior Salish, Chinese, and pioneer artifacts.
2. Take the historic walking tour along Vermilion and Bridge, which includes eight stops of interest, from a bridge to a cave.
3. On a hot day take a swim at Bromley Lake Provincial Park, just off Hwy. 3, east of town.
4. Celebrate at Tulameen Days in August.
5. Paddle down the Similkameen from Princeton to the US border—check locally first, it can be treacherous.
6. Cast a line into one of the 30 or more good trout lakes within an 80-km radius of Princeton. Ask at the Info Centre where they're biting. Or show up for the Otter Valley Fishing Derby in June.
7. Search for agates, petrified wood and fossils in the hills near Vermilion and McCormack Flats.
8. Visit a ghost town.
9. Browse the Fall Fair in September.
10. Hike or bike the Trans Canada Trail.

*The gold, silver and copper ores played out in Hedley in 1955. However, gold panners still work the nearby Similkameen River.*

Princeton is also a ranching town, serving the Nicola and the Similkameen valleys. Outdoor recreation (fishing, hiking, snowmobiling, gold panning, rockhounding) is also important to the local economy.

## Ghost Towns of the Tulameen

**About 60 million years ago**, the Tulameen area north of Princeton was a shallow lake about 24 km long, filled with plant life that later decomposed to form peat bogs. Over time, coal was formed. The town of **Blakeburn**, established in 1917, once produced one tonne of coal per minute and employed 365 men. Now a ghost town, Blakeburn's story is particularly tragic. In 1930, 45 miners died in an underground explosion, one of the worst mining disasters in BC history. The mine closed in 1940.

**Coalmont**, about 18 km northwest of Princeton, was founded in 1911. The original hotel is still operating, and the people who live here have retained a sense of humour. Among the goods for sale at the local store: instant water! Bicycles and boats are available to rent for a closer exploration of the area.

Another 2 km along the road is **Granite City**, where a cowboy with the fortuitous name of John Chance bent over to get a drink of water in the Tulameen River one day in 1885 and found a gold nugget. By 1886 Granite City was a bustling gold-rush town with 13 saloons and a population of 2000, making it the third largest town in BC. In three years, miners took out $350,000 in gold, but by 1888 the boom was over.

The Similkameen and Tulameen rivers are good places for river panning. You can still find platinum and gold, if you know where to look (Granite Creek area) and when (early spring and late fall). The Princeton Info Centre has information on regulations and good places to look.

## Hedley

40 km (25 mi.) east of Princeton. Population: 402.

Approaching Hedley from the west, the highway rounds a bend to reveal Lookout Mountain towering 1922 metres above the tiny town. From the highway viewpoint, you can see remains of the Nickel Plate Mine's 3-km long aerial tramway—the longest in the world when it was built (ca. 1903). The tramway was used to transport ore to a stamp mill at the bottom of the mountain.

One story about the mine's origin says that in 1890, two keen young men on a quest for gold met with some grizzled old prospectors nearby. The greenhorns politely asked the veterans where the best place might be to find gold. With sly smiles, the old-timers directed the newcomers to the top of

## Princeton Castle

**Just north of town** on Osprey Lake Road, stone ruins stand in the trees. What seems to be a medieval castle is in fact the remains of a Portland cement factory. The plant opened in 1913, but closed almost immediately. The construction cost several million dollars, four years, and several workers' lives. Today romantics speculate about hoaxes, blunders, and swindles, but the more practically-minded suggest that a lack of limestone, coal, and financing caused the failure. The site now exists as a modern well-appointed resort, with cabins, an RV park and recreational activities (Princeton Castle: 1-888-228-8881).

the steepest mountain they could see. The young men dutifully crawled and clawed their way up the rock face and discovered a rusty red outcrop of rock – and gold. They sold their claim that year for $60,000, and between 1904 and 1955 the mountain yielded $47 million worth of gold, as well as copper, silver, and arsenic. The mining operation currently visible beside Highway 3 east of town reworks old tailings to recover leached gold.

It's worth while to stop here for gas or to stretch your legs while taking a walk along the main street. (It's pretty hard to get lost.) Many of the town's historic buildings have been spruced up and there are some charming restaurants and B&Bs. And if you want to know more about the history of mining in Hedley, stop in at the Heritage House mining museum.

## Hedley to Keremeos: Wildlife Viewing

**Between Hedley** and Keremeos the highway passes through dry grassland and steep mountain slopes. Motorists can often spot mountain goats, especially in spring and fall. The route follows the Similkameen River and there are plenty of pull-offs for watching the goats as well as golden eagles, marmots, and other wildlife. The only venomous snake in BC, the Pacific rattlesnake, lives in the dry vegetative areas of the southern Interior, so if you're hiking, watch where you place your hands and feet.

*Pictographs, typically painted with red ochre and depicting mythological and supernatural motifs, can be found throughout the Interior. This one is on the Old Hedley Road near Princeton.*

## Alternate Route: The Old Hedley Road

**If you're heading east** to Hedley and Keremeos, you may find the Old Hedley Road an interesting alternative to Highway 3. (Go through Princeton on Bridge Street, cross the bridge, turn right on Tulameen Ave, and cross Highway 5A to the Old Hedley Road.) This route existed for hundreds of years, long before the fur traders and prospectors came through. Look for Native pictographs on the rocks between 10 and 20 km east of Princeton. Also visible are traces of the Dewdney Trail, constructed in the 1860s to connect Hope with the Interior in a bid to minimize US economic and political domination. The Welby stage ran coaches along this route three days a week from Princeton to Penticton until 1910. Rustic Forest Service camping and picnic spots overlook the river.

## Ghost Towns on the Crowsnest

**Ashnola**—On the west side of Similkameen River, 13 km south of Princeton. The door post of the Ashnola Hotel (built in 1902 but destroyed by fire in 1945) carried the inscription: "James MacLaren invested $50,000 in venture and bang went sixpence."

**Fort Steele**—now a provincial heritage site; east of Cranbrook.

**Granite City**—In the Tulameen region northwest of Princeton. At one time it was considered the third-largest settlement in BC. By 1900 all the streams and creeks were completely mined and the town had twice been swept by fire.

**Phoenix**—Near Greenwood off Highway 3. A major centre in the boom years of the 1890s. Today a strip mine covers the townsite.

**Waldo**—In 1905 this was a lumbering town with two mills and 700 people, located 46 km southwest of Fernie. The town was flooded by Lake Koocanusa after the Libby dam was built in 1972.

*A colourful variety of wild plants grow along Interior roadways.*
*From top left, clockwise: oxeye daisy, Saskatoon berries, mountain ash berries, and tansy.*

## Cathedral Lakes Provincial Park

Three km west of Keremeos is the turnoff (south) onto the 23-km access road to Cathedral Lakes Provincial Park. The 33,000-hectare park is in the Cascade Mountains and features some truly spectacular rock formations and alpine scenery. Long recognized as a prime wilderness area—Archduke Franz Ferdinand of Austria, whose 1914 assassination triggered World War I, reportedly made a lavish hunting trip to the area in the early 1900s—the park attracts those truly interested in wilderness recreation. (Hollywood has also discovered the magnificent scenery. Several scenes of the 1986 movie, *Clan of the Cave Bear*, were shot here.)

At the core of the park, surrounded by pinnacled peaks, are six turquoise alpine lakes. There is restricted motor vehicle access to Cathedral Lakes Resort (1-888-CLL-HIKE) on one of the lakes, but otherwise the core is reached only by three hiking routes. (Contact the resort to arrange transportation to the core, even if you're not staying there.) Anglers catch cutthroat and rainbow trout in the lakes and steams. Mule deer, mountain goat, and California bighorn sheep are plentiful. Birdwatchers can look for whiskey jacks, Clark's nutcrackers, golden eagles, and ptarmigan. In summer, over 200 species of flowers bloom. Best hiking is from July to October.

Along the same access road, the Ashnola Mountains Conservation Reserve is home to one of Canada's largest herds of California bighorn sheep.

### SuperGuide's Top Ten Wildlife Viewing Areas on the Crowsnest

(In alphabetical order)

1. Cathedral Lakes Provincial Park

2. Creston Valley Wildlife Centre

3. Elk Lakes Provincial Park, past Elkford

4. Flathead Valley, near Sparwood

5. Hedley to Keremeos— Hwy. 3

6. Kikomum Creek Provincial Park, near Elko

7. Manning Park

8. Pend'Oreille River between Waneta and Nelway

9. Syringa Creek Provincial Park, Castlegar

10. Vest Pocket Desert, Osoyoos

# Keremeos

29 km (18 mi.) east of Hedley. Population: 1178. Info Centre: 415-7th Avenue, Highway 3, PO Box 452, V0X 1N0. 250-499-5225. Web: keremeos.net/. Seasonal. First learn to say it: care-eh-mee-ose. Then enjoy the fact that you are in the "Fruit Stand Capital of Canada." Fruit and vegetables are available at roadside stands throughout the Okanagan, but with 25 here (some open year-round), more just down the road in Cawston, and early ripening dates, Keremeos is a good place to stock up.

Although now known primarily for its orchards, Keremeos was on the route of early fur traders like Alexander Ross, the first European to visit the area in 1811. Taking advantage of the luxurious golden bunch grass that once covered the area, the Hudson's Bay Company established a fort here to pasture oxen, horses, and cows. The first homestead was established in the early 1860s, and the first commercial orchard was planted in 1897 by Frank Richter, a pioneer cattleman.

## Harvest Times in the Keremeos Area

| Fruit | Blossom | Ripening |
| --- | --- | --- |
| Apples | late April to early May | mid-July to late Sept. |
| Apricots | early to mid-April | mid-July to mid-August |
| Cherries | mid to late April | late June to late July |
| Grapes | late April to mid-May | early Sept. to mid-Oct. |
| Peaches | mid-April | late July to mid-August |
| Pears | mid to late April | mid-July to late October |
| Prunes/Plums | mid-April | mid-August to late Sept. |

| Vegetables | Ripening |
| --- | --- |
| Asparagus | May 1 to June 10 |
| Tomatoes | August 5 to October 20 |
| Corn | July 1 to first frost |
| New Honey Crop | August 1 to mid-Sept. |

## Old Grist Mill

**Off the beaten track**, but a definite must-see, is the Old Grist Mill. Now a provincial historic site, the mill was built in 1877 by wealthy young Englishman Barrington Price, and today is one of the best examples of its kind in the country. Included are hands-on interpretive displays, a Victorian garden, a tea room, and a resource centre.

If you're there in October, plan to attend the Giant Zucca Reunion. It may be your only chance to attend a zucca reunion. The zucca, widely grown in the area between 1934 and 1955, was believed to be extinct until staff tracked down seed from a farmer in the US. The giant fruit can weigh as much as 70 kilo-

*Horticultural displays at the 1877 Grist Mill in Keremeos include heritage apples, historic varieties of wheat and an Edwardian herb garden.*

grams. (Take Highway 3A east, then follow the signs to Upper Bench Road. Open daily in summer and in winter by reservation.

Upper Bench Road, 250-499-5528; www.keremeos.com/grist-mill/index.html)

*Spotted Lake, an ancient First Nations site with spiritual significance, has recently been restored to the stewardship of the Okanagan Band.*

## Spotted Lake

Spotted Lake, 35 km east of Keremeos on the south side of the road, always attracts attention. Its large white rings are deposits of magnesium and sodium salts, formed when the lake water evaporates. The curative power of Epsom salts for a variety of ailments is widely accepted. First Nations people called the lake *Klilok* ("Medicine Lake"), and used to soak in its soft mud for relief from rheumatism and arthritis, as well as venerating it as a place of spiritual significance. The lake had been the source of blockades in the 1990s, when private owners wanted to develop it as a spa and/or export its mud. In 2001, the Okanagan Band and the federal government purchased the land, so its legacy to the First Nations people can be protected.

### While You're In Keremeos ... Top Seven

1. Poke around Keremeos Museum (6th Avenue and 6th Street). Housed in a former jail, it features pioneer artifacts and police memorabilia (250-499-5445).
2. Search for agate, jasper and opal in the nearby hills.
3. Hike into Keremeos Columns Provincial Park (3 hrs.; strenuous) to view 30-metre natural basalt columns, formed by cooling lava over 30 million years ago.
4. Sample wine at local wineries—Crowsnest Vineyards in Cawston (250-499-5129) and St. Lazlo Estate Winery in Keremeos (205-499-5600).
5. Join in the fun at the Elks Rodeo in May and the Chopaka Rodeo on Easter weekend.
6. Spend an afternoon at the Grist Mill.
7. Buy fruit and vegetables at a fruit stand.

## Osoyoos

120 km (75 mi.) east of Princeton. Population: 4379. Info Centre: junction of Highways 3 and 97, next to the Husky station. Box 227, V0H 1V0. 250-495-7142; Fax: 250-495-6161. Toll free: 1-888-676-9667. Email: tourism@osoyooschamber.bc.ca. Web: www.osoyooschamber.bc.ca

Like many modern communities along this route, Osoyoos was an important Native camping place for thousands of years before European settlement. The name comes from the Salish word *soyoos* meaning "crossing point" or

*Osoyoos lies at the southern end of the Okanagan Valley, a broad glacial trough noted for its warm summer temperatures and fertile agricultural land.*

"the place two lakes come together", a reference to the natural land bridge that almost divides Osoyoos Lake in two.

The site was a stopping point along the early Fur Brigade Trail between Fort Okanagan (at the head of navigation on the Columbia River) and Fort Kamloops. Later it was an important way station for gold miners. By 1890, cattle ranchers had taken over, and in 1906 the first orchards were planted. Like Keremeos, Osoyoos boasts the earliest fruit ripening dates in the Okana-

gan, and there are several roadside stands along the highway. Osoyoos Lake, claimed by locals to be the warmest freshwater lake in Canada, has made the town a

popular resort and retirement centre.

Haynes Point Provincial Park, 2 km south of town and 2 km north of the US border, is a popular place. The sandspit

## Osoyoos Special Events –Best Bets

**June**–Cherry Fiesta Days

**August**–High Country Blues Festival; Mt. Kobau Star Gazing Party

**September**–Rock Creek Fall Fair

## While You're In Osoyoos ... Top Ten

1. Explore Canada's only true desert, the "Vest Pocket Desert" on the northeast side of Osoyoos Lake, accessible from both Osoyoos and Oliver.
2. Hear a naturalist's talk at Haynes Point Provincial Park.
3. Take in the spectacular view from Mount Kobau, a favourite spot for hikers and amateur astronomers. Access is by a forestry road 11 km west of Osoyoos. Watch for signs off Hwy 3.
4. Stop at a roadside stand for fresh fruit and vegetables.
5. Pop in at a local winery for a tour and a taste.
6. What the heck—parasail! Or rent a boat and go water-skiing. Or keep it simple and go for a swim.
7. Hit the slopes at Mount Baldy ski area (250-498-4087).
8. Stroll along the waterfront on the Pioneer Walkway.
9. Cycle the 20-km route between Osoyoos and Oliver along the Okanagan River. (Head east on any of the turnoffs from Hwy 97 between McAlpine Bridge and Road 22.)
10. Delve into the past at the Osoyoos Museum (250-495-6090) at Community Park. It is housed in the 1891 log cabin that was the town's first schoolhouse and later its jail and courthouse.

that makes up the park stretches three quarters of the way across Osoyoos Lake and used to be a favourite shortcut for early ranchers. Now the beachfront campsites are in high demand, making reservations necessary.

The border crossing south of town is open 24 hours.

## Okanagan Highland

East of Osoyoos, Highway 3 winds its way around several hairpin turns up Anarchist Mountain (summit elevation: 1233 m). Viewpoints at the top give a spectacular panoramic view of Washington state and the Okanagan Valley—definitely stop and take a look. In the spring, the blossoming orchards are an added bonus. The mountain was named after an Irish settler, Richard Sidley, who apparently headed for the hills when his politics were branded too revolutionary for his government employers.

Highway 3 passes through the ranchland and wheat fields of the Okanagan Highland.

## Vest Pocket Desert

**One of the more fascinating** natural attractions in the south Okanagan is the "Vest Pocket Desert," Canada's only true desert and an extension of the Great Basin Desert of the United States.

Part of this small geographical anomaly has been designated as a provincial ecological reserve, on the east side of Osoyoos Lake between Oliver and Osoyoos. Supporting unique plants and wildlife, the desert is home to several species not found anywhere else in the country. The desert, which receives less than 20 cm of precipitation annually, supports a large concentration of birds of prey. Canada's smallest bird, the calliope hummingbird, also lives here. So does the kangaroo rat, whose body is 65 percent water, although it never takes a drink.

The habitat also supports Great Basin spadefoot toads, western skinks (small lizards), western painted turtles, Pacific rattlesnakes and praying mantises.

Prickly pear cactus and rabbit brush are among the plant life. Native pictographs and remains of *kekuli* can be seen as well. April and May are good times to see desert flowers.

Access from Osoyoos: Follow the signs to the Inkameep Campground (250-495-7279), run by the Osoyoos Indian Band. They can give permission to travel across their land to the desert. (In winter, call the band office: 250-498-3444.)

Access from Oliver: south of town turn east on Road 22, cross the Osoyoos River, drive north past the deserted Haynes Ranch, and then take a sharp right to the ecological reserve.

The Osoyoos Desert Society (1-877-889-0897; Web: www.desert.org/) offers interpretive tours (south of Hwy. 97 at 146th Street) of a protected area of desert on the other side of the lake. Seasonal. Admission charged.

Many old homesteads are visible from the highway and there are several guest ranches in the area. Tours to the floor of Rock Creek Canyon, just east of the bridge, offer explanations of the flora, fauna, and history of the area. Visitors can also rent horses or four-wheel drive vehicles. (Gold Canyon Highlands Tourism Association, RR 1, Rock Creek, V0H 1Y0, 250-446-2455.)

Just west of the bridge is the turnoff to Mt. Baldy (250-498-4087), a family-oriented ski area also accessible from Oliver in the Okanagan

(16 runs, 2 lifts, 522 vertical metres). The road also travels by the site of Camp McKinney, one of the earliest lode gold camps in the province. The area that stretches from here to Christina Lake was home to a number of rip-roaring gold mining towns beginning in the 1890s. Cascade, Anaconda, Deadwood, and Eholt are just a few of the places that once housed thousands, and no longer exist.

Rock Creek is picturesquely situated in the Kettle River Valley. Prospectors discovered gold here in 1859, and the tiny

town still has the flavour of a frontier settlement. Although a massive influx of miners didn't materialize, Governor James Douglas in Victoria anticipated one, and contracted 24-year-old Edgar Dewdney to build a trail from Hope to Rock Creek. The Dewdney Trail, surveyed by the Royal Engineers, was pushed through to Princeton in the fall of 1860 and to Rock Creek in the fall of 1861, just as the gold began to peter out. (If you're driving through in September, plan to stop at the Rock Creek Fall Fair.)

## Kettle Valley Railway

**Of the many railways** that appeared in the Interior during the 1890s and early 1900s, the Kettle Valley Railway is the one that seems to have captured the imagination of railway buffs.

Construction of the line faced the challenge of rugged terrain, political and physical battles, declining markets, slides, avalanches, and washouts. The two greatest railway tycoons of the century—Canadian J.J. Hill, who controlled the Great Northern Railroad (US), and American William Van Horne, who controlled the Canadian Pacific Railway—made the Kettle Valley Railway a personal battleground. Both were vying for control over the lucrative market in the southern Interior, brought about by the mining boom in the Kootenays.

The Crowsnest Agreement of 1897 gave the CPR rights to a rail line from the east across the southern Interior to Nelson. But J.J. Hill was determined to maintain control of the area by buying and building spur lines that connected to the US. In 1905, workers from the two sides actually came to blows over a right-of-way dispute near Midway.

Work finally began on the line connecting Midway to Hope in 1910. Despite a lack of skilled workers and the First World War, the railway was completed in 1916.

It was finally the internal combustion engine that spelled the end of the Kettle Valley line with the opening of the Hope-Princeton Highway in 1948.

The railway closed forever in 1964. Today many portions of the railway have been reclaimed for recreational use in the "rails to trails" movement. (For trail information: www.planet.eon.net/%7Edan/kvr.html).

Highway 33 north of here is an alternate route to Kelowna and Big White ski area along the West Kettle River. The Kettle Valley Recreation Area, just north of Rock Creek, is a popular spot for hikers and bikers wanting to explore the old Kettle Valley Railway line. The Kettle River offers good canoeing, inner tubing, and fishing.

## Midway

50 km (31 mi.) east of Osoyoos. Population: 682. Info Centre: at the CPR Station Museum on the highway. Box 32, V0H 1M0. Phone and Fax: 250-449-2614. Web: midway-bc.cjb.net

"Midway between what and what?" you might ask. This small community is about halfway between Vancouver and the Alberta border. It was also about halfway on the Dewdney Trail. And some say it was named after the midway at the Chicago World's Fair. Take your pick!

This used to be part of the camping and hunting grounds of the Okanagan people. When the 49th parallel was established as the boundary

### Edgar Dewdney

*The Dewdney Trail as it looks today near Highway 3. Some sections are maintained as hiking trails.*

**Road Builder and Lieutenant-Governor**

Englishman Edgar Dewdney was only 24 years old when he arrived in Victoria in May 1859. The energetic civil engineer was never to dig for the gold that had brought him here, but he made an immense contribution to the development of the Interior. Loyal, single-minded, and unafraid of confrontation, he was involved in most of the major transportation projects in the Interior over the next 50 years.

He is best remembered for his work on the Dewdney Trail, begun in 1859, and continued in 1860 with surveyor Walter Moberly (who later found the Eagle Pass through the Selkirk Mountains and did extensive surveying for the CPR). The next year gold was discovered at Rock Creek just west of present-day Osoyoos, and Moberly and Dewdney extended the road there.

From 1862 to 1864, Dewdney was involved in building the Cariboo Wagon Road. When gold was discovered at Wild Horse Creek in the East Kootenay in 1864, Dewdney was contracted to continue the road from Rock Creek east.

"I shall never forget what pleasure and enjoyment I had when walking over the frozen summits on a bright sunshiny early morning, the sun dazzling in the snow, which seemed studded with millions of diamonds, and the air bracing and seeming to give fresh life with every breath you drew", he later wrote.

*Edgar Dewdney's long career in British Columbia included stints as road builder and lieutenant-governor.*

In 1868, Dewdney began a career in government, appointed as provincial representative for the Kootenays in Victoria. In 1872, following Confederation, he became a federal Member of Parliament. In 1879 he was appointed Indian commissioner for the North-West Territories and the area's lieutenant-governor in 1881. After another term as an MP, he was appointed lieutenant-governor of British Columbia in 1892.

When he retired in 1897, Dewdney returned to engineering, helping to choose the Kettle Valley Railway route. He died in 1916, the year the railway was completed.

between the US and Canada in 1846, however, no thought was given to First Nations people who lived on both sides of the newly established border. Members of the band entwined two saplings to symbolize the spiritual unity of the Okanagan people. The trees live to tell the tale today in a town park.

In 1905, Midway was the site of a railway battle between workers of the CPR and its rival, the US-owned Great Northern Railway (GNR). The feud, based on a bitter conflict between CPR's William Van Horne and GNR's J.J. Hill, occurred when CPR workers blocked the GNR crew's attempt to lay line over CPR ground. The GNR group attacked the barricade and the CPR workers' tent camp. The CPR brought in reinforcements and began ripping up enemy track. GNR rolled out the barbed wire. Both sides fought off the autumn chill with good stiff drinks, gained courage, and had at each other with fists, shovels, and picks.

*The sole surviving example of the large frame courthouses once found throughout the Interior, this 1902 building is now used as Greenwood's city hall.*

Luckily no one was killed, and the dispute was settled in court with GNR winning expropriation rights over the disputed land. Eventually, however, the CPR gained control of the rail lines to Hope. Midway's railroading days ended in the 1990s, when the CPR shut down its route to Castlegar.

## Greenwood

13 km (8 mi.) east of Midway. Population: 758. Info Centre: 214 South Copper Street, Box 399, V0H 1J0. Phone/Fax: 250-445-6355.

Seasonal. Email: musuemgwd@direct.ca. Web: www.greenwood-heritage.bc.ca

Greenwood, like most towns in this area, was created by a mining boom that began in 1886. Hidden among the trees on the mountainside are some beautiful turn-of-the-century homes. Their domes, bay windows, and verandas are reminders of the town's more prosperous days. The Info Centre has a driving/walking tour brochure describing over 40 heritage homes and buildings.

## While You're In Midway ... Top Three

1. Visit the original railway station, beside the highway just west of town, which houses the Info Centre and the Kettle River Museum (250-449-2229).
2. Picnic beside the Entwined Trees (Sixth Avenue and Haynes).
3. Hike or bike the Trans Canada Trail, accessible here. This is "mile zero" of the famed Kettle Valley Railway trails.

## While You're In Greenwood ... Top Ten

1. Explore the eerie moonscape of Lotzkar Park—not your usual run-of-the-mill park beside a river.
2. Drop in at the Greenwood Museum, right on Highway 3 (it's also the Info Centre).
3. Enjoy Greenwood hospitality at the Strawberry Social in May.
4. Take a side trip to a ghost town such as nearby Phoenix or Deadwood.
5. Hike or bike the Trans Canada Trail—Greenwood is a designated "Gateway Community."
6. Cast a line at Jewel Lake, 9 km east, for year-round fishing, or at Wilgress Lake Rest Area, 15 km east.
7. Thrill to the annual Demolition Derby in June.
8. Do some birdwatching on the Boundary Creek Nature Walk.
9. View the heritage buildings on the self-guided tour.
10. Cheer for your favourite at the annual soapbox derby in July.

*"Golden Heights," a Grand Forks landmark, was built by travelling dentist George Averil in 1895 for a cost of $6000. The showplace home included a carriage house, maids' quarters, a private ballroom, and Michelangelo-style gilt ceilings.*

## While You're In Grand Forks ... Top Ten

1. Learn about Doukhobor history and culture at Mountain View Doukhobor Museum on Hardy Mountain Road.
2. Attend a Doukhobor choir festival. Traditional Doukhobor singing is a capella and the harmonies are extraordinary. Ask at the Info Centre.
3. Stop for lunch at a restaurant offering borscht, perogis, and other typical Russian dishes.
4. Take a walking tour to view the beautiful turn-of-the-century buildings.
5. Explore the Boundary Museum (7370 - 5th Street, 250-442-3737) for displays and information about the area's multi-layered history.
6. Shop for gifts at Grand Forks Art Gallery (7340 - 5th Street, 250-442-2211), which features local and touring exhibitions.
7. Dig for quartz, amber and other gems at the Rock Candy Mine (book through Info Centre: 250-442-2833).
8. Stroll the Farmers Market at Grand Forks City Park, every Tuesday and Thursday in the summer.
9. Ski Phoenix Mountain (250-442-2813), 21 km west of town on Highway 3.
10. Drive the picturesque road up one side of the Granby River and down the other.

The large brick tower standing sentry at the west of town is a remnant of the BC Copper Company smelter. This once-busy facility processed ore from the Phoenix, Mother Lode, and other area mines, employing 400 men from 1901 to 1918. Visitors can tour the eerily beautiful slag piles of Lotzkar Memorial Park, which has been described as one of BC's great industrial ruins. (Cross the bridge at Washington Street on the west side of town.) The heritage brick building next to the park that until recently housed West Kootenay Power is slated to become a mining interpretive centre.

Although it now bills itself as "the smallest town in Canada", at one time Greenwood had a population of 10,000, and along with Phoenix, was considered to be a city of major significance. Although almost a ghost town by 1930, 1200 Japanese-Canadians were interned here during World War II. Several remained after the war to call it home. Fittingly, several scenes in the American feature film *Snow Falling on Cedars* were shot here in 1998.

## Grand Forks

35 km (22 mi.) east of Greenwood. Population: 4297. Info Centre: 7326 - 5th Street, Box 1086, V0H 1H0. 250-442-2833; Fax: 250-442-5688. Email: gfchambe@sunshinecable.com. Web: www.boundary.bc.ca
Ideally situated in the "Sunshine Valley" where the Granby and Kettle rivers meet, this broad, lush flatland has

housed people for hundreds of years.

The huge Granby smelter once dominated the town, processing ore from Phoenix and other area mines in the mining boom of the 1890s. Agriculture and logging are now the major industries.

Visitors driving into town from the west will notice the large brick buildings across the highway to the south. This is the remnant of one of many Doukhobor communal settlements, the large farms created by Russian peasants who immigrated to Canada in the 1890s. Although the commu-

nal experiment was largely abandoned in 1937 when the community went bankrupt, many Doukhobor people still live in the area, maintaining to varying degrees the customs and traditions of their forefathers (and mothers).

## The Blueberry-Paulson

Highway 3 continues past Grand Forks to the popular summer resort town of Christina Lake. One of the warmest lakes in Canada, the town has a variety of campgrounds, motels, and boat launching sites. Pictographs

on the rock cliffs at Texas Creek Provincial Park on the east side of the lake attest to ancient occupancy of the area. Ole Johnson Marine Park, accessible only by boat, has excellent fishing for kokanee, rainbow trout, whitefish, and carp.

The Blueberry-Paulson stretch of Hwy. 3, between Christina Lake and Castlegar, climbs to Bonanza Pass (1535 m) through remote forest land of the Monashee Range before dropping back down to Castlegar on Lower Arrow Lake. Old log trappers' cabins can be glimpsed occasionally along

## Doukhobors

**In the late 19th century**, 7400 Russian peasants known as Doukhobors left their homeland looking for a new place to live. Persecuted from the time they separated from the Russian Orthodox Church in the 17th century, they were condemned as "spirit wrestlers" by an early church official. The Doukhobors adapted the name to mean "those who wrestle for and with the Holy Spirit". Their motto became "toil and peaceful life".

They espoused pacifism, rejecting church liturgy and secular government. An oral culture, their teaching was passed down through a "living Bible" of psalms and hymns.

In 1898, with the aid of novelist Leo Tolstoy and the Quakers, the Doukhobors settled on communal farms in the area now known as Saskatchewan. Although they received special dispensation regarding education and military service, in 1905 this

special status was revoked.

In 1908, led by Peter "the Lordly" Verigin, 6000 Doukhobors trekked to BC, rebuilding their communal farms in the Grand Forks and Castlegar areas. But the group's troubles were far from over.

In 1924, Peter Verigin was killed when the train on which he was riding was allegedly bombed. During the 1930s, lending institutions foreclosed and the communal lands went into receivership.

In the 1950s and 1960s, government again put pressure on

the Doukhobors, forcing their children into public schools. A radical sect, the Sons of Freedom, gained notoriety through protest methods that included arson and nude marches. Although less active today, Sons of Freedom members still protest what they perceive to be a corruption of the original vision.

Many Doukhobor people continue to live in the West Kootenay. A substantial number continue to speak Russian and maintain cultural traditions such as pacifism, vegetarianism, and religious customs.

*Rossland was a booming mining town from 1887 to 1916. Today, Red Mountain's nearby slopes attract outdoor enthusiasts from around the world for hiking, biking and skiing.*

## Nancy Greene–Gold Medal Skier

**"She's great,"** said US ski team coach Bob Beattie of Nancy Greene in 1967. "She'll fight you to win. I've been trying to get her to defect for five years." Luckily, for Canada, the Rossland-based skier stayed home.

Described by *Sports Illustrated* in 1968 as "friendly but frank" with "the instincts of a

Canadian Mountie", Greene was known for her aggressive skiing style. Her nickname was "Tiger".

Born in Ottawa, Greene learned to ski on Rossland's Red Mountain at age three, but didn't begin competitive racing until 1958 when she was 14. She skied in her first Olympics at age 16, in Squaw Valley.

In 1967 and 1968, Greene turned the skiing world on its ear by breaking the stranglehold of the French and Austrians on world championships. Among her awards were two world cups in 1967 and 1968, and Olympic gold and silver medals in 1968. She was named Canada's 1968 athlete of the year.

Greene retired form competitive skiing in 1968. She married her coach, Al Raine, and is now director of skiing at Sun Peaks Resort near Kamloops.

the route. Motorists often see deer and black bear.

A variety of forestry and logging roads provide good access to off-road exploration, snowmobiling, and cross-country skiing.

## Rossland

28 km (17 mi.) south of junction with Highway 3 on Highway 3B. Population: 3825. Info Centre: Junction of Highways 3B and 22. Box 26, V0G 1Y0. 250-362-7722; Fax: 250-362-5379. Toll free: 1-888-448-7444. Seasonal. Web: www.rossland.com/. Email: museum@rossland.com
Rossland experienced a major gold rush in the 1890s, and today the main street, combining the town's mining roots with its popularity as a ski destination, is reminiscent of jet-set ski resorts in Colorado, without the jet-set price tags. Billing itself "BC's Mountain Biking Capital", this charming

## Alternate Route: Rossland and Trail via Highway 3B

**Nancy Greene Provincial Park**
Forty-seven km east of Grand Forks, Nancy Greene Lake sits at the junction with Highway 3B to Rossland. The park and the nearby recreation area to the south are named after Rossland's Olympic ski champion, Nancy Greene.

The park's alpine lake is a great place for a picnic, and features a self-guided nature trail also used for cross-country skiing in the winter. No motorized boating is allowed on the lake. Fishing is for rainbow trout.

*This scale model of a 20-metre high Picasso sculpture overlooks the Columbia River in downtown Trail.*

town offers no end of outdoor recreation thrills.

During its prime from 1887 to 1916, Rossland boasted a population of 7000, supporting 42 saloons, 17 law firms, 4 newspapers, 3 breweries, and a daily train to Spokane. It was BC's third largest city in 1897 and produced one-half of the province's gold. Red Mountain's rich deposits of gold, copper, and silver contributed to the establishment of Cominco, a major Canadian mining conglomerate with a smelter in nearby Trail.

Red Mountain hosted a number of mines. In its heyday the 548-metre LeRoi shaft was the deepest mine in Canada, producing nearly $75 million worth of gold in its lifetime, which ended in 1929. Tours take you 100 metres below the surface. Staff say it is the only genuine hardrock gold mine in Canada open to the public.

Another legacy of the prosperous mining days can be found in the stained glass and other fine detail of the area's heritage homes and buildings. Built in 1897, the Miner's Hall was the first union hall in the province. In the summer, Tuesday to Sunday in the hall, local performers present a light opera production based on Rossland's early days.

The historic town is also the site of renowned Red Mountain (1-800-663-0105). Located in Nancy Greene

## While You're In Rossland ... Top Ten

1. Take the LeRoi Underground Mine Tour (junction of Highways 22 and 3B. 250--362-7722).
2. Stop at the Rossland Historical Museum (250-362-7722), which houses the Western Canada Ski Hall of Fame, on the same site.
3. Hike the old Dewdney Trail between Rossland and Christina Lake (part of the Trans Canada Trail) or take an easy walk along the Railgrade at the south end of town.
4. Catch the Gold Fever Follies at the Old Miners Hall (summer).
5. Frolic in the snow at the annual Rossland Winter Carnival in January (running since 1897).
6. Join in the celebrations at the Rubberhead Mountain Bike Challenge in September.
7. Ski Red Mountain.
8. Tap your feet at the Rossland Light Opera Society's annual presentation in February and March.
9. Bike a variety of trails—ask at the Info Centre.
10. Stroll along Columbia Avenue and browse through the shops.

*Built as a small facility in 1895, the Teck-Cominco smelter in Trail now dominates the landscape.*

## Trail

8 km (5 mi.) east of Rossland, 27 (17 mi.) km south of Castlegar on Highway 22. Population: 7728. Info Centre: 200 - 1199 Bay Avenue, V1R 4A4. 250-368-3144; Fax: 250-368-6427. Toll free: 1-877-636-9569. Email: tcoc@netidea.com. Web: www.trailchamber.bc.ca

Trail has been a major force in BC's economy for decades. Originally a river port shuttling supplies to miners, in 1895 it became a modest facility to process Red Mountain ore, and later home to Cominco (now Teck Cominco), operator of the largest lead-zinc smelter in the world. Today the smelter processes more than 300,000 tonnes of zinc and 120,000 tonnes of lead annually from mines around the world. Its 120-metre-high smokestacks, perched high above the downtown area on the banks of the Columbia, dominate the landscape.

Many of the men who came to work in the mines and on the railway in the 1890s and early 1900s were Italians who stayed to work in the smelter. This Italian heritage is strongly present in Trail to this day.

Provincial Recreation Area just north of the city, the area attracts Nordic and alpine skiers from around the world to its 850 metres of vertical drop and 83 runs. No johnny-come-lately of the ski world, it hosted the first Canadian Downhill Championships in 1897. Besides being the home slope of Nancy Greene, Red Mountain raised Kerrin Lee-Gartner, a gold medallist in the 1992 Winter Olympics. Other outdoor destinations include 2400-metre Old Glory Mountain, popular with hikers and berry pickers.

## Deer

**The most abundant** big-game animals in North America, deer are members of a family of hooved ruminants *(Cervidae)* that includes 40 species worldwide.

The two North American species are the white-tailed deer and the black-tailed deer. The only variety of whitetail in BC is the northwest whitetail, most commonly found in the southeastern Interior. The only variety of black-tail in the Interior is the mule deer, found from the Coast Mountains to the Rockies.

Deer are very common on Interior highways, and at night they can be a genuine hazard. Attracted to headlights, they will leap into the path of oncoming vehicles, causing serious accidents. If you see eyes staring at you from the side of the road, slow down, turn down your high beams, and keep alert.

*Mule deer*

**93**

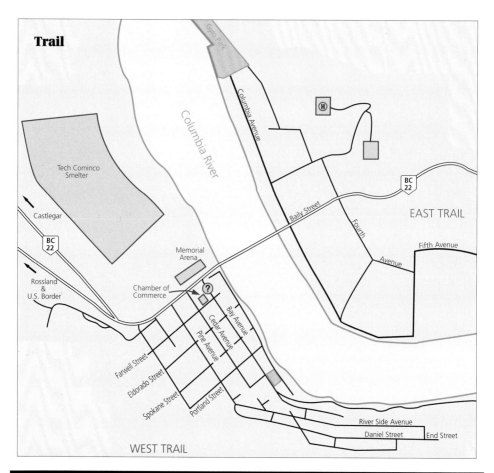

**Trail**

Gyro Park

Columbia River

Columbia Avenue

Tech Cominco Smelter

Castlegar

BC 22

Baily Street

Fourth

EAST TRAIL

BC 22

Fifth Avenue

Avenue

Rossland & U.S. Border

Memorial Arena

Chamber of Commerce

?

Bay Avenue

Cedar Avenue

Pine Avenue

Farwell Street

Eldorado Street

Spokane Street

Portland Street

River Side Avenue

Daniel Street

End Street

WEST TRAIL

## While You're In Trail ... Top Ten

1. Browse the archives of the Columbia Lodge (584 Rossland Avenue; 250-364-2052). It offers summer tours of its archives, depicting the history of Italian immigrants—one of the strongest collections on the continent.

2. Join in the fun on Silver City Days, held every May.

3. Enjoy authentic Italian restaurants—our favourite is the Colander (1475 Cedar Avenue, 250-364-1816). Be prepared to sit at long family-style tables and get to know your neighbours.

4. Pick up a historical walking tour brochure at the Info Centre.

5. Search out memorabilia from the Trail Smoke Eaters' world-championship hockey teams from the 1950s and 1960s at the City of Trail Museum at the Memorial Centre.

6. Enjoy Gyro Park's beautiful gardens; walk the 3-km trail along the east bank of the Columbia River.

7. Take a tour of Waneta and Seven Mile dams on the nearby Pend'Oreille (pon-dor-eye) River on Highway 22A southeast of Trail (250-367-7521). Waneta's generators produce enough power to supply a city of 250,000.

8. Canoe Champion Lakes Provincial Park, 12 km east on Highway 3B.

9. View wildlife along the Pend'Oreille River between Waneta and Nelway. It's the only habitat for preying mantis in the province outside the Okanagan.

10. Tour the smelter. (Tours start at the interpretive centre above the TD Bank at 1199 Bay Avenue. Free; some restrictions; 250-368-3144.)

*Alexander Zuckerberg built a replica of a Russian chapel on his island retreat in Castlegar in the 1930s.*

## While You're In Castlegar ... Top Ten

1. Visit Verigin's Tomb, the burial spot of Doukhobor spiritual leader, Peter "the Lordly" Verigin, on the mountainside above Brilliant.

2. Explore the Doukhobor Village Museum (just across from the airport on Highway 3) and its re-creation of a typical communal farm.

3. Wander through Zukerberg Island Heritage Park, the retreat of a Russian mystic, Alexander Zuckerberg, who came to Castlegar in 1931 to teach Doukhobor children.

4. Shop for gifts at the Kootenay Gallery of Art, History and Science (250-365-3337) gift store.

5. Enjoy a look at the past at the Railway Station CPR Museum (400 - 13th Street, 250-365-6440), the focal point of Castlegar from 1902 until daily passenger service was discontinued in 1949.

6. Take in the events at the Pass Creek Fall Fair every September.

7. Walk the Waldie Island Trail across the river at Robson, with interpretive displays of local and natural history.

8. View wildlife at Syringa Creek Provincial Park across the lake to the northeast. Rocky Mountain bighorn sheep, elk, whitetailed and mule deer, mountain goats, and a number of bird species inhabit the area.

9. Go fishing on the Arrow Lakes.

10. Sample fresh fruit and vegetables in season across the river at Robson.

## Castlegar

94 km (56 mi.) east of Grand Forks on Highway 3. Population: 7427. Info Centre: 1995 - 6th Avenue, V1N 4B7, next to the Recreation Centre. 250-365-6313; Fax: 250-365-5778. Email: cdcic@look.ca. Web: www.kootenay.org. Also: www.castlegar.com.

Castlegar, like Trail, is primarily an industrial town. But its strategic location on a plateau at the confluence of the Kootenay and Columbia Rivers has made it an important settlement site for centuries.

The earliest residents were the Interior Salish. For 3500 years, they used the area now known as Zukerberg Island as a camp while fishing for Pacific salmon. Fur traders subsequently moved into the area, followed by miners, farmers, and orchardists. The Columbia River and Arrow Lakes were an early transportation route to Revelstoke for rivermen and sternwheelers.

As in Grand Forks,

**95**

Doukhobors settled in the nearby communities of Brilliant and Ootischenia in 1904. Here again, the remains of their communal farms and abandoned orchards can still be seen from the highway. Castlegar is also a centre for outdoor recreation, including wildlife viewing, biking, snowmobiling, hiking and cross-country skiing. Castlegar bills itself as the "gateway to the Arrow Lakes", and offers access to almost 100 km of freshwater fishing and boating.

The Keenleyside Dam, just north of town, was built as part of the 1964 Columbia River Treaty between Canada and the US. This controversial document legislated the flooding of the Arrow Lakes for flood control and generation of hydroelectric power. Many small towns and farms along the shores of the lake were submerged amid a great deal of controversy, which lasts to this day.

From Castlegar, Highway 3A continues along the Kootenay River to Nelson (see West Kootenay section). The Crowsnest route carries on to the village of Salmo.

## Salmo

43 k (27 mi.) east of Castlegar on Highway 3. Population: 1253. This small town is worth a stop for its heritage buildings and stonework murals. From the west, travellers pass a small ski hill and the "oldest telephone booth in the world".

The Salmo River, which follows Highway 3 south of here, was known as the Salmon River long before the days of the hydroelectric dams and

downstream power benefits. As a result of damming on the Columbia system, today this river has no salmon, but still hosts Dolly Varden trout.

On Sheep Creek Road, 8 km south of town, lie the ruins of several old mines with typically evocative names: Kootenay Bell, Reno, and Goldbelt. This and other secondary roads in the area are good for wildlife viewing and cross-country skiing.

## Western Red Cedar

*Arbor vitae*

There are no true cedars native to North America. The species here are *Arbor vitae,* which means "tree of life".

A mainstay of BC's lumber industry, cedar, while lightweight and brittle, is easy to split, and resistant to rot. It is valued for shingles, posts, and exterior siding.

The tree's tiny scale-like leaves form flat, lacy sprays that are highly aromatic. The cones bear up to 400,000 seeds per pound, making the tree one of the most prodigious seed producers of the evergreen species.

Mature trees, with their tapered trunks, and shallow, widespread root systems, can reach heights of 60 metres and measure three to four metres in diameter. The largest red cedars are believed to be about 1000 years old.

Native cultures in the Northwest relied heavily on cedar for housing, totem poles, decorative carving, and dugout canoes. The bark of mature trees was peeled off in strips that were used to make clothing, floor coverings, and baskets.

*The abandoned Brilliant Bridge, made of hand poured concrete by Doukhobors in the early 1900s, crosses the Kootenay River east of Castlegar.*

## The Kootenay Skyway

The route between Salmo and Creston over the Selkirk Range is known as the Kootenay Skyway. When the weather is fine, the drive over 1774-metre high Kootenay Pass is spectacular. Snow, avalanches, and limited visibility contribute to frequent closures during the winter. The alternate route is through Nelson and Highway 3A. Listen to the radio or ask locally for current information.

At the summit, enjoy the pure mountain air at Stagleap Provincial Park while you picnic at or walk around picturesque Bridal Lake. You can observe the transition

### Columbia River: Ten SuperGuide Facts

1. 2044 km long, 763 km in BC.
2. Headwaters: Columbia Lake near Canal Flats in East Kootenay.
3. The Big Bend Highway, which opened in 1940, followed the Columbia River between Revelstoke and Golden. It was the shortest highway route through the Rockies until the Rogers Pass portion of the Trans-Canada Highway opened in 1962.
4. Major tributaries include the Kootenay and Okanagan rivers in BC and the Snake River in the US.
5. Its drainage basin is 155,000 square km—one of the largest in North America. Over 100,000 square km are in BC.
6. Spanish explorers originally named it Rio de San Roque, but it was renamed by early explorer Captain Robert Gray after his ship *Columbia*.
7. David Thompson was the first to chart the entire river, arriving at its mouth in 1811.
8. The Hudson's Bay Company built Fort Vancouver on the Columbia (now Vancouver, Washington) in 1824-25, creating the major transportation route from the south into the Interior.
   Canada and the US ratified the Columbia River Treaty in 1964. The controversial terms included a one-time payment for power benefits of $254 million (US).
9. The treaty resulted in Duncan Dam (1967) on Kootenay Lake, Hugh Keenleyside Dam (1968) on Lower Arrow Lake, Mica Dam (1973) on the Big Bend, and Revelstoke Dam (1984). The treaty cannot be renegotiated until 2024.
10. Number of dams in BC: 14.

*Overleaf: The Creston Valley Wildlife Centre is a bird-watcher's paradise, with over 240 bird species to observe.*

between ecological zones. The west side of the Selkirks tends to be more like the coast—wetter, with thicker vegetation—but moving east, the drier vegetation of pine and spruce take over.

Creston is in the Mountain Time Zone. Sometimes. People in Creston don't like to interfere with time, so in the summer, Creston is on Pacific Daylight Saving Time. Ask locally.

## Creston

83 km (52 mi.) east of Salmo. Population: 5161. Info Centre: 1711 Canyon Street, Box 268, V0B 1G0. 250-428-4342; Fax: 250-428-9411. Email: crescofc@kootenay.com. Web: www.crestonbc.com/chamber

Creston is an agricultural and logging community located on a rich floodplain south of Kootenay Lake.

The big attraction in the "Valley of the Swans" is the Creston Valley Wildlife Centre (250-428-3260), located on the west side of Creston and south of Highway 3. The Centre is a 6800-hectare project managed by federal, provincial, and private agencies to conserve vital wetlands for migratory waterfowl. Over 240 bird species, including swan, osprey, and hummingbirds, make this a birdwatcher's paradise. On guided canoe tours or self-

guided nature walks you may also glimpse deer, elk, coyote, and moose. Although the interpretive centre is open in the summer only, the site can be toured in winter by snowshoe or cross-country ski.

The Ktunaxa (Kutenai) people were earlier residents of this area, and surveyor and fur trader David Thompson was likely one of the first Europeans to visit the area in the early 1800s. Unlike many West Kootenay towns, Creston did not begin with the discovery of a precious metal. It was put on the map by the extension of the Dewdney Trail into the mining town of Wild Horse further east, where gold was discovered in the 1860s. The coming of the CPR and Great Northern lines, and the paddlewheelers that sallied forth from here to Kootenay Lake communities like Ainsworth and Kaslo, made Creston a transportation centre.

Logging was a vital part of

the early economy, but no one thought to plant fruit trees on these rich lands until 1908. Today, the fruits, vegetables, and honey sold at roadside stands are a highly valued part of the economy. Creston's two grain elevators are the only ones found in the southern interior.

## Moyie River

About 36 km east of Creston, Highway 3 intersects with Highway 95. A 24-hour border crossing is 11 km south at Kingsgate.

For most of the route to Cranbrook, Highway 3 crosses back and forth over the Moyie River. Forty km east of Creston is a tiny town with the unlikely name of Yahk, a booming lumber and railway centre until the 1930s. Some experts say the town got its name from *yaak*, a Ktunaxa word meaning "bow", referring to the shape of the Kootenay River. Others suggest it comes from the word for arrow, *a'ak*. The town's first hotel, built in 1912,

## Creston Special Events —Best Bets

**April**—Osprey Festival
**May**—Blossom Festival
**July**—Creston Valley Garden Festival
**September**—Fall Fair

## While You're In Creston ... Top Ten

1. Walk the boardwalks and trails or paddle a canoe around the Creston Wildlife Centre. You absolutely have to stop here. It is superb.
2. Go to the drive-in! Yes—Creston boasts one of the few remaining drive-in movie theatres in Canada.
3. See the Ktunaxa canoe at the Stone House Museum (219 Devon Road, 250-428-9262). Its unusual design suggests a link with indigenous people in Russia.
4. Tour the Columbia Brewery or the Kootenay Candle Factory. (Contact the Info Centre for these and other industrial tours.)
5. Wander through the Wayside Gardens and Arboretum, 1/2 mile east on Hwy. 3. (250-428-2062). Seasonal.
6. Camp in a 300-year-old cedar grove at Summit Creek Park.
7. Enjoy the larger-than-life murals on the downtown streets.
8. Shop at roadside stands for fresh produce and honey.
9. Take a gander at the Gateway Ostrich Ranch (BC's largest) in Canyon. (250-428-7239).
10. Golf at the Creston Golf Club. (18 holes; 250-428-5515).

*Moyie's original firehall still stands.*

*Moyie was thriving in 1907 when 400 people were employed at its St. Eugene mine, the largest producer of lead and zinc in the country.*

mines helped establish Cominco's dominance over the mining industry in this area.

The original discovery was made by a Ktunaxa man, Pierre, who was awarded a house, cattle, farm implements, and five dollars a month for his share of the claim. Father Coccola, one of Pierre's partners, built churches at Moyie and St. Eugene Mission near Cranbrook with the $12,000 he received. Between 1898 and 1911, the mine produced $11 million worth of ore.

Paddlewheelers once travelled the waters of Moyie Lake. Today, travellers can stop for a swim, fish for Dolly Varden, kokanee, eastern or brook trout, or examine the intermingling of the dry- and wet-zone ecology in Moyie Lake Provincial Park at the north end of the lake. Popular with locals, the park also offers interpretive services and hiking trails. David Thompson passed this way looking for the mouth of Columbia River in 1808, and was almost turned back by the swollen waters of the Moyie River at spring runoff.

If you've managed to pass this far through mining country without a touch of gold fever, more power to you. Those who are falling prey to the stories of undiscovered mother lodes will be glad to hear that rumours still exist of isolated pay streaks in the Moyie River. Gold panners might also try the Negro and Palmer Bar creeks, both tributaries of the Moyie. Ask locally for directions, regulations, and hot tips.

still operates today, and a small museum offers local history. It is here that you can buy the internationally cherished T-shirt, "I've been to Yahk and back".

Moyie, 34 km east of Yahk, is another Kootenay town that had its glory days in the 1890s. Just west of town on Hwy. 3 you can still see remains of the St. Eugene Mine. In 1907 it was the largest lead-silver mine in Canada and employed 400 men. Establishment of the mine influenced the CPR's decision to build its Crowsnest line across the southern Interior. St. Eugene's consolidation with two Red Mountain

*The restored St. Eugene Church near Cranbrook was originally built when Father Coccola sold his share of the St. Eugene Mine claim in the 1890s.*

## While You're In Cranbrook ... Top Ten

1. Have tea on the luxurious "Argyle" car at the train museum. If you're there at Christmas, go for the gala dinner.

2. Stroll through town on the self-guided walking tour of heritage buildings. Pick up a brochure at the Info Centre or Museum of Rail Travel.

3. Ogle at the priceless hand-painted Italian stained-glass windows, scalloped louvers and buttresses at St. Eugene Mission Church, the finest gothic style mission church in the province (at St. Mary's Reserve on the old airport road 9 km north on Hwy. 95A).

4. Look local fauna in the eyes at the Wildlife Education Centre (250-426-5914) in the Chamber of Commerce building (2279 Cranbrook Street N.).

5. Watch the experts do their thing at the Aasland Museum of Taxidermy (2200 Highway 95A; 250-426-3566).

6. Boat or fish to your heart's content at over 100 lakes within 80 km of town. Those over 65 or under 12 can fish at Idelwild Park just outside town.

7. Celebrate Sam Steele Days in June.

8. Hoot and holler at the Wycliffe Rodeo in August.

9. Relive history at Fort Steele Heritage Town (east on Hwy. 95).

10. Golf at two 18-hole championship courses: Cranbrook Golf Club (1-888-211-8855) and St. Eugene Mission Golf Resort (1-877-417-3133).

## Cranbrook

106 km (66 mi.) east of Creston. Population: 19,874. Info Centre: 2279 Cranbrook Street North, Box 84, V1C 4H6. 250-426-5914; Fax: 250-426-3873.1-800-222-6174. Email: cbkchamber@cyberlink. bc.ca. Web: www.cranbrookchamber.com

Located in a spectacular setting with the Rockies and Purcells looming in the background, Cranbrook was put on the map when developer and politician Colonel James Baker convinced the CPR to build its Crowsnest line through Cranbrook instead of Fort Steele. Since the Colonel owned a great deal of land in the area, the CPR's decision likely made him a very happy man.

Not surprisingly, Cranbrook's major attraction is the Cranbrook Museum of Rail Travel (250-489-3918; www.crowsnest.bc.ca/cmrt) downtown at 1 Van Horne Street. An entire train, the

*Opposite: At one time, paddlewheelers took passengers along Moyie Lake, now a popular recreation destination in the East Kootenays*

"Trans Canada Limited", is on display, as are many other meticulously restored luxury cars and a number of heritage buildings. Several different tours are available, and some include meals or refreshments.

Fitting right in with this heritage train display are the many turn-of-the-century homes and buildings in and around town. Cranbrook also serves as an outdoor recreation centre for hiking, fishing, camping, rockhounding, and a variety of other activities.

Just beyond Cranbrook, you have a choice: Highway 95A heads northwest to Kimberley while Highway 93/95 goes to the heritage town of Fort Steele.

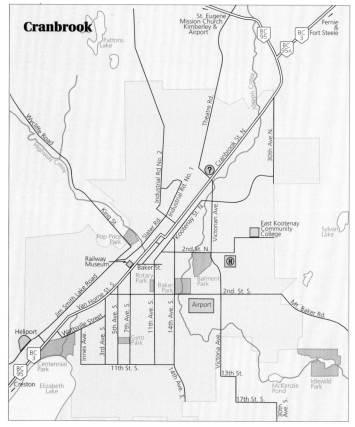

Cranbrook owes its prosperity to the railway—and to Colonel James Baker, who successfully lobbied the CPR to have the Crowsnest line bypass Fort Steele in favour of his town.

Workers have spent many hours carefully restoring the old train cars now on display at Canadian Museum of Rail Travel in Cranbrook.

## Western Painted Turtle

*Chrysemys picta bellie*
Commonly seen in the southern Interior, the western painted turtle is always near water, often basking for hours on floating logs. Their shells are olive green with yellow and red markings, and can measure up to 25 cm.

Turtles eat both plants and animals. Food includes trout fry, tadpoles, water snails, insects, water lilies, and bulrushes.

Nest-building begins in May, usually on a southern slope close to water. The female turtle digs a hole with her rear legs, laying about a dozen small (2 cm) eggs. The young hatch in the fall and stay in the nest until spring.

Good viewing spots are the Okanagan, the Creston Valley Wildlife Centre and Kikomun Creek Provincial Park on Lake Koocanusa.

## Wardner

32 km southeast of Cranbrook
Nearly nine million fish are caught in BC's freshwater lakes and streams each year. Just north of the once-busy lumber town of Wardner on the Wardner-Fort Steele Road, the Kootenay Trout Hatchery and Visitor Centre (250-429-3214) gives you a chance to find out where those fish come from. This facility, the second largest in the province, raises six million rainbow, brook, and cutthroat trout every year. Its extensive interpretive area, which includes aquariums, educational models and displays, and self-guided tours, could very well tell one everything one ever wanted to know about trout—or the endangered white sturgeon, currently being raised at the hatchery.

## Lake Koocanusa

Just north of Wardner, the Kootenay River enters the Lake

## Fore! SuperGuide's Picks on the Crowsnest

**Champion Lakes Golf & Country Club**. 9 holes. Par 72. 5891 yards. Box 158, Fruitvale BC V0G 1L0. 250-367-7001.

**Christina Lake Golf & Country Club**. Semi-private. 18 holes. Par 72. 6680 yards. 250-447-9313. www.christinalakegolfclub.com

**Cranbrook Golf Club**. Semi-private. 18 holes. Par 72. Designed by Geddes, Finlay & Fergie. 6575 yards. www.golfcranbrook.com. 1-888-211-8855.

**Creston Golf Course**. Public. 18 holes. Par 72. 6433 yards. 1800 Mallory Rd., V0B 1G2. 250-428-5515. Email: rpanton@kootenay.com. Web: www.crestonvalley.com/golfcreston/index.html

**Fernie Golf & Country Club**. Semi-private. 18 holes. Par 70. 6556 yards. Box 1507, V0B 1M0. 250-423-7773.

**Osoyoos Golf & Country Club**. Semi-private. 27 holes. Par 72. 6318 yards. Box 798, V0H 1V0. 250-495-7003

**Princeton Golf Course**. 18 holes. Par 72. Box 1346, Darcy Mountain Rd., V0X 1W0. 250-295-6123. Information on all courses in this region: www.bcgolfguide.com.

**St. Eugene Mission Golf Resort**. Semi-private. 18 holes. Opened in 2000. Designed by Les Furber. 250-417-3417; 1-877-417-3133. www.golfsteugene.com

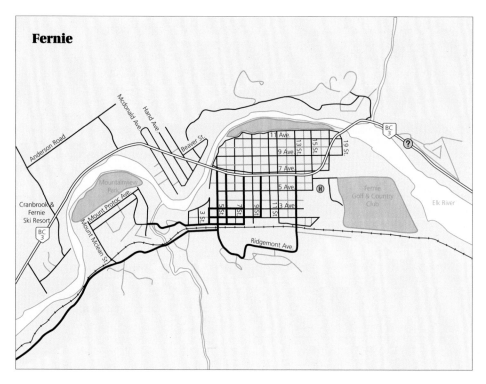

Fernie

Koocanusa reservoir, which drains south into Montana. The 128-km-long lake was created in 1972 when Libby Dam was built in Montana. Although the word "Koocanusa" may seem like some exotic Native word, in fact it is a merging of "Kootenay", "Canada", and "USA." The lake offers excellent fishing and paddling, and is off limits to powerboats.

Kikomum Creek Provincial Park, on the east side of the lake and accessible from Jaffray or Elko, connects several small lakes with paved roads, making it ideal for cycling. Painted turtles, heron rookeries, and fish-spawning channels are among the other attractions.

From Elko, Highway 93 heads 38 km south to the border crossing of Roosville, open 24 hours a day.

## Fernie

87 km (54 mi.) east of Cranbrook. Population: 5272. Info Centre: Highway 3 and Dicken Road, V0B 1M0. 250-423-6868; Fax: 250-423-3811. Email: fernie@elkvalley.net. Web: www.chamber.fernie.bc.ca

If you weren't watching closely, you may not have noticed, but this town is happenin'! The BC Recreation and Parks Association designated it "Best Little Town in BC" in 2001. And if that weren't enough, *Rolling Stone* magazine considers Fernie "the coolest town in North America". With the redevelopment of the old ski hill into the top-flight Fernie Alpine Resort and the upgrading of the Fernie Golf and Country Club into a championship 18-hole course, it's fast becoming a popular tourist/recreation destination.

Originally called Coal Creek, Fernie was established in 1898 with the construction of the CPR's Crowsnest route. The town has had a lot of bad luck over the years, which some trace to a curse set on founding father William Fernie.

The story goes that Mr. Fernie met a group of Natives during a prospecting trip and noticed the chief's daughter was wearing a necklace of coal. In exchange for information about the source of the coal, Fernie agreed to marry the young woman. However, once he found out where the coal deposits were, he backed out, and the woman's mother put a curse on the valley.

It may be that some of Fernie's fluctuating fate has had more to do with world markets than bad karma, but among the disasters were an explosion in 1902 that killed 128 miners, and a fire in 1908 that destroyed 1000 buildings and claimed ten lives. A flood in 1916 and several mining accidents followed.

In 1964, at the invitation of local citizens, the chief of the Tobacco Plains Band lifted the curse in a special ceremony. It is also worth noting that when Mr. Fernie retired to Victoria in 1906, he remained a bachelor and devoted his life to philanthropic pursuits. Curse or no curse, events like the development of coalfields in the northeastern part of BC and unstable world prices have challenged Fernie's economy in recent years.

While some residents are cautious about the town's changing identity, the addition of smart cafés, shops, and adventure tourism companies to downtown streets indicates that Fernie's bad breaks are a thing of the past.

## Sparwood

32 km (20 mi.) east of Fernie. Population: 4167. Info Centre: Highway 3 and Aspen Drive, PO Box 1448, V0B 2G0. 250-425-2423; Fax: 250-425-7130. Toll free: 1-877-485-8185. Email: spwdchamber@titan-link.com

Sparwood is a relatively new town, created in 1966 to replace the turn-of-the-century mining communities of Natal, Michel, and Middleton. Billing itself as "the Clean Coal Capital of the World", it sits atop one of the largest soft coal deposits in North America. Sparwood has one of the largest open-pit mines in Canada (potential annual output: 8 million tonnes) and the world's largest dump truck, the 350-tonne Terex Titan. But there's more to Sparwood than coal and trucks. Check at the Info Centre for the best spots for hiking, canoeing, biking, ATV-ing, cross-country skiing, and more.

The Flathead Valley and the Akamina-Kishinena Provincial Park is accessible via a secondary road 10 km

## While You're In Fernie ... Top Ten

1. Take the self-guided walking tour of heritage buildings. An interesting architectural feature is the atypical brick and stone, designated as building materials after the fire of 1908. The courthouse, the Leroux Mansion, and the Holy Family Catholic Church are examples of this late-Edwardian style.

2. Stroll the trail along the Elk River through town. Take your fishing rod.

3. Ski the powder and see what all the fuss is about at the newly redeveloped Fernie Alpine Resort. (Winter: 102 trails, 5 alpine bowls, tree skiing; 857 vertical metres; longest run 5 km. Summer: fishing, hiking, mountain biking, whitewater rafting, horseback riding. 1-800-258-7669; www.skifernie.com).

4. Play a few rounds at the championship Fernie Golf & Country Club (1-888-754-7325).

5. Soak up local culture at the Elk Valley Art Walk, held each year in July and August.

6. Poke through old photos at the Fernie Heritage Museum (corner of Fifth Avenue and Fifth Street, 250-423-6512).

7. Celebrate snow with what appears to be an almost continuous round of races, derbies, carnivals and special events (November through April). Griz Days Winter Carnival is in March.

8. Tap your feet at The Gathering music festival in August or the Fernie Blues Festival in September.

9. Search for fossils at Mount Fernie Provincial Park (3 km west), which also offers wildlife viewing, old-growth cedar and Lizard Creek water fall.

10. Go whitewater rafting.

## While You're In Sparwood ... Top Five

1. Follow the footprints for the mural walking tour. (Starts at the chamber of commerce building and ends at the Greenwood Mall.)

2. Take a coal mine tour (250-425-2423).

3. Watch for wildlife on the many area trails (eagle, osprey, deer, moose, elk). Drive the Lower Elk Valley road and watch for wild buffalo and elk.

4. Fish: for kokanee at Emerald Lake, for trophy trout in the Elk River.

5. Kick up your heels at Coal Miner Days in June.

east of Sparwood on Highway 3. This is isolated wilderness that promises very good wildlife viewing. Grizzly bear, black bear, elk, moose, and deer are among the species, as well as a significant number of endangered plant species. Home to a large self-sustaining grizzly populations in North America, the park borders on Alberta's Waterton Lakes National Park to the east and Montana's Glacier National Park to the south. Together they form the unique "Crown of the Continent" area of the Rocky Mountains. Conditions are primitive and there are no services. Visitors should be well-prepared, but trails are rated for all levels of ability. No motorized vehicles are allowed in the park.

## Side trip: Elkford

35 km (22 mi.) north of Sparwood on Highway 43. Population: 2866. Info Centre: 4A Front Street, PO Box 220, V0B 1H0. 250-865-4614; Fax: 250-865-2442. Toll free: 1-877-ELK-WILD. Email: ecofc@titan-link.com. Web: www.chamber.elkford.bc.ca

A coal town incorporated in 1970, Elkford bills itself as the "Wilderness Capital of British Columbia". One of the largest bighorn sheep populations

### While You're In Elkford ... Top Five

1. Mush on at the Annual Wilderness Classic Sled Dog Derby in January.
2. Hike, bike, paddle, snowmobile and cross-country ski to your heart's content—get the map from the Info Centre.
3. Tour the backcountry on horseback.
4. Go on up the road to 17,325-hectare Elk Lakes Provincial Park, an easily accessible subalpine wilderness in the middle of the Rockies, for hiking, wildlife viewing or just going gaga over Mother Nature. Hike in. No facilities.
5. Marvel at the great outdoors on the Forest Falls and Lakes Walk. It's only 40 minutes to spectacular Josephine Falls from the parking lot.

### Downhill Ski Resorts on the Crowsnest

(In alphabetical order)

**Fernie Alpine Resort**. 102 trails, 5 alpine bowls, tree skiing; 10 lifts, 13,716 skiers per hour capacity; 857 m vertical; longest run 5 km. Alpine village. Dog sledding, snowboard park, snowmobiling, cross-country, rentals, shopping, night skiing, ski shop, daycare. 1-800-258-7669; www.skifernie.com.

**Gibson Pass Ski Area**. Cascade Mountains, Manning Park (near Hope). 437 m vertical, 24 runs, 4 lifts. Accommodations, rentals, snowboard park, ice rink, shopping, daycare, ski shop. 250-840-8822.

**Kimberley Alpine Ski Resort**. 67 runs, 9 lifts on 1800 skiable acres, 750 m vertical, 23 km of Nordic trails. Alpine village. Four seasons. Snowboard park, cross-country, ice rink, shopping, night skiing, rentals, ski shop, daycare. 1-250-427-4881. www.skikimberley.com/

**Mount Baldy Ski Area** (near Oliver). 16 runs, 2 lifts. 586 m vertical. Accommodations. Cross-country, rentals, restaurants, shopping, ski shop. 250-498-4087.

**Phoenix Mountain** (near Grand Forks). 11 runs, 2 lifts. 244 m vertical. Longest run 1.5 km. Rentals, snowboard park, restaurant, cross-country, night skiing. Family skiing. 250-442-2813.

**Red Mountain**, Rossland. 83 runs, 5 lifts, 2 mountains, 1200 acres. Accommodation, rentals, snowboard park, restaurants, snowmobiling, cross-country, ice rink, shopping, daycare, night skiing, ski shop. 1-800-663-0105; www.ski-red.com/

**Salmo Ski Area**. 4 runs, 2 lifts, 304 m vertical. Rentals, snowboard park, restaurant, cross-country, shopping, night skiing, ski shop. Family skiing. 250-357-2323; home.wkpowerlink.com/~bsaill/ski/

**Whitewater Resort**, Nelson. 38 runs, 3 lifts. 396 m vertical. Accommodations, rentals, snowboard park, cat skiing, restaurants, snowmobiling, cross-country, ice rink, shopping, daycare, ski shop. 250-354-4944, 1-800-666-9420; www.skiwhitewater.com/

and the highest concentration of elk in North America live in the area. The Elk River is noted for trout fishing. Elkford has a 40-km interpretive trail system close to town with a variety of hikes and walks. In winter, cross-country skiers use the same trails. Wapiti Ski Hill (250-865-2020) is the local downhill destination.

## Alberta Border

The Crowsnest Pass (1357 m) and the Alberta border are only 19 km east of Sparwood. The Crowsnest Pass is a centuries-old Ktunaxa route through the Rockies. The Ktunaxa traded with the Plains Natives and made the trip through the pass three times a year to hunt buffalo on the Prairies. The Native word for the large rounded mountain in the pass is *Kah, ka-coo-wut-tskis-lun* ("nesting place of the raven"). Another story says the pass got its name when Blackfoot warriors massacred a group of Crow camped here.

### Elk

*Cervus elaphus*

Also known as wapiti, elk are the most highly evolved of the old world deer, crossing over from Siberia into North America.

Half again as large as an adult deer, a bull elk stands 1.5 metres tall at the shoulder. Wapiti means "white rump" in Shawnee, and this marking helps in identification. The rest of the coat is light brown with darker hair on the neck and legs and a shaggy fringe on the underside of the neck.

Elk are social animals, tending toward open terrain. Females spend most of the year in the valley bottoms with offspring and immature males, sometimes forming herds of 50 or more.

The mating ritual begins in late summer. The males try to attract as many females as possible, and the locking of antlers is a major part of the show. (Elk in rut are very unpredictable; observers should keep their distance.) Gestation is long—up to 240 days. Calves are born in June.

The male's antlers begin to grow in April. The number of points on an antler rack can indicate the age of the animal. Six points, the usual maximum, means the animal is at least four years old. The rack of a mature animal may be as long as 1.5 metres, and as wide as 1.8 metres.

Excellent viewing opportunities exist in the East Kootenay.

# Coquihalla-Nicola

*Nicola Valley lakes boast some of the finest inland fishing in the country.*

The opening of the Coquihalla Highway (Hwy. 5) in 1986 gave easy access to an area that had previously been very out of the way. The controlled-access highway, with its 110-km/hr speed limit, puts Merritt just three hours from Vancouver. Peachland is another hour east over the Okanagan Connector (Hwy. 97C), and Kamloops another 40 minutes north. The rolling grasslands and subalpine forests are appealing, however, and travellers will have to steel their hearts to make that kind of time. No hustle and bustle here; the area's quiet allure lies in its lakes, its remoteness, and its fascinating history.

Stretching from the Cascade Mountains in the south to the Thompson Plateau in the north, the region includes a variety of landscapes, from coastal rain forest and subalpine slopes to rolling grasslands. On the map, it is roughly the area east and south of Highway 1, west of the Okanagan Valley, and north of Highway 3.

(If you want to take a look at what the highway looks like, try logging on to the government's web cam site, where you'll see a minutes-old photograph showing current road and weather conditions: www.th.gov.bc.ca/bchighwaycam/).

Early inhabitants of the Nicola Valley were the Athapascans, who were eventually pushed out or absorbed by the Okanagan and Thompson Salish people. Although initially nomads, about 3000 years ago they became more settled, over-wintering in *kekuli* or pit houses around Merritt, Nicola Lake, and Douglas Lake. Some say that "Nicola" is derived from the name of Chief N'Kwala, who was a Native leader in the area for many years.

*Opposite: Making hay; BC's cattle industry employs about 12,000 people.*

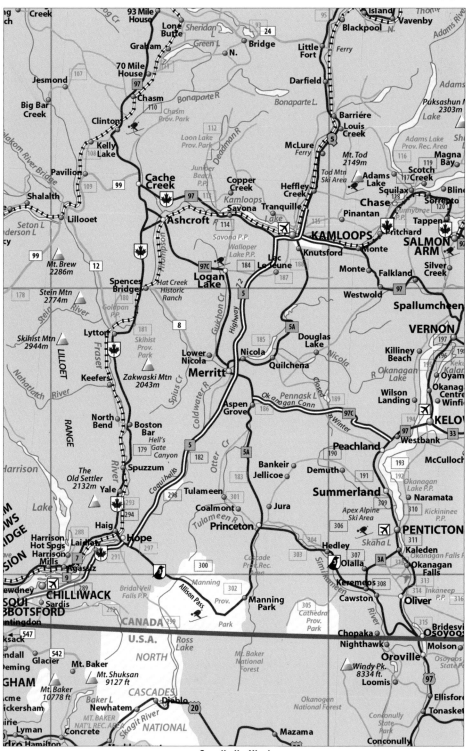

*Merritt is still a low-key ranching town, despite its location at the crossroads of several highways.*

# Coquihalla Highway

Kw'ilk'iya:la (Coquihalla) is a Sto:lo word meaning "stingy container." Apparently there is a rock at the mouth of the Coquihalla River that used to be a good place to spear salmon. On bad fishing days, Sto:lo legend held that the underwater people pulled the salmon off the spears, not allowing their precious fish out of the river.

It seems the provincial government didn't know about the "stingy" legacy when they built the superhighway. What with budget overruns and complicated bookkeeping, it is not clear exactly how much it cost to build, but one estimate at the time put the 210-km route at over $600 million. The first phase, between Hope and Merritt, was completed in 1986, and has 46 bridges and more than 20,000 tonnes of steel in its various structures. The second phase, between Merritt and Kamloops, has only eight bridges, but over 450,000 cubic metres of earth were displaced. During the building of the third, "Okanagan Connector" phase, which opened in 1990, over 700,000 cubic metres of rock had to be moved. Cost estimates near the 1728-metre-high Pennask Summit on this portion were as high as $3.5 million per km—creating a genuine "million-dollar view".

The Okanagan Connector, Highway 97C, features some wonderfully scenic vistas, as well as the longest chain-link fence in North America. The 100-km barrier is designed to prevent wildlife from crossing the highway.

The Coquihalla Highway starts just east of Hope at the junction with Highway 3, and roughly follows the route of the old Kettle Valley Railway. The Kawkawa Lake exit is an alternate route to the Othello-Quintette Tunnels, abandoned by the railway when it closed in 1961. (See Hope.) Several signs displaying a picture of a railway engine with names like Lear, Falstaff, and Juliet appear along the route. These denote former sidings so named by Andrew McCulloch. As well as being the engineering genius who designed the route, McCulloch had a passion for Shakespeare.

Just before the Coquihalla Summit (elevation: 1244 m), the massive sheer granite face of Zopkios Ridge emerges—truly a magnificent sight. At the toll booth just east of here, cars and recreational vehicles continuing north must pay a $10 fee. (This is BC's only toll highway.)

## Gone Fishin' ...

**Over 150 small lakes** dot the terrain, making the Nicola Valley the preferred destination for 50 percent of BC's freshwater anglers. "A lake a day for as long as you stay" is the local promise. Many experts feel the best fishing is in the area roughly east of Highway 5 and north of the Okanagan Connector. Species include Dolly Varden, kokanee, rainbow, mountain whitefish, and freshwater ling cod.

A seasonal road south of Quilchena travels to 1450-metre-high Pennask Lake Provincial Park, highly recommended for rainbow trout fishing. The Pennask Lake trout are considered so superior that their eggs are used for the provincial trout-stocking program.

Hope, Roche, Douglas and Chataway lakes are just a few anglers' favorites. Ice fishing is a popular wintertime activity.

*Rodeos are popular in the Nicola Valley. Cowboys have been working area ranches since the 1860s.*

# Merritt

115 km (71 mi.) north of Hope on Hwy. 5, 90 km (56 mi.) north of Princeton on Hwy. 5A. Population: 8073. Tourist information: 190 Mamette Ave., Box 1649, V1K 1B8. 250-378-5634; Fax: 250-378-6561. The way some historians tell it, the area's first non-Native resident was a Mexican packer, Juan Garcia, who stopped here with a herd of sheep and cattle on his way to the Cariboo in 1860. Other settlers followed, exploiting the natural grasslands, and developing a ranching industry. When the CPR was built in the 1880s, it was a double blessing to the area— Merritt had an eager market for its coal, and a way to transport its beef to markets farther afield.

Downtown, the Coldstream Hotel with its domed copper roof and old-time veranda was a centre for the prosperous and thriving community. "Serving the thirsty since 1908" is the proud motto etched in the sidewalk in front of the hotel today. Build by Murdoch McIntyre for the princely sum of $6000, the hotel was *the* place for honeymooners (bed and breakfast, $1.50). Its rooms with attached bathrooms made the Coldstream one of the finest establishments in the Interior.

The good times didn't last, however. In 1930, Nicola Pine Mills went bankrupt, and so did the town, remaining in receivership until 1952. The coal mine produced its last lumps in 1946, but the traditional industries of logging, mining, and ranching, along with tourism, are once again supporting the region. One recent tourism developer, the ambitious Active Mountain

## The Douglas Lake Cattle Ranch

**The 200,000-hectare** Douglas Lake Cattle Ranch is the largest working ranch (by deeded acres) in the country and well worth a visit.

The ranch was originally homesteaded in 1872, but the company expanded with the construction of the CPR in the 1880s. In 1886, 19-year-old Dan McGinnis' job was to drive about 150 head of cattle from Douglas Lake to Hope twice a month, on a road so narrow in places that the animals could barely walk single file. "On one side rose a wall of rock, and on the other side was a sheer drop of 300 feet," the cowboy wrote in a letter home. "I lost as many as eleven steers in one trip."

Currently running up to 18,000 head of cattle and employing 60 people, the ranch offers tours of the spread via four-wheel-drive Jeep, and has several fishing resorts on its property. (250-350-3344; www.douglaslake.com)

Around Douglas Lake visitors can also notice the path of retreating glaciers. Erractics, eskers, drumlins, moraines, and the north-south direction of the lakes were created by the moving and melting ice sheets.

*Murray Church was built in 1876 at Upper Nicola. The earliest settlers in the valley arrived in 1867.*

Entertainment Corporation, is determined to make Merritt a major tourist destination. It began the Merritt Mountain Country Music Festival in 1990, attracting well-known performers and thousands of fans to its annual four-day event each July. The company plans to open the Active Mountain Raceway in 2002, with a full season of motor-sport events. Future plans include a hotel spa complex, 18-hole championship golf course, and an amusement park.

Merritt is the hub of activity for the region, with highways spreading out from its centre like spokes on a wheel. Senior citizens volunteer at the Chamber-of-Commerce-run tourist information centre downtown, and they have a wealth of information about places to see, local history, and where to catch the biggest fish. The huge log structure on the

## While You're In Merritt ... Top Ten

1. Celebrate with the locals at the Nicola Valley Pro Rodeo and the Nicola Valley Fall Fair on Labour Day Weekend.
2. Have tea at the heritage Baillie House, every Sunday in July. (2202 Voght Street; 250-278-0349).
3. Stroll the farmers market, Saturdays during the summer, at the Railyard Mall.
4. Search for pictographs and other archeological goodies at Monck Lake Provincial Park. The park is also a great place for windsurfing.
5. Take a picture of Murray Church in nearby Nicola. Built in 1876, it's one of the oldest and most-photographed churches in the province.
6. Stop at the old Quilchena Hotel on Highway 5A (toward Kamloops)—for lunch or for a few days. Built in 1908, it's still operated (May to October) by descendents of the original owner, Joseph Guichon. Ahead of its time, the hotel implemented a drinking-and-driving policy well before breathalyzers. The test was simple. There were no chairs in the bar. If a cowboy fell over, he'd had too much. (250-378-2611; www.quilchena.com/)
7. Hike the old fur brigade routes or bike the old Kettle Valley Railway lines (ask at the tourist centre).
8. Spend a few days on a guest ranch.
9. Go birdwatching—over 200 species fly around these parts. Try Highway 5A north of Merritt (particularly Beaver Ranch Flats) and the Kane Valley Lakes.
10. Browse the Nicola Valley Museum and Archives' displays, which feature early mining and ranching history. (2202 Jackson Avenue, 250-378-4145; www.sonotek.com/nvmuseum.html)

*Sunset at 1728-metre Pennask Summit on Highway 97C.*

highway (junction of Highways 5 and 97C) houses the provincially-run Info Centre, which offers regional tourist information. A short nature walk, the Godey Creek Trail, starts just behind the log house.

During the first half of the 19th century, fur brigades—great clanging processions of men, women, and horses—carried supplies and furs in and out of the Interior. In 1846, the Hudson's Bay Company established the first fur brigade trail to lie entirely within the province, through the Cascades and into the Nicola Valley.

The main outdoor recreation activities are fishing, horseback riding, cross-country skiing, rockhounding, snowmobiling, windsurfing, and hiking. Visitors can pursue these activities on their own or at one of the many area resorts and guest ranches.

## Logan Lake

42 km (26 mi.) north of Merritt. Population: 2350. Info Centre: 31 Chartrand Avenue, PO Box 1060, V0K 1W0. 250-523-6322; Fax: 250-523-6678. 1-800-331-6495. Seasonal. Off season: 250-523-6225. Email: loganlake@telus.net. Web: www.district.loganlake.bc.ca. Lava from early volcanoes, fossils found pressed into the sedimentary rock, and coal beds are part of the geology of the Coquihalla region. Besides coal, metals such as gold, silver, lead, iron, zinc, copper, and molybdenum have traditionally been mined. The motherlode that supports metal mining is the Guichon Creek Batholith, 200-million-year-old granitic rocks that stretch from Merritt to Cache Creek. The batholith contains some of the largest deposits of low-grade copper and molybdenum in the province.

### While You're In Logan Lake ... Top Four

1. Tour one of the largest open-pit mines in the world, Highland Valley Copper (250-575-2443).

2. Spend a day at Lac Le Jeune Provincial Park, 26 km east on Hwy. 5. Sandy beaches, excellent fishing, and hiking trails. In winter, cross-country ski on 56 km of groomed trails.

3. Attend the improbable Lobster Festival in May.

4. Sample local fare at the Logan Lake Fall Fair in September.

# Highway 5A South

South of Merritt, Highway 5A travels to Princeton through an area rich in history. Aspen Grove, at the junction with 97C to Peachland, is where quiet, genteel George Edwards lived in the early 1900s. Edwards' friends and neighbors assumed he was independently wealthy until he was arrested for train robbery in 1906. It was then they learned he was the notorious outlaw Bill Miner, one of America's most-wanted bad guys.

Cross-country skiers will appreciate Kane Valley, 18 km south of Merritt. The area has 40 km of trails for beginning and intermediate skiers, with covered rest areas along the routes.

The highway also passes by several old homesteads and ghost towns like Granite City, Tulameen, and Coalmont. (See Princeton.) Kentucky-Alleyne Provincial Park is noted for its trout fishing and turquoise lakes, but also has a "kame and kettle" topography. These hills and depressions are yet more evidence of ancient melting glaciers. Wildlife includes black bear, coyote, deer, and birds such as hawks, falcons, and grebes.

## Bill Miner, "The Grey Fox"

**$500 Reward**

The above reward will be paid for the arrest and detention of WILLIAM (Bill) MINER, alias Edwards, who escaped from the New Westminster Penitentiary, at New Westminster, British Columbia, on the 8th August, 1907, where he was serving a life sentence for train robbery.

**DESCRIPTION:**

Age 65 years; 138 pounds; 5 feet 8½ inches; dark complexion; brown eyes; grey hair; slight build; face spotted; tattoo base of left thumb, star and ballet girl right forearm; wrist joint-bones large; moles centre of breast, 1 under left breast, 1 on right shoulder, 1 on left shoulder-blade; discoloration left buttock; scars on left shin, right leg, inside, at knee, 2 on neck.

Communicate with

**LT.-COL. A. P. SHERWOOD,**
Commissioner Dominion Police.

**Bill Miner, "the master criminal** of the American West", began his career in 1859 as a 16-year-old searching for fortune in California. Broke, Miner and three companions robbed a stagecoach, netting $75,000. Bill was hooked.

Credited with originating the expression "Hands up!", Miner spent the next 55 years alternately robbing stagecoaches and serving time in prison. His victims always described him as a gentleman—soft-spoken, courteous, apologetic. To the slew of police and Pinkerton men who pursued him, the elusive Miner became known as "The Grey Fox".

After 34 years in and out of San Quentin, Miner was released in 1903, aged 60. Bungling his first attempt at train robbery, he "retired" to BC's Nicola Valley as grey-haired, mild-mannered George Edwards. During this time, several train robberies occurred in the Pacific Northwest. All the while genial "George" charmed small children and grandmothers in the Nicola Valley.

On May 8, 1906, Miner's luck ran out. He robbed the wrong CPR train near Kamloops, netting only $15. While escaping, Miner and his companions lost their mounts. Confronted by the police, the engaging George Edwards had almost convinced his accusers of their mistake when one of his companions panicked and opened fire. The photograph above shows Miner on his way to the Kamloops jail.

Miner was sentenced to imprisonment in the penitentiary at New Westminster. However, as a newspaper reporter noted at the trial, "He claims to be 63, but looks like a man of 50, and moves like one of 30." Fourteen months later the Grey Fox escaped and took up where he left off.

He was arrested and imprisoned three times more, escaping twice. The years finally took their toll, and on September 2, 1914, Bill Miner died in prison, aged 71.

# Okanagan

*Wood Lake provides locals with a relief from the heat on a typical summer day in the Okanagan.*

W ith its semi-arid landscape, 2000 hours of sunshine a year, and many kilometres of sandy beaches, the Okanagan has a definite California ambience. The population doubles and even triples between June and September as vacationers enjoy water sports,

cycling, hiking, wildlife viewing, and rock-hounding. Golf season stretches from March to November, or sometimes even year-round. Several communities host rodeos. Culture-seekers enjoy galleries, museums, and theatre performances. And the annual wine festival every fall is a "must-do", consistently voted one of the top tourist events in North America. In the wintertime, skiers flock to three major resorts—Apex Alpine in Penticton, Big White in Kelowna, and Silver Star in Vernon.

The 160-km-long Okanagan Valley is a glacial trough on the Interior Plateau containing 145-km-long Okanagan Lake and several smaller lakes. The Okanagan river system drains southward into the Columbia River in Washington state. The main route through the valley is Highway 97.

Human history in this region starts with early residence by the Okanagan and Secwepemc (Shuswap) people, followed by fur traders, missionaries, miners, and ranchers. Fur traders established a brigade route in the early 1820s that ran from Fort Okanagan, at the junction of the Columbia and Okanagan rivers, to Fort Kamloops and beyond to Fort Alexandra on the Fraser River. Although it was not in the interests of the fur companies to encourage settlement, both Westbank (near Kelowna) and Osoyoos were favourite stopovers.

In the late 1850s, the Okanagan Valley became a route for American miners to the Fraser

*Opposite: An Okanagan sunset*

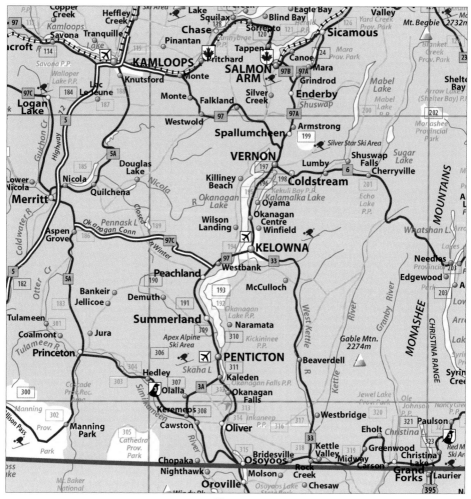

*Okanagan*

and Cariboo goldfields. Some entrepreneurs, realizing that they could make a better living supplying the miners than digging for gold, established ranches and farms in the fertile valley instead.

The orchard industry began in the 1860s when Father Charles Pandosy planted the first fruit trees. In the 1890s Lord and Lady Aberdeen harvested the first commercial apple crops, precipitating a land boom that made Penticton, Kelowna, and Vernon prominent centres. Land that sold for a dollar an acre in 1898 was snapped up for a thousand dollars an acre in 1910. Today, the Okanagan produces a fifth of Canada's commercial peach crop, a third of its apples, half of its cherries, pears, and plums, and all of its apricots. In season, roadside stands along the highway sell fresh fruits and vegetables.

Vintners from around the world recognize the quality of Okanagan wine. Every fall, the entire valley celebrates the Okanagan Wine Festival (250-490-8866), but most wineries offer tours and samplings year round (www.bcwine.com/).

Despite its value as an agricultural area, the Okanagan is the fastest-growing region in the province. In the early 1990s, the area's population increased by more than 30 per cent. Although the influx of people is diminishing, it is still

*Haynes Lease Ecological Reserve is part of the Okanagan's Vest Pocket Desert, one of 131 ecological reserves in the province.*

the most rapidly growing area in the Interior.

As in almost every other part of the province, logging is an important part of the economy, particularly in the central and northern Okanagan.

## Osoyoos Oxbows

East of Highway 97 on Road 22 north of Osoyoos.

Located between Osoyoos and Oliver, the Osoyoos Oxbows area is an excellent area for wildlife viewing, and is designated as an Important Birding Area (IBA) by Birdlife International. Just north of Osoyoos Lake, this marshland provides a dramatic contrast to the otherwise semi-arid landscape—one of the hottest and driest areas of Canada. The habitat supports songbirds, waterfowl, western painted turtles, and a variety of small mammals. On the east side of the Osoyoos River you'll see some abandoned farm buildings—the original homestead of the Haynes Ranch. Judge John Haynes was the earliest customs officer in the area and the patriarch of a prominent early ranching family.

Past the ranch site, signs mark a wildlife habitat reserve and the access road to the provincial Haynes Lease Ecological Reserve, which protects a portion of the "Vest Pocket Desert". About 3 km north along Black Sage Road, look for signs on the west side of the road marking the Burrowing Owls Enhancement Area. The Ministry of Environment has imported burrowing owls here from Washington state in an effort to restore this endangered species.

## Okanagan Fruit and Blossom Schedule

| Fruit | Blossom | Ripening |
| --- | --- | --- |
| Apricots | April 7 to 30 | July 15 to Aug. 10 |
| Cherries | April 15 to May 10 | June 25 to July 20 |
| Peaches | April 15 to May 10 | July 30 to Sept. 1 |
| Pears | April 20 to May 16 | Aug. 15 to Sept. 15 |
| Prunes | April 20 to May 16 | Sept. 1 to 20 |
| Apples | April 25 to May 20 | Aug. 1 to Oct. 10 |
| Grapes | April 25 to May 20 | Sept. 5 to Oct. 10 |

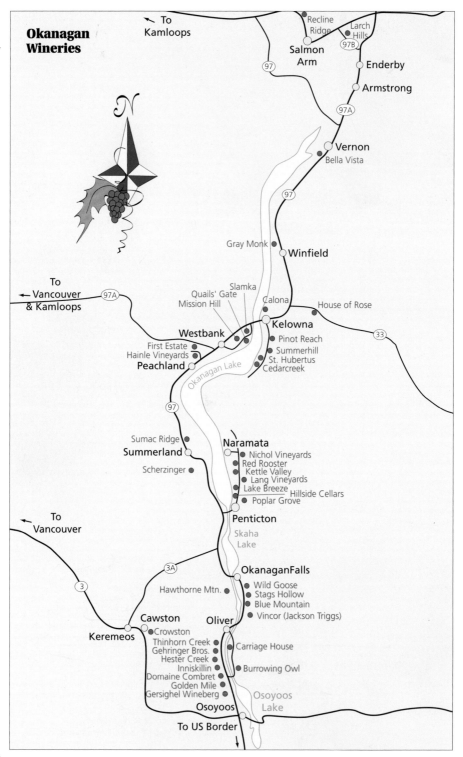

**Okanagan
Wineries**

To
Kamloops

Recline
Ridge
Larch
Hills
97B

Salmon
Arm
97

Enderby

Armstrong

97A

Vernon
Bella Vista

97

Gray Monk
Winfield

To
Vancouver
& Kamloops
97A

Slamka
Quails' Gate
Mission Hill
Calona

House of Rose

Kelowna
33

Westbank

First Estate
Hainle Vineyards
Peachland

Pinot Reach
Summerhill
St. Hubertus
Cedarcreek

Okanagan Lake

97

Sumac Ridge
Summerland
Scherzinger

Naramata
Nichol Vineyards
Red Rooster
Kettle Valley
Lang Vineyards
Lake Breeze
Hillside Cellars
Poplar Grove

Penticton

Skaha
Lake

To
Vancouver

3A

Okanagan Falls

Hawthorne Mtn.
Wild Goose
Stags Hollow
Blue Mountain
Vincor (Jackson Triggs)

3

Cawston
Crowston
Keremeos
Thinhorn Creek
Gehringer Bros.
Hester Creek
Inniskillin
Domaine Combret
Golden Mile
Gersighel Wineberg

Oliver

Carriage House

Burrowing Owl

Osoyoos
Lake

Osoyoos

To US Border

**122**

## Okanagan Wine Festivals

**Stomp some grapes**, tour a winery, picnic in a vineyard. Enjoy gourmet dining, formal tasting sessions, and cooking demonstrations. If you're over 19, all this can be yours at one of the four major wine festivals held each year in the Okanagan.

Although grapes have been grown in this region since the 1800s, it wasn't until the 1960s that Okanagan wineries began to seriously sell their products. In recent years, the industry has come of age. At present, there are over 30 wineries in the Okanagan planting 3000 acres of premium grapes. Their wines are winning prizes around the world.

The industry celebrates its success with several wine festivals every year. The oldest and largest is the Fall Festival, held over ten days every September–October since 1980. It is consistently listed as one of the top 100 events in North America by Destination magazine. Its 110 events attracted over 83,000 visitors in 2001.

An Icewine Festival is held in January, a Spring Festival in May, and a Summer Festival in August.

Okanagan Wine Festivals, organizers of these events, offers tour packages. For dates, events, and other information, contact them at 1527 Ellis Street, Kelowna BC V1Y 2A7; 250-861-6654; www.owfs.com/

## Fore! SuperGuide Recommends

The Okanagan has more golf courses than anywhere else in the Interior. And most courses are open year-round. Here's a selection:

**Kaleden**
**Twin Lakes Golf Resort**. Semi-private. 18 holes. Par 74. 6867 yards. Design: William Robinson. S26B, C8, R.R.1, V0H 1K0. 250-497-5359. Email: twinlakesgolf@telus.net. Web: www.twinlakesgolfresort.com

**Kelowna**
**Gallagher's Canyon**. Semi-private. 18 holes. Par 72. 6792 yards. Rated as one of Canada's top 100 courses by Score Magazine in 2001. 4320 Gallaghers Dr. W., V1W 3Z9. 250-861-4240. Email: info_gallaghers@golfbc.com. Web: www.gallaghersgolf.com

**Harvest Golf Club**. 18 holes. Par 72. 7109 yards. Design: Graham Cooke. Rated as one of Canada's top 100 courses by Score Magazine in 2001. Several other awards. 2725 K.L.O. Rd., V1W 4S1. 800-257-8577. Email: proshop@harvestgolf.com. Web: /www.harvestgolf.com

**Kelowna Golf and Country Club**. Semi-private. 18 holes. Par 72. 6276 yards. 1297 Glenmore Dr., V1Y 4P4. 250-762-2736. Email: golf@kgcc.bc.ca. Web: www.kgcc.bc.ca

**Kelowna Springs**. Semi-private. 18 holes. Par 72. 6180 yards. Four stars from Golf Digest 1996-97. 480 Penno Rd., V1X 6S3. 250-765-4653. Email: golf@kelownasprings.com. Web:www.kelownasprings.com

**Okanagan (The Bear Course & The Quail Course)**. Semi-private. 18 holes each course. Both par 72. 3200 Via Centrale, V1V 2A4. 250-765-5955. 1-800-898-2449. Email: smeyer_okanagan@golfbc.com. Web: www.okanagangolfclub.com

**Sunset Ranch Golf & Country Club**. Semi-private. 18 holes. Par 72. 6518 yards. 4001 Anderson Rd., V1X 7V8. 250-765-7700. Email: sunset@silk.net. Web: www.sunsetranchbc.com

**Oliver**
**Fairview Mountain**. Semi-private. 18 holes. Par 72. 6578 yards. Design: Les Furber. Rated as one of Canada's top 100 courses by Score Magazine in 2001. On Golf Course Road. Box 821, V0H 1T0. 250-498-3521. Web: www.fairviewmountain.com/

**Osoyoos**
**Osoyoos Golf & Country Club**. Semi-private. 27 holes. Par 72. 6318 yards. Box 798, V0H 1V0. 250-495-7003

**Peachland**
**Ponderosa Golf and Country Club**. 18 holes. Par 72. 6006 yards. 4000 Ponderosa Dr., V0H 1X0. 250-768-7839. Email: teetimes@golfponderosa.com. Web: www.golfponderosa.com

**Penticton**
**Penticton Golf and Country Club**. Semi-private. 18 holes. Par 70. 6131 yards. On West Eckhardt Avenue. Box 158, V2A 6K8. 250-492-8727

**Summerland**
**Summerland Golf & Country Club**. Semi-private. 18 holes. Par 72. 6555 yards. "One of the most challenging back nines in the province." 2405 Mountain Ave., V0H 1Z0. 250-955-7955.

**Vernon**
**Predator Ridge Golf Resort**. Semi-private. 27 holes. Par 72. 7144 yards. Design: Les Furber. Rated as one of Canada's top 100 courses by Score Magazine in 2001. Other awards. 301 Village Centre Place, V1H 1T2. 1-888-578-6688

**Spallumcheen Golf & Country Club**. 27 holes. Par 71. 6423 yards. 9401 Hwy 97 N., V1T 6M2. 250-545-5824. Email: spallumcheen_estates@telus.net. Web: www.spallumcheengolf.com

**Vernon Golf & Country Club**. Semi-private. 18 holes. 6610 yards. 800 Kalamalka Lake Rd., V1T 6V2. 250-542-9126. Email: pro@vernongolf.com. Web: www.vernongolf.com

*All courses are public, unless indicated. Some are playable all year.*
*For information on all courses in this region: www.bcgolfguide.com*

# Oliver

20 km (12 mi.) north of Osoyoos. Population: 4285. Info Centre: Box 460, V0H 1T0. 250-498-6321; Fax: 250-498-3156. Email: info@oliver-chamber.bc.ca. Web: www.oliver-chamber.bc.ca

"Honest John" Oliver, the premier of BC from 1918 to 1927, is the namesake of this town. Remembered for his progressive irrigation policies, Oliver's foresight has served the Okanagan well. His program, designed to attract returning veterans from WWI, changed the area from a dry desert to a thriving agricultural community.

Mining enjoyed a frenzied but brief prominence in the late part of the 19th century. Today, an interpretive sign and a cross mark the site of Fairview (5 km southwest on the Oliver-Cawston Road), the greatest gold mining camp in the Okanagan, which operated from 1892 to 1902. None of the original buildings remain, but a kiosk on the site gives the lowdown on how it was back then. You can still take a look at the original jail, reconstructed downtown.

Oliver declares itself the "wine capital of Canada", so if you've come to the Okanagan for wine tasting, this is a good place to start. Just south of town, the "Golden Mile" hosts several wineries. Grapes grown here are prized across the province for wine making.

## Oliver Wineries

**Black Hills Estate Winery.** 30880 - 71 Street (Black Sage Road). 250-498-0666. www.blackhillswinery.com.

**Burrowing Owl Vineyards.** #100 Burrowing Owl Place, Black Sage Road. 250498-0620. 1-888-498-0621. www.bowwine.com.

**Carriage House Wines.** 32764 - 71 Street (Black Sage Road). 250-498-8818.

**Domaine Combret Estate Winery.** 131 Street, Road 13. 250-498-6966.

**Fairview Cellars.** 13147 - 334 Avenue (Old Golf Course Road). 250-498-2211.

**Gehringer Brothers Estate Winery.** 326 Avenue (Road 8). 250-498-3537.

**Gersighel Wineberg.** 29690 Hwy 97. 250-498-3319.

**Golden Mile Cellars.** 316A Avenue, Road 13. 250-498-8330.

**Hester Creek Estate Winery.** 13163 - 326 Avenue, Road 8. 250-498-4435. www.hester creek.com.

**Inniskillin Okanagan Vineyards.** 32074-123 Street, Road 11. 250-498-6411. 1-800-498-6211. www.inniskillin.com.

**Silver Sage Winery.** 32032 - 87th Street, Road 9. 250-498-0310.

**Tinhorn Creek Vineyards.** 32830 Tinhorn Creek Road, Road 7. 250-498-3743. 1-888-484-6467. www.tinhorn.com.

**Vincor International.** 38691 Hwy 97 North. 250-498-4981.

## While You're in Oliver ... Top Ten

1. Browse through the Oliver Museum (106 West 6th Avenue, 250-498-4027). The old Fairview jail is right next door.
2. Walk or bike on the 18-km trail beside the river. (Park at the CPR station.)
3. Visit the Chamber of Commerce tourist offices in the restored CPR station. In the summer months, take in the displays of local arts and crafts.
4. Ski at Mount Baldy (250-498-4086). Thirty km east of town, this family ski area has 17 runs, one double chair, one T-bar and 550 metres of vertical drop.
5. Sample local wine on the "Golden Mile". There are 13 local wineries. Several have tours, and all have wine shops.
6. Enjoy the view of Vaseux Lake from McIntyre Bluff and Canyon (north of town on Hwy 97, accessible from Sea Crest or River roads), the site of an early battle between the Shuswap and Okanagan people. Be on the lookout for native rock paintings at the base of the bluff.
7. Enjoy a quiet paddle on Vaseux Lake. No motorized vessels allowed—it's a bird sanctuary and wildlife viewing area (trumpeter swans, chukar partridge, California bighorn sheep). The Wildlife Centre at a pull-off on Hwy 97 has a good interpretive display.
8. Golf at two 18-hole courses within a few minutes of downtown: Fairview Mountain or Inkameep Canyon.
9. Cast your line at Sawmill (Burnell), Madden, Tuc-el-Nuit, Bear, and Osoyoos lakes, to name a few.
10. Take a dip at Rotary Beach.

*Female red wing blackbird*

# Okanagan Falls

20 km (12 mi.) north of Oliver. Population: 1100. Chamber of Commerce: PO Box 246, V0H 1R0. In the 1890s, a man named Snodgrass dreamed of making this pretty town—then called Dogtown—the centre of the Okanagan. (Neighboring Skaha Lake was called Lac du Chien, French for "Dog Lake".) He built the first steamboat on Skaha Lake and the Okanagan River, but transportation problems proved too complicated, and his dream died. The area was used primarily as ranchland until the 1930s. Then orchards were planted, and the powers that be opted for the tonier name of Okanagan Falls. You might wonder why, since there don't appear to be any falls around. Apparently there were some once, but they were destroyed in the 1950s when the dam was installed.

## While You're in Okanagan Falls ... Top Five

1. Space out at the National Research Council Dominion Radio Astrophysical Observatory (250-493-2277; www.drao.nrc.ca/index-eng.shtml). Go north on Highway 97 and follow signs at White Lake Road. Scientists here study radio signals through extremely powerful telescopes. Visitor centre is open year-round, weekdays only. From 2 to 5 on Sundays during July and August, scientists are on hand to answer questions. White Lake is great for birdwatching.

2. Shop for jade.

3. Explore Okanagan Falls Provincial Park (west of town on Green Lake Road), a lush ecological zone in an otherwise arid landscape. Great wildlife viewing.

4. Stroll downtown to see Bassett House Museum (1145 Main Street, 250-497-5308), an authentically restored and refurbished 1909 mail-order house.

5. Tour a local winery.

## Okanagan Falls Wineries

**Blue Mountain Vineyards & Cellars**. Allendale Road. 250-497-8244. www.bluemountain-winery.com

**Hawthorne Mountain Vineyards**, Green Lake Road. 250-497-8267. www.hmvineyard.com

**Stag's Hollow Winery & Vineyard**. 12 Sun Valley Way. 250-497-6162

**Wild Goose Vineyards and Winery**. 2145 Sun Valley Way. 250-497-8919. www.wilgoosewinery.com/

*Wild roses are a common site along the side of Interior highways.*

# Penticton

20 km (12 mi.) north of Okanagan Falls. Population: 32,219. Info Centre: 888 Westminster Avenue West, V2A 8S2. 250-493-4055; Fax: 250-492-6119; 1-800-663-5052. Email: vic@img.net. Web: www.penticton.org

Many towns in BC are at the confluence of two rivers, but Penticton is a meeting place of two lakes: Okanagan and Skaha. The deep blue waters of Skaha Lake were once part of Okanagan Lake. Over time, silting built up the delta that is the present site of Penticton.

When Tom Ellis came here in 1866, this spot had been an Okanagan Native settlement for centuries. First Nations people called it *Pen-tak-tin*, "a place to live forever". Mr. Ellis agreed, and built a ranching empire encompassing 12,000 hectares. His roundup covered the area from Naramata to Osoyoos, and he drove his cattle all the way to Hope over the Dewdney Trail. Most historians credit Ellis with planting the first fruit trees in the area, but one early account says he was only copying the Natives, who cultivated wild species.

The townsite was laid out in 1905 when the Southern Okanagan Land Company bought the Ellis holdings. By 1910 only 400 people had settled in the area, despite the elegant CPR paddlewheelers launched in 1892 to attract tourist dollars. Rumors of the Kettle Valley Railway caused a land boom in 1912. Twenty-two real-estate firms set up shop, selling land at up to $3000 an acre. By 1915 the railway was completed.

Today Penticton is a popular summer resort area, bookended by beaches, surrounded by outdoor recreation opportunities, and offering some nice shops and restaurants.

Rockhounds should have a field day in this area. Evan G. Cameron, an Okanagan geologist, has claimed that "all of the common and uncommon types of rocks existing in the world are found within a radius of approximately 40 miles (65 km) of Penticton."

## Penticton Wineries

**Benchland Vineyards.** 170 Upper Bench Road. 250-770-1733

**Hillside Estate.** 1350 Naramata Road. 250-493-4424

**King Family Farms.** 801 Carder Rd. 250-492-7646

**La Frenz.** 740 Naramata Road. 250-492-4575

**Paradise Ranch Wines.** 1465 Ellis. 604-683-6040. www.icewines.com/

**Poplar Grove.** 1060 Poplar Grove Road. 250-492-2352

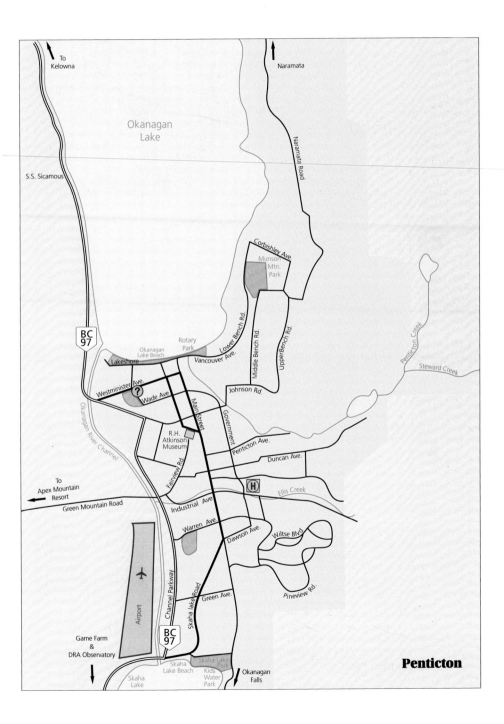

To
Kelowna

Naramata

Okanagan
Lake

Naramata Road

S.S. Sicamous

Corbishley Ave.

Munson
Mtn.
Park

BC
97

Rotary
Park

Okanagan
Lake Beach

Lakeshore

Lower Bench Rd.

Middle Bench Rd.

Upper Bench Rd.

Penticton Creek

Steward Creek

Vancouver Ave.

Westminister Ave.

?

Wade Ave.

Johnson Rd.

Okanagan River Channel

Main Street

Government

R.H.
Atkinson
Museum

Penticton Ave.

Duncan Ave.

Fairview Rd.

To
Apex Mountain
Resort

Green Mountain Road

H

Ellis Creek

Industrial Ave.

Warren Ave.

Dawson Ave.

Wiltse Blvd.

Airport

Channel Parkway

Skaha Lake Road

Pineview Rd.

Green Ave.

Game Farm
&
DRA Observatory

BC
97

Skaha
Lake Beach

Skaha Lake
Park

Kids
Water
Park

Okanagan
Falls

Skaha
Lake

**Penticton**

## S.S. Sicamous

**One of the original** CPR paddlewheelers on Okanagan Lake, the luxurious S.S. *Sicamous* now sits in Lakeshore Park in Penticton. (Open daily; 250-492-0403.) Steamboat service began on the lake in 1886. But when the CPR trunk line was completed from Sicamous to Vernon in 1892, the CPR began operating a regular service on the lake. Its luxury paddlewheelers attracted tourists, and the agricultural community found a way to transport their produce. The economy was changed forever.

With a name meaning "shimmering waters" in Shuswap, the S.S. *Sicamous* was launched in 1914, replacing the S.S. *Aberdeen*. Able to carry 500 passengers plus freight, the ship's deluxe embellishments included stained glass skylights, brass chandeliers, Burmese teak, and Australian mahogany. Passengers had access to 40 staterooms, four salons, a smoking lounge, and observation lounges. Dinner was tastefully served in a 20-metre-long dining room by uniformed waiters.

Despite their romantic associations, sternwheelers have a long and valiant history in the Interior, providing basic transportation when there were no roads or railroads. In April 1931, the CPR terminated sternwheeler service on the lake.

## While You're In Penticton ... Top Ten

1. Take a day to browse through the R.N. Atkinson Museum (785 Main, 250-490-2451), which features the largest collection of Western Canadiana in the Interior. Included are displays on the Okanagan people, early settlers, the Kettle Valley Railway, mining, orcharding, and natural history.

2. Shop for the work of local artists at the Art Gallery of the South Okanagan (on the lakefront, east of the Info Centre, 250-493-2928).

3. Take a class at the Okanagan Summer School of the Arts (250-493-0390; www.img.net/ossa). Operating since 1960, the school runs throughout July. Distinguished faculty have included Robert Silverman, Tony Onley, W.O. Mitchell, Jan Rubes, Ingrid Suderman, Ann Mortifee, and Judith Dampier.

4. Windsurf on Skaha Lake (30-knot winds are possible in August). Parasail! Bungee jump!

5. Swim, swim, swim on almost 3000 metres of beaches.

6. Inner tube down the 6-km long Penticton River Channel between Okanagan and Skaha lakes. There's a walking/cycling path beside the channel and it's a good spot for wildlife viewing.

7. Go rockhounding. Ask at the Info Centre or check the display at the R.N. Atkinson Museum for good spots.

8. Ogle at over 120 different species of imported and native wildlife on the 224-hectare Okanagan Game Farm (250-497-5405).

9. Savour local wines. Many wineries have signs on the highway, or you can ask locally for tours, or look online (www.welcometopenticton.com/wine.htm) for an updated list.

10. Ski Apex Mountain Resort, named as "Best Small Destination Resort" by Ski Canada Magazine. A half-hour drive west of Penticton, it features an alpine village and four-season activities (250-292-8222; 1-877-777-2739; www.apexresort.com).

**Director**, International School of Writing, En'owkin Centre, Penticton-Okanagan Band

I guess I'm biased like everyone else about where they grew up. I think this is probably the most beautiful area in the country. I am so familiar with it, I feel like it's very much a part of my internal landscape. When I have tried living in other cities, I have felt a huge loss.

I stay here principally because I am Okanagan, and I define myself as that. I have very close ties to the land here and very strong ties to the community, the language, the body that makes up my whole self, which is my family. Without that around me I'm not whole.

I grew up on the Penticton Indian Reserve. My early years were spent on the reserve in a very different lifestyle than people in the non-Native community. I really didn't participate in the non-Native community other than high school.

It did create problems for me and others because we weren't easily accepted, we were different. But I came from a strong family background that had a lot of pride in being Native, and I didn't see anything wrong with my culture.

The Penticton-Okanagan people and the Okanagan Native people in general have always had a great pride in their culture. Our understanding, which is ingrained in our cultural teachings, is that every person has the right to be what they are, and every culture has the right to be what they are. We seek to create peace and harmony as a result of that value. Every time there is a debate, confrontation, conflict, or whatever, the Okanagan people have risen as the peacemakers.

I like to define myself as an activist in a creative sense, rather than as a writer. Principally I see my creative arts as a way to activate change in my community and in the wider community.

For the local community, the En'owkin Centre is a source of pride and recognition for ourselves of what is possible. We are one of the leading Native organizations in the country, in terms of future development in the literary arts. So we've become a measurement, a standard, in excellence. That's a real source of pride.

*The En'owkin Centre was formed in 1979 to house the activities of the Okanagan Indian Education Resource Society, which represents all Native organizations in the Okanagan valley. Lot 45, Green Mountain Road, RR #2 Site 50, Comp. 8, Penticton, V2A 6J7; 250-493-7181; www. geocities.com/enowkin/2.html.*

## Penticton Special Events–Best Bets

**February**–Apex Winter Triathlon & Carnival (1-877-777-2739; www.apexresort.com)

**January, May, August, October**–Okanagan Wine Festivals (250-861-6654; www.owfs.com). The big one is in the fall, but try the Tour de Vine–a bike tour through the wineries of the south Okanagan, and Bacchanalia–a food and wine extravaganza in May.

**May**–Meadowlark Festival (250-497-6889; meadowlarkfestival.bc.ca)

**July**–Penticton Highland Games (250-493-1257); Beach Blanket Film Festival (1-866-696-7777)

**August**–Square Dance Jamboree (250-492-5204; www.squaredance.bc.ca); Annual Peach Festival (since 1947!) (250-493-7385; www.peachfest.com); Subaru Ironman Canada Triathlon (the real thing: 1700 elite athletes from 30 countries). (250-490-8787; www.ironman.ca)

**September**–Annual Pentastic Hot Jazz (1-800-663-1900; www.pentasticjazz.com)

## Side Trip: Naramata

16 km (10 mi.) northeast of Penticton. Population: 2000. www.discovernaramata.com/faq.htm

A visit to charming Naramata provides a chance to stay near the lake but get away from the crowds. The town was established by prominent land promoter John M. Robinson, who also was the developer behind Summerland. He reportedly named the town after a Sioux Indian chief who visited him during a seance and spoke of the love of the chief's life, Narramatah.

This lovely low-key spot is home to a number of artists and craftspeople as well as several wineries and "Canada's largest retreat and experiential learning centre", Naramata Centre. If you want nightlife and shopping, Penticton's your best bet, but if you're looking for outdoor

### Naramata Wineries

**Elephant Island Fruit Winery**. 2730 Aikens Loop. 250-496-5522. .www.elephantisland wine.com/

**Hillside Estate Winery**. 1350 Naramata Road. 250-493-6274. www.hillsideestate.com

**Kettle Valley Winery**. 2988 Hayman Road. 250-496-5898

**Lake Breeze Vineyards**. Sammet Road. 250-496-5659

**Lang Vineyards**. 2493 Gammon Road. 250-496-5987

**Nichol Vineyard**. 1285 Smethurst Road. 250-496-5962

**Red Rooster Winery**. 910 Debeck Road. 250-496-4041. www.redroosterwinery.com/

recreation, try the lake (swimming, canoeing, kayaking, wakeboarding) or the hills (hiking and cycling on the old Kettle Valley Railway bed).

The stretch from the Okanagan Highland down to Penticton was one of the most difficult challenges facing Andrew McCulloch when he was surveying the Kettle Valley Railway (KVR). He solved the

### Pacific Rattlesnake

*Crotalus viridis oreganus*
The Pacific rattlesnake, the only poisonous snake in BC, is found in the dry areas of the southern Interior, usually near cliffs and talus slopes. Normally about 80 cm long, this species can grow up to 1.5 metres. The distinguishing feature is the segmented tail or rattle.

The venom of the Pacific rattlesnake is dangerous, but this species is not aggressive. If given a choice, they'll retreat rather than attack. However, if surprised or stepped on, they'll strike without rattling a warning. When hiking in dry areas of the southern Interior, always watch where you place your hands and feet, and listen for the rattle.

problem by creating a series of switchbacks on the mountain above Naramata, creating the longest 2.2 percent grade in Canada. Portions of the now-defunct line have been planted over, but hikers can walk to old station sites like Arawana, Glenfir, Adra, and Chute Lake. Ask locally or follow the road to Rock Ovens Park, a former KVR

Wear long pants and sturdy footwear.

If bitten, keep calm and still, and get to a hospital. Penticton Hospital is equipped to treat snakebite patients.

Although Pacific rattlers are not social creatures, they do spend the winter in communal dens in talus slopes or caves. As many as a hundred rattlers might live in one den, which they will likely share with other creatures.

The snakes go into the den in mid to late September, and they are out in late March or early April. They mate in late summer, and the young are born in September.

*Fruit boxes*

## Summerland

16 km (10 mi.) north of Penticton. Population: 11,150. Info Centre: 15600 Highway 97, Box 130, V0H 1Z0. 250-494-2686; Fax: 250-494-4039. Email: schamber@vip.net; Web: www.summerlandchamber. bc.ca/

Back on Highway 97 north of Penticton, Giant's Head Mountain, a once-active volcano resembling the profile of a man, towers over the orchards and vineyards of Summerland. Since the Native word "Okanagan" derives part of its meaning from the word "head," some surmise that similar shapes on rock faces up and down the valley may be how the area got its name.

Along with Naramata, Summerland also owes its existence to John M. Robinson. An owner of several Manitoba newspapers, he came to the Okanagan looking for mining opportunities in the late 1800s. After tasting local peaches, he developed an irrigation scheme instead, and sold land parcels, claiming "Heaven on earth with summer weather forever!" By the early 1900s, Summerland boasted the first hydroelectric plant in the valley, its own light and telephone system, and orchards containing a million fruit trees.

construction camp, 4 km past the old Glenfir station.

Besides peaches, apples and other delicious produce, Naramata also provides you with access to Okanagan Mountain Provincial Park— the longest undeveloped shoreline on Okanagan Lake. Accessible by road north of Naramata or south of Kelowna, no thoroughfares cross the 10,462-hectare park. It has 24 km of hiking tails, some of them former fur-brigade routes. As always when hiking in the Okanagan and Similkameen regions, beware of rattlesnakes. They are not aggressive, but hikers must wear sturdy shoes and watch where they put their hands.

### While You're In Summerland ... Top Five

1. Climb Giant's Head Mountain for a spectacular view of the valley.
2. Learn all about trout at the Summerland Trout Hatchery (Lakeshore Drive, 250-494-0491). Tours are not normally available, but the public can view the site and a small display.
3. Picnic at the Ornamental Garden at the Federal Agricultural Research Station (250-494-7711) just off the highway opposite Sun-Oka Provincial Park. (The development of the Spartan apple is one result of the centre's research.) One of the largest steel girder bridges of its kind in North America crosses Trout Creek Canyon here. The 200-metre-high, 500-metre-long structure was part of the Kettle Valley Railway.
4. Explore local history at the Summerland Museum (9521 Wharton Street, 250-494-9395), which features local history; an art gallery upstairs displays work of local artists.
5. Climb on the Kettle Valley Steam Railway for a one-and-a-half-hour tour. 250-494-8422. Seasonal.

### Summerland Wineries

**Calliope Wines**. 6816 Andrew. 250-494-7213, 1-866-366-0100. www.calliopewines.com/

**Sumac Ridge Estate Winery**. 17403 Hwy. 97. 250-494-0451. www.sumacridge.com Thornhaven Winery. 6816 Andrew. 250-494-8683. www.thornhaven.com/.

*Commercial orcharding began in the Okanagan in the 1890s.*
*In 1999, total sales from Okanagan-Similkameen-Kootenay orchard fruit was $64.8 million.*

Today the town celebrates its old country heritage with simulated British cottage architecture and its own town crier.

## Peachland

25 km (16 mi.) north of Summerland. Population: 5018. Info Centre: 5812 Beacon Avenue, Box 383, V0H 1X0. 250-767-2455. Fax: 250-767-2420. Email: peachland chamber@cablelan.net
More than two kilometres of public beach line the main

### Peachland Wineries

**Hainle Vineyards Estate Winery**. 5355 Trepanier Bench Road. 250-767-2525, 1-800-767-3109. www.hainle.com

**First Estate Cellars**. 5031 Cousins Road. 250-767-9526, 1-877-377-8788.

street of this orchard community, making it a popular summertime destination. Originally named after miner Gus Hewitt in the late 1800s, the name was changed to Peachland after the Lambly family grew the first Okanagan peaches here. Right on Okanagan Lake, it's a great place for

### While You're In Peachland ... Top Five

1. Browse the old photos of the Kettle Valley Railway at the Peachland Museum (5890 Beach Avenue, 250-767-3441), an unusual, eight-sided structure that used to be a church.

2. Boat across to Okanagan Mountain Provincial Park, directly across the lake. Watch out for the legendary lake monster Ogopogo off the park's Squally Point!

3. View spawning salmon at Antler's Beach at the south end of town.

4. Go fishing at Eneas Lakes or Darke Lake provincial parks.

5. Hike the trails at Hardy Falls.

water sports, camping and hiking.
Trepanier Creek, at the north end of town, reportedly got its name from the surgical procedure of trepanning, or cutting a hole in the skull. The story goes that while hunting in 1817, Chief Short Legs' scalp was badly torn by a grizzly

bear. The chief was not recovering, so after several days, fur trader Alexander Ross operated, removing several pieces of bone from the chief's skull. "In fifteen days by the aid of Indian medicine he was able to walk around," Ross wrote. "And at the end of six weeks from the time he was wounded, he was on horseback, again at the chase."

Three kilometres north of Peachland, the Okanagan Connector (Highway 97C) is the fastest route to the Lower Mainland or Kamloops via the Nicola Valley.

## Ogopogo

**Ogopogo**, the Loch Ness Monster of Okanagan Lake, is considered tourist hype by some, but there are many people who take its existence very seriously. In 1990 and 1991, a Japanese television network sent film crews and an underwater submersible to prepare documentaries on the legendary creature. The NBC program *Unsolved Mysteries* has also covered the story.

Okanagan Natives described N'ha-a-itk, the lake monster that lived in a cave near Squally Point, to early pioneers such as Susan Allison in the mid 1800s. Since the monster often came out of the water during storms and claimed lives, the Natives carried small animals to sacrifice when approaching the point.

In 1914, Mr. F.M. Buckland, a prominent Okanagan citizen, was among a group of campers on the lake who discovered the decomposing remains of a strange animal they'd never seen before. He described it as close to two metres long and weighing about 200 kilograms. The neckless creature had a thick hide, tusks, and flipper-like arms. Apparently bones from the animal were on display for several years in the area. One scientist who examined them concluded they belonged to a prehistoric creature. Unfortunately, the bones have since disappeared.

Although skeptics still claim Ogopogo is an invention of the tourism industry, some scientists take the creature seriously. The International Society of Cryptozoology, based in Washington, DC, is dedicated to the investigation of "all matters related to animals of unexpected form and size or unexpected occurrence in time and space." Just because the existence of an animal seems impossible, they say, it doesn't mean it is impossible. No one believed that the two-metre-long fish, the coelacanth, still existed until it was caught off the South African coast in 1938. Or that a clam without a digestive system could exist, until John Reid discovered it off Vancouver Island in 1979.

Comparisons with Scotland's Loch Ness monster are inevitable. People have postulated that Nessie is a plesiosaur, an aquatic reptile, thought to be extinct for 65 million years. It is possible Ogopogo is, too.

Another explanation involves a huge creature that was sighted off the Oregon coast in the 1930s, possibly an extinct whale. Some theorize that this creature could have travelled up the Columbia River to the Okanagan.

From time to time various promoters offer large cash prizes for proof that the monster is real. But no one has ever won—yet.

For more information, read Arlene Gall's book, *Ogopogo* (Surrey, BC: Hancock House, 1985).

*One of Kelowna's attractions is its many parks: a dozen are right on the lake, including City Park in the heart of downtown.*

## Kelowna

60 km (37 mi.) north of Penticton. Population: 100,433. Info Centre: 544 Harvey Avenue (Highway 97), V1Y 6C9. 250-861-1515; Fax: 250-861-3624. 1-800-663-4345. Email: kcofc@kelownachamber.org. Web: www.kelownachamber.org

In 1958, when Princess Margaret opened Okanagan Lake's 1400-metre-long Floating Bridge, it was the first of its kind in North America. The unusual 640-metre-long pontoon structure floats up and down with lake levels. The view of wild waves to the north and calm waters to the south often greets travellers crossing the bridge. This paradox may typify the heart and soul of modern Kelowna.

Attracted by the legendary good weather and laid-back lifestyle, people from across the country are flocking to the Okanagan, and Kelowna in particular. Experts estimate

## While You're In Kelowna ... Top Ten

1. See how the Abderdeens lived. Stroll through Guisachan Heritage Park (Cameron Avenue, just off Gordon Drive). The Abderdeens' restored colonial style bungalow now operates as a first-class restaurant (250-863-9368). Visit Benvoulin Heritage Church, also built by the Aberdeens, the oldest standing church in Kelowna.

2. Soak up the past at Father Pandosy's Mission (250-860-8369).

3. See the *Tyrannosaurus rex* skull at the Kelowna Museum (470 Queensway, 250-763-2417).

4. Learn all about apples at the Provincial Orchard Industry Museum 1304 Ellis, 250-763-0433), Kelowna's first restored heritage building. The Winery Museum is right next door.

5. Browse both local and touring exhibits at the impressive Kelowna Art Gallery (1315 Water Street, 250-762-2226).

6. Tour an orchard, farm, packing plant or local forest. Many places cater to families and have child-friendly facilities like playgrounds, petting zoos and picnic tables. (Ask at the Info Centre.)

7. Tour the wineries.

8. Golf at one of the area's several top-rated courses.

9. Ski Big White in the winter or hike the trails in the summer. (250-765-8888; 1-800-663-2772).

10. Hop on the Okanagan Valley Wine Train for a scenic day-excursion to Vernon. Seasonal. 250-712-9888, 1-888-674-8725.

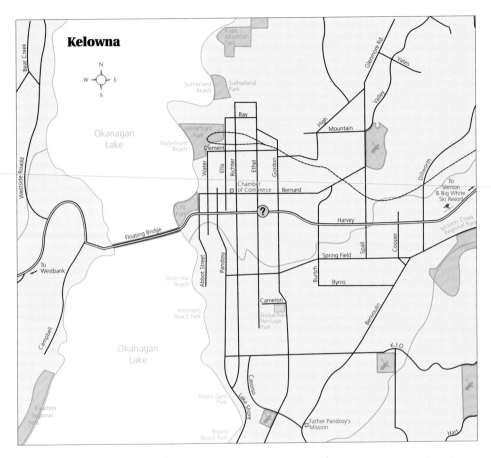

Kelowna

that by 2018, the Central Okanagan's population will have risen to 269,000. Some fear the increase will bring about changes that will alter the community's essence as the increased demand for housing and facilities encroaches on agricultural land.

The luxury homes that now nestle on prime lakeview lots are a far cry from August Gillard's earth home in 1862. Apparently, when the red-bearded, gruff-mannered Gillard emerged from his half-underground dwelling one day, he reminded his Native neighbors of a crotchety bear after a long hibernation. They called the man and the place *kim-am-tou-che* (brown bear), which was later refined to *kelowna* (grizzly bear).

Despite its great summer weather and glorious beaches, this growing city is not just another resort town. The largest city in the Interior, Kelowna is a centre of business and light industry. Calona wines is based here—the oldest winery in the province. This is also the headquarters of the Okanagan Wine Festival, a highly successful organization that has made the October event one of the most popular in North America.

Kelowna is also a cultural centre, with galleries, performing arts, and a university college. It is the focal point for a number of outdoor recreation activities, from hiking and skiing to watersports of all kinds. And it is an area rich in history, providing visitors with many opportunities to steep themselves in the past.

The Earl and Countess of Aberdeen are responsible for many of Kelowna's heritage sites. They arrived in 1891 on a cross-Canada tour, and fell in love with Hudson's Bay Company trader John McDougall's ranch, renaming it Guisachan when they bought it. Theirs was the first large-scale planting of fruit trees and hops in the central Okanagan. The Earl and Countess were very busy people—she was the founder of both the World Council of Women and the Victorian Order of Nurses, and he was Governor General of Canada from 1893 to 1898.

## Kelowna: A City of Parks

**Kelowna is blessed** with over sixty parks totaling 240 hectares, either in the city or close by, with seven of them right on the lake.

**Kelowna City Park**, right downtown, is easy to find on hot a day, and has a great beach.

**Boyce-Gyro Park**, south of the Floating Bridge, is very popular with locals.

**Knox Mountain Nature Park** at the north end of Ellis Street gives first-time visitors a great view of the city and a sense of where things are. The park also has nature trails, a nature pavilion, and a picnic area.

**Mission Creek Regional Park** (not far from Orchard Park Shopping Centre on Springfield Road). Its attractions include spawning kokanee in the fall, 100 species of flowering plants between April and August, numerous trails, and an interpretive centre.

**Woodhaven Nature Conservancy Park** (end of Raymer Road in Okanagan Mission) encompasses three bio-geoclimatic zones in 21 acres, as well as 59 bird species.

## Best Bets for Hiking and Biking

*The old Kettle Valley Railway Line is popular with hikers and bikers. This is one of the trestle bridges over Myra Canyon, east of Kelowna.*

**Kettle Valley Railway**—Several chunks of this historic track have been reclaimed for recreational use. "Never saw a railway built on any such hillside as this," was what chief engineer Andrew McCulloch had to say about this portion of the line, and these hiking/biking routes get you up close and personal with 18 impressive trestle bridges.

**Myra Canyon**—Follow KLO Road to McCulloch Road past the end of the pavement for 2 km. Take the Myra Forest Road for 8 km to the parking area. It will take you five hours to see the 18 trestles.

**June Springs**—Follow KLO Road to McCulloch Road, turning right on June Springs Road, continuing as it turns into Little White Forest Service Road. Park in the small area to the left where the KVR, looking like a dirt road, crosses the road.

Continue left to Myra Canyon. 12 km one way.

**Chute Lake**—Take Lakeshore Road south from Kelowna onto Chute Lake Road, turning left onto Headmen and right onto Billiard Forest Service Road. When the KVR (looking like a plain old turn road) crosses this road, park. The first trestles are about 5 km to your left.

**Okanagan Mountain Provincial Park**—Take Lakeshore Road south. Wild Horse Canyon is very popular, but there are several other trails, beginner to advanced.

**Bear Creek Provincial Park**—across the lake on Westside Road. The spectacular Canyon Rim Trail goes along Bear Creek.

There are many, many other choices. Ask locally or call Tourism Kelowna at 1-800-663-4345.

## WAC "Wacky" Bennett: Hardware Premier

**"The finest music** in the country is the ringing of cash registers," according to William Andrew Cecil Bennett, BC's longest-reigning premier.

The Kelowna-based politician was premier of BC during a time of general prosperity. His tenure from 1952 to 1972 was a time of major development in the Interior, including the expansion of the road system and the provincial railway (now BC Rail), and the construction of hydro-electric projects on the Peace and Columbia rivers. Bennett was the first premier from a Social Credit party that was to dominate provincial politics for

50 years. He survived disastrous political scandals and several colourful cabinet ministers during his years in office.

Born in New Brunswick in 1900, young William was raised in a strict Presbyterian family. At the end of World War I, he moved west to Edmonton, married, and opened a hardware store. When the Depression came, he moved to BC, first to Victoria, and then to Kelowna, where he started another hardware business, and, as author Derek Pethick notes in *Men of British Columbia,* "pondered the paradox of poverty in a land of plenty."

Elected to the provincial legislature in 1941, Bennett became premier in 1952. Because of his leadership, the Social Credit Party was to become a major force in BC politics until 1991.

Although WAC Bennett was defeated in the polls in 1972, his son Bill became premier in 1975. WAC Bennett died in Kelowna in 1979.

## Kelowna Special Events–Best Bets

**January**–Parade of Lights & Snowfest
**April**–Classic and Antique Boat Show
**May**–Black Mountain Rodeo; Rutland May Days; Spring Wine Festival
**June**–Kelowna Gardens Tour; BC Old Time Fiddlers Contest
**July**–Folkfest; Kelowna Regatta
**August**–Downtown Mardi Gras; Molson Thunderfest (hydroplanes)
**September**–Dragon Boat Festival
**October**–Okanagan Wine Festival
**December**–Christmas Light Up

## Kelowna Wineries

**Calona Vineyards**. (BC's oldest winery.) 1125 Richter Street. 250-762-9144, 1-888-246-4472; www.calona.kelowna.com/.

**Cedar Creek Estate Winery**. 5445 Lakeshore Road. 250-764-8866, 1-800-730-9463; www.cedarcreek.bc.ca

**Mission Hill Winery**. 1730 Mission Hill Road (Westbank). 250-768-7611; www.missionhilwinery.com

**Mount Boucherie Estate Winery**. 829 Douglas Road (Westbank). 250-769-8803, 1-800-663-5086; www.mtboucherie.bc.ca

**Pinot Reach Cellars**. 1670 Dehart Road. 250-764-0078; www/pinotreach.com/

**Quail's Gate Estate Winery**. 3303 Boucherie Road. 250-769-4451, 1-800-420-9463; www.quailsgate.com

**St. Hubertus Estate Winery**. 5225 Lakeshore Road. 250-764-7888, 1-800-989-WINE; www.st-hubertus.bc.ca

**Slamka Cellar**. 2742 Cordova Way. 250-769-0404; www.slamka.bc.ca/

**Summerhill Estate Winery**. 4870 Chute Lake Road. 250-764-8000, 1-800-667-3538; www.summerhill.bc.ca/

*Agricultural and housing needs are increasingly in conflict in the Okanagan, with the fastest-growing population in the province.*

# The North Okanagan

The North Okanagan enjoys slightly cooler temperatures and lusher vegetation than the south. Although early attempts were made to duplicate the soft-fruit orcharding success of the southern Okanagan, farmers realized the land was better suited to dairy farming and hardier fruits and vegetables.

A secondary road travels the west side of Okanagan Lake to Vernon via Fintry and Westside Road. Highway 97 travels north past Duck Lake, Wood Lake, Oyama, and Kalamalka Lake through picturesque country alternating dry grasslands with irrigated orchards.

Approaching Vernon from the south, Kalamalka Lake is dazzling on a bright cloudless day. One interpretation of its name is "lake of many

## Pandosy Mission

Established in 1860 by Father Charles Pandosy (right) and colleagues from the Oblate order, the Pandosy Mission was the first permanent European settlement in the Okanagan valley and the first non-Hudson's Bay Company settlement in the province. In 1859, the Oblate Fathers spent their first winter on Duck Lake, north of present-day Kelowna, but almost starved and froze to death. In the spring, the group established a mission on its present site, with a garden and cattle, chickens, ducks, and geese. The Oblates are also credited with planting the first vineyard and orchard, and building the first school. Three of the original log buildings are still standing: the chapel, the root house, and the living quarters. The mission now operates as a provincial heritage site and is open year-round, weather permitting. (Benvoulin and Casorso roads; 250-860-8369.)

*Idyllic Polson Park is in the centre of Vernon, the Interior's oldest incorporated city.*

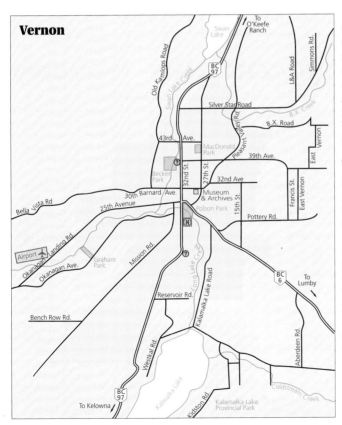

colours". Glacial deposits at several places along the shore cause the water to shimmer and shine in an array of blues and greens. Access to Kalamalka Lake Provincial Park is south of Vernon on the east side of the lake.

## Vernon

55 km (34 mi.) north of Kelowna. Population: 34,678. Info Centre: 701 Highway 97 South, Box 520, V1T 6M4. 250-542-1415, 1-800-665-0795; Fax: 250-542-3256. Email: info@vernontourism.com. Web: www.vernontourism.com Vernon sits at the centre of four valleys (Priest, Pleasant, Coldstream, and Mission) within easy reach of two large lakes (Okanagan and Kalamalka). Although early fur traders discouraged settlers, once gold fever hit, the friendly

**139**

## Ken Mather—Manager, O'Keefe Ranch, Vernon

**I came here in 1984.** I'm just somebody who has worked in heritage sites for a long time, appreciates what they represent, and loves the work. I've been doing it for almost 30 years.

I'm probably stuck here because it's a really hard place to leave. It's beautiful. We live right here on the site. We have our own milk cow, our own chickens. It's awfully hard to say, "Well, gee, I'm going somewhere else for better money." I mean the fact is you'll never find a style of life like this in what I do. It's very much a love.

There's a field across there that we've just planted to oats. In August we'll thresh that with the old binder. We'll tie up the stooks and then we'll use horse-drawn wagons and load up the bundles. We've got a great big steam tractor that has a long belt attached to it, and we'll actually thresh-out the old way. There was a lot of wheat grown on O'Keefe Ranch because the Okanagan was the breadbasket for a long time, before the Prairies took off.

There seems to be a resurgence of interest in this sort of thing. Part of it is the search for something genuine in an age that tends to be fairly artificial. People are looking at the whole cowboy thing and liking what they see. In the States people are scouring the country for old cowboy gear. If you could find an old pair of boots or something like that, they'd sell for hundreds of dollars. And a good pair of angora chaps is worth thousands of dollars. Because it's heritage, it's nostalgia, but also people are seeing a real value to it.

## While You're In Vernon ... Top Ten

1.  Spend an afternoon at O'Keefe Ranch (250-542-7868; www.okeeferanch.bc.ca).

2.  Experience Sen 'Klip Native Theatre's performance of First Nations legends every weekend from July to September. (One hour before dusk at Komasket Park off Westside Road; 250-542-1247.)

3.  Tour the local winery (Bella Vista Vineyards, 3111 Agnew Rd; 250-558-0770) or sample local brew at the Okanagan Spring plant (250-542-2337).

4.  Stroll through picturesque Polson Park with its meandering stream, swans, historic sites, flower garden and other delights, right in the middle of the city. Stop in at the Interior Space and Science Centre (250-545-3644) and enjoy their hands-on displays of rocks, fossils, illusions and environmental issues.

5.  Explore local history at the Greater Vernon Museum and Archives (3009 - 32nd Avenue, 250-542-3142).

6.  Go birdwatching at Swan Lake Bird Sanctuary (north at junction of Highways 97 and 97A).

7.  Ski Silver Star—59 alpine runs, 760 m vertical drop, 70 km groomed Nordic trails. (250-542-0224; 1-800-663-4431). The chairlift runs year-round, so it's also a good spot for hiking. Or bike Silver Star's Mile High Descent (25 km, 1535 m vertical drop).

8.  Golf at several excellent courses.

9.  Go birdwatching at Swan Lake Bird Sanctuary (north at junction of Highways 97 and 97A).

10. Sample local produce at western Canada's largest outdoor farmers market (Mondays and Thursdays from April through October, Vernon Recreation Centre parking lot).

## O'Keefe Ranch

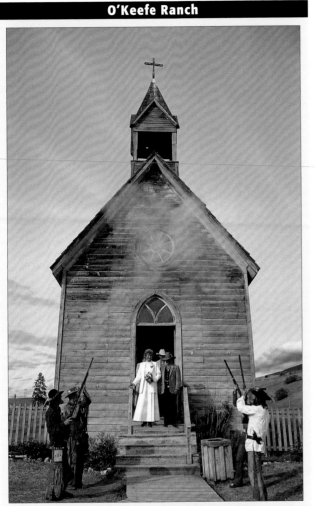

*St. Anne's Church, built at O'Keefe ranch in 1889, still has its original pews and pump organ. It's a popular place for weddings.*

**At the north end** of Swan Lake, Highway 97 heads west to Kamloops, past the O'Keefe Ranch (250-542-7868; www.okeeferanch.bc.ca), a lovingly restored history lesson and a major attraction. Established in 1867 by Cornelius O'Keefe and Thomas Greenhow, the ranch was totally self-sufficient, with a church, store, and a still-functioning blacksmith shop. The buildings date back to the 1870s, and some, like the mansion, contain original furnishings. A working ranch until 1977, the facility is now operated as a historic site. In 1997 it began a preservation and reproduction program for rare and endangered breeds of domestic livestock. Open for viewing during the summer months, the ranch has a year-round restaurant.

climate and lush natural grasslands made this an attractive settlement area.

Originally called Priest's Valley, after Oblate Father Durieu who built a cabin in the area in the 1860s, the city of Vernon was eventually named after early rancher Forbes Vernon. Along with his brother Charles, Forbes founded Coldstream Ranch, one of the largest in western Canada. In 1891, Lord and Lady Aberdeen bought out the Vernons and planted the first orchard in the area. The CPR had been completed north of here in 1885, so when a branch line was extended to Sicamous in 1892, fruit marketing became feasible. The town incorporated that same year.

Although at one time it was a major hop grower in the province, Coldstream Ranch became one of the largest producers of fruit in the British Empire. In 1917, the orchards produced 800 boxcars of apples and 200 boxcars of other fruit, which were shipped to England at a value of over a million dollars.

Others attracted to the

## Vernon Special Events –Best Bets

**January**—World Cup Dog Sled Races, Monte Lake
**February**—Vernon Winter Carnival (largest in western Canada)
**May**—Falkland Rodeo
**July**—Bella Vista Triathlon
**August**—Okanagan Summer Wine Festival, Silver Star; O'Keefe Ranch Cowboy Festival; Okanagan Nation traditional games (Komasket Park; 250-542-4328).

area's good agricultural land included Cornelius O'Keefe and Thomas Greenhow, who, while driving cattle from Oregon during the gold rush in the 1860s, were so impressed with the knee-high bunch grass that they decided to stay. The restored O'Keefe Ranch north of town is a major area attrac-

tion with restored buildings, demonstrations, and special events.

Many Chinese miners opted for the wealth of the soil rather than the elusive promises of gold, and they numbered among early settlers as well. Today agriculture remains an important part of

the economy of the North Okanagan.

Highway 97 continues on a very scenic drive through Falkland and Monte Lake to Kamloops. Highway 97A travels north of Vernon through Armstrong and Enderby and meets the Trans-Canada at Sicamous or Salmon Arm.

## Kalamalka Lake Provincial Park

*Kalamalka Lake features western Canada's only freshwater dive site.*

**South of Vernon**, across the lake from Highway 97, the virgin grasslands of 890-hectare Kalamalka Lake Provincial Park give a sense of how the landscape seduced early ranchers like the Vernons and Cornelius O'Keefe. It used to be like this all the way to Osoyoos, 140 km to the south.

In order to protect the fragile ecosystem, some areas of the park are restricted, but there is much to enjoy, including spectac-

ular views of the lake and colourful wildflowers in spring. The turquoise water makes swimming particularly exotic at Jade, Juniper, and Cosens bays. And the park features western Canada's only freshwater underwater marine park—good news for scuba divers.

Four distinct ecological zones exist here—arid grassland, woodland, forest, and wetlands—containing ten plant species rare in

BC. Pacific rattlesnakes also live in these parts, but they are shy creatures that prefer to be left alone. Other hazards include unexploded bombs left over from target practice during World War II—a military base is just across the lake. (Metal objects along trails should be left undisturbed and reported to RCMP.) Please stay on the paths.

*The Armstrong Hotel, built in 1892, still operates.*

# Armstrong

23 km (14 mi.) north of Vernon. Population: 4257. Info Centre: 3350 Bridge Street, Box 118, V0E 1B0. 250-546-8155; Fax: 250-546-8868. Email: armstrong_chamber @telus.net. Web: www.armstrong bc.com/chamberofcommerce.

Armstrong's history is wrapped up in agriculture and railroading. The first settlers called the settlement Aberdeen, honouring the illustrious couple who introduced commercial orcharding to the Okanagan. But the town was renamed when William Heating Armstrong's London banking house helped finance the Shuswap and Okanagan Railway.

Historically the "breadbasket" of the northern Okanagan, Armstrong is actually located in the Spallumcheen Valley, and is well-known for its hardy fruits, asparagus, and celery. Local dairy cows provide the milk for the famous Armstrong cheese.

Armstrong has an old cowtown feel to it, with its wide main street, railway running down the middle, and turn-of-the-century architecture. The Armstrong Hotel, built in 1892, is still in operation.

# Enderby

13 km (8 mi.) north of Armstrong on Hwy. 97A. Population: 2920. Info Centre: 706 Railway Street, Box 1000, V0E 1V0. 250-838-6727, 1-877-213-6509; Fax: 250-838-0123. Email: echamber@jetstream.net. Web: www.enderby.com/chamber.

The volcanic Enderby Cliffs tower over this thriving agricultural and logging community. The highest in the Okanagan, they look down over the Shuswap River as it meanders through the town below.

The river has long been important to area residents. Natives used it as a transportation route. Lambly's Landing, near the present site of Enderby, used to be the head of navigation for steamers coming from Sicamous on Shuswap Lake. Farmers soon planted grain on the rich soils of the flood plain, and a grist mill was built in 1887. Today farmers raise dairy cows and other crops, and agriculture, along with logging, continues to be important to the economy.

# Side trip: The Monashee Highway

East of Vernon, the Monashee Highway (Hwy. 6), travels through an area rich in history

## While You're In Armstrong ... Top Five

1. Tour the Armstrong Cheese Factory (Pleasant Valley Road, 250-546-3084).
2. Get a sense of the past at the Armstrong Spallumcheen Museum (Railway Avenue, 250-546-8318, seasonal).
3. Catch a show at the unique Caravan Farm Theatre during the summer months. . In the winter it offers special Christmas productions and sleigh rides (250-546-8533).
4. Watch the birds at Otter Lake Wildlife Preserve.
5. Join in the festivities at the annual Kinsmen Rodeo in August and the Interior Pacific Exhibition in September.

and beautiful scenery, popular with anglers and hikers. The landscape varies from rolling farmlands to forested hills, and you will cross the geologically mature Monashee Mountains before encountering the younger and more angular ranges to the east.

Lumby, considered the logging centre of the North Okanagan, attracted settlers from Quebec in the late 1800s. Originally called White Valley, the town was renamed after Moses Lumby, an early miner and farmer who came to BC in 1862, settling in the Spallumcheen area in 1870. Lumby became vice-president of the Shuswap and Okanagan Railway and Vernon's government agent in 1891.

Inspired by stories of gold in Barkerville, miners were in the Cherryville area as early as 1863. Farming and logging took over in the 1880s, but mining continued until the 1930s. Travellers who look

closely will see the remains of the Chinese workings and water canals along the river. And if they look closer, maybe they'll see something glinting and beckoning in the water of Cherry Creek—the mother lode was never found.

Highway 6 past Lumby and Cherryville is a beautiful but winding drive east through the Monashee Mountains to the Arrow Lakes. A free ferry takes travellers across the lake from Needles to Fauquier. North are Nakusp, Revelstoke, and the Trans-Canada Highway. East of Nakusp, Highway 6 continues south through the Slocan Valley.

## While You're In Enderby ... Top Ten

1. Hike up the Enderby Cliffs.
2. Look at the collection of old photos and other displays at the Enderby Museum, on Highway 97 in the city hall complex. 250-838-7170; www.sjs.sd83.bc.ca/museum/index.htm).
3. View heritage buildings with the self-guided walking tour (available at the museum or tourist centre).
4. Drive out to Gunter Ellison Lookout (west) for a spectacular view of the area.
5. Kayak or canoe on the Shuswap River or Mabel and Mara lakes.
6. Picnic at Gardom Lake.
7. Visit a farm—bisons, llamas or deer (ask at the Info Centre).
8. Tour the Kingfisher Community Fish Hatchery and Environmental Interpretive Centre, 26 km east on Mabel Lake Road, where they raise about 500,000 salmon and trout each year. (250-838-0004 or 250-838-6569).
9. Take in the Kayak Rodeo held every year in June.
10. Watch a movie at the Starlight Drive-In Theatre.

## Enderby Wineries

**Larch Hills Winery**. 110 Timms Road, Salmon Arm. 250-832-9419; www.larchhillswinery.bc.ca
**Recline Ridge Vineyards & Winery**. 2640 Skimikin Road, Tappen, near Salmon Arm. 250-835-2212; www.recline-ridge.bc.ca/

## Monashee Highway Special Events

**May**—Gold Panning Championships
**September**—Lumby Horseplay Days; Cherryville Zucchini Daze

## While You're On Monashee Highway ... Top Five

1. Browse the outdoor logging display at the Lumby Museum (250-547-6285).
2. Hang-glide from Cooper's Launch (Trinity Valley Way via Defies Creek) or several other local mountains .(250-547-2169) or just hike up and enjoy the view.
3. Spend the day at BC Hydro's Shuswap River Recreation Area. Picnic at Shuswap Falls. After lunch, canoe the river. Or view Brenda Falls from Sugar Lake Dam Viewpoint.
4. Search for pictographs on the western shore of Mabel Lake. Or just go for a swim in the warm water and laze on the sandy beaches.
5. From Cherryville, drive up to remote Monashee Provincial Park, a 7513-hectare wilderness area. Appropriate for experienced hikers, the many alpine lakes, rock formations in Valley of the Moon, and 3000-metre peaks have a strong appeal.

*Rainbow Falls at Monashee Provincial Park can only be enjoyed by backpackers or fly-ins. This wilderness area has no road access.*

## Top Ten Okanagan Wildlife Viewing Spots

1. Inkameep Provincial Park (Oliver)—birds

2. Kalamalka Lake Provincial Park (Vernon)—birds, small mammals, rattlesnakes

3. Lions Park (Kelowna)—spawning salmon

4. Okanagan Falls Provincial Park—birds, mammals, bats

5. Osoyoos Oxbows—birds, turtles, deer, small mammals

6. Peachland Creek—spawning salmon

7. Skaha Lake (east side; Penticton)

8. Swan Lake (Vernon)—birds

9. Vaseaux Lake (Penticton)—birds, reptiles, bighorn sheep, small mammals.

10. White Lake (Okanagan Falls)—birds

## SuperGuide's Top Okanagan Ski Resorts

**Alpine Apex**, Penticton—67 trails, 5 lifts, 610 m vertical. Named "Best Small Destination Resort" by Ski Canada Magazine. New ski lodge. Four-season activities. Accommodations, dog sledding, rentals, snowboard park, restaurants, snowmobiling, cross-country, shopping, daycare, night skiing, ski shop, tube park. (250-292-8222; 1-877-777-2739; www.apexresort.com)

**Big White**, Kelowna—112 designed trails, 13 lifts, 777 m vertical, lift capacity of 23,400 skiers per hour, and a fully developed ski village. Top rated kids' programs. Voted "Best Place to be Abandoned by Your Parents" by Ski Canada Magazine. Recent expansion of facilities. Dog sledding, rentals, snowboard park, restaurants, snowmobiling, cross-country, ice rink, shopping, daycare, night skiing, ski shop, tube park. (250-765-8888; 1-800-663-2772; www.bigwhite.com/)

**Silverstar**, Vernon—108 alpine runs. 10 lifts, 760 m vertical drop, 70 km groomed Nordic trails, alpine village. Two mountain faces. New lifts. Varied terrain. Four seasons. Numerous awards, including "Outstanding Ski Area Of The Year" by the Far West Ski Association (USA). Dog sledding, rentals, snowboard park, restaurants, snowmobiling, cross-country, ice rink, daycare, night skiing, ski shop, tube park. (250-542-0224; 1-800-663-4431; www.silverstarmtn.com/)

# West Kootenay

*Glacier-fed Kootenay Lake is over 200 km long and contains Dolly Varden, Kokanee salmon and record-sized rainbow trout.*

The West Kootenay region has often hosted people who were "different." The earliest known inhabitants, the Ktunaxa (Kutenai), were more closely allied to the Plains Natives than to the Interior Salish. The Ktunaxa regularly crossed the Rocky Mountains to hunt buffalo and

were thus more influenced by their contact with these people to the east than by the coastal tribes. Living structures, dress, artifacts and other life details reflect this alliance.

When the English orchardists settled here in the early 1900s they also were "different". Looking for new opportunities, they built homes, ranches and farms around the Kootenay and Arrow lakes, growing prize-winning cherries and apples while beating the wilderness back with parasols. At the same time, Doukhobors settled around Castlegar, escaping persecution in Russia (and Saskatchewan) for their pacifist views. And during World War II, hundreds of Japanese-Canadians from coastal BC were

forced to relocate to internment camps here. In the late part of the twentieth century an international array of "back to the landers" pursued their dreams of an alternate lifestyle by building homesteads and pursuing counterculture values, following the pattern of previous waves of newcomers.

David Thompson travelled this way on his route to the Pacific in 1808, but the West Kootenay didn't receive much attention from Europeans until the discovery of copper and silver at Toad Mountain near Nelson in 1886. Then prospectors filed claims throughout the "Silvery Slocan" Valley and Kootenay Lake region, and settlers and business people built towns and

*Opposite: The Slocan Valley provides spectacular views of the Valhalla Range of the Selkirk Mountains.*  **147**

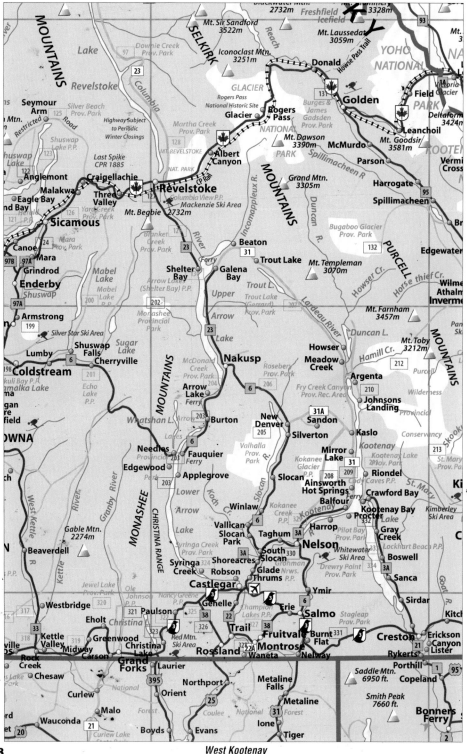

railways. By the mid-1950s large-scale logging was viable in the Interior, and forestry became important to the economy.

The West Kootenay is made up of several valleys encompassing three north-south river systems: the Arrow Lakes/Columbia, the Slocan, and the Kootenay. Throughout the southern Interior, the natural corridors provided by the rivers, lakes, and valleys encouraged north-south trade with the Americans. This was a worry to early politicians such as Governor James Douglas—in early mining days, the American Fourth of July was as common a holiday as the Queen's Birthday. The building of the Dewdney Trail in the 1860s and the Crowsnest rail

line in the 1890s were attempts by business and political leaders to prevent American domination.

The cold temperatures of the glacier-fed lakes and the abundant precipitation have prevented the West Kootenay from becoming a major tourist destination like the Okanagan or Shuswap regions. But outdoor enthusiasts appreciate the area's wide range of recreational activities, and "adventure tourism" is establishing itself as an important contributor to the local economy. Water sports, snow sports, hiking, and fishing, as well as artistic and cultural attractions, draw visitors here from around the world.

Exploring the West Kootenay is not a straightforward

journey. SuperGuide's route heads east from Castlegar to Nelson, north beside Kootenay Lake to Kaslo, west to the Slocan Valley, and south to Hwy. 3A. Then the tour heads back to Nelson, crossing Kootenay Lake via the free ferry at Balfour and travelling south along the east side of the lake to Creston.

## Dams and Osprey: Castlegar to Nelson

Travelling east from Castlegar, Hwy. 3A follows the Kootenay River, a major tributary of the Columbia. The headwaters of both rivers are in the Rocky Mountains, but they flow in opposite directions – the Kootenay south to Montana,

## Osprey

The migratory osprey are found throughout the Interior, from early spring to autumn near lakes, rivers, and sloughs. Dark brown on the upper body with white forehead, chin, neck, and underparts, the average osprey weighs about 1.5 kilograms and has a wingspan of 1.6 metres.

Their distinctive nests are often seen on dead trees, telephone poles, pilings, or other man-made structures. Made of twigs, branches, and sticks, the bulky structures range from half a metre to 2.5 metres in diameter and can be up to two metres high.

Although it is not uncommon for osprey nests to be commandeered by other species such as Canada geese and great horned owls, in the Kootenays one osprey pair was observed

returning to the same nest for eleven consecutive seasons.

Osprey usually lay two to four eggs in May and June; the young hatch in five to six weeks and remain fledglings for six to eight weeks.

Sometimes known as the

"fish hawk," osprey are unique among hawks in their ability to capture and handle fish. A bird may dive from 10 to 20 metres for a fish swimming one metre under water. Tenacious creatures, they have been known to drown rather than release a fish that is too big to lift from the water.

At the top of their food chain, osprey can serve as indicators of environmental problems. In the 1960s, the population underwent a serious decline in some areas because of the presence of organochlorine pesticides such as DDT. Since restrictions of such substances have come into effect, osprey populations have increased.

The Creston Valley Wildlife Centre sponsors an Osprey Festival every April (250-428-3260).

*Gyro Park in Nelson provides a great view of Kootenay Lake.*

the Columbia north around the Big Bend – finally joining together at Castlegar.

There are several dams and power plants along this stretch of highway that keep all our electric lights and pizza warmers humming. Old-timers in the area tell stories about pulling big salmon out of the Kootenay, Slocan, and Columbia rivers before the hydroelectric projects were installed. Several pull-offs along the road have interpretive signs and impressive views. The Bonnington Falls are the reason the river was unnavigable between the Kootenay and Columbia systems. But it was a favourite salmon fishing spot for Natives, who were likely camping here four thousand years ago.

Just past Taghum, the road crosses the river. Watch for osprey nests on poles and trees along the side of the road. In the spring, it is possible to see little beaks flapping over the edge of their mud and twig homes, demanding lunch. Osprey sometimes return to the same nest year after year. When the bridge was being built in the 1980s, crews had to replant one of the poles so as not to disrupt the tenants' breeding habits.

Grohman Narrows Provincial Park, 4 km west of Nelson, is a day-use park with a short trail beside a small marsh.

## Nelson

43 km (27 mi.) east of Castlegar. Population: 9585. Info Centre: 225 Hall Street, V1L 5X4. 250-352-3433, 1-877-663-5706. Fax: 250-352-6355. Email: chamber@ netidea.com. Web: www.discover Nelson.com/core.html

When the Hall brothers discovered silver on Nelson's Toad Mountain in 1886, the event attracted the attention of prospectors and mining syndicates. This seemed to spearhead a mining boom, as other discoveries quickly followed, from Greenwood to Kimberley.

The town was incorporated in 1897. Calling itself the "Queen City," it soon grew to prominence as a cultural, transportation, and business centre. When it opened in 1899, Nelson's electric streetcar system was the only one in the West outside of Vancouver and Winnipeg—and the smallest in the British Empire. In the 1980s, local visionaries pushed a major heritage revitalization program, restoring over 350 homes and office buildings. (Hollywood, always quick to spot a pretty face, chose the town as the location for two movies in 1987, *Roxanne* and *Housekeeping*.)

Some say there are more artists and artisans per capita

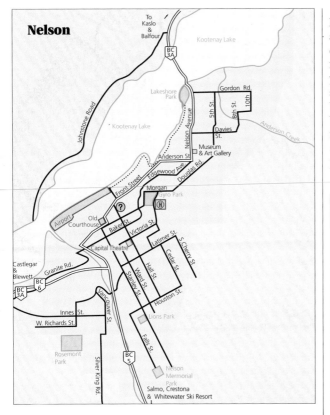

Nelson

living in the Nelson area than anywhere else in Canada. It's definitely become a magnet for escapees from city life, as you'll see by the many craft stores and outdoor recreation businesses in the area. Hiking, biking, skiing, hang-gliding, fishing, and boating are among the popular outdoor pastimes.

## Nelson Special Events —Best Bets

**Summer**—Street Fest: jugglers, acrobats, street performances. (250-352-7188; www.street-fest.bc.ca)

**Summer**—Artwalk (250-352-2402)

**July-mid Summer**—Curling Bonspiel. (http://curl.2.50megs.com/)

## While You're In Nelson ... Top Ten

1. Ride the fully restored Streetcar 23 along the waterfront from Prestige Inn to Lakeside Park (250-352-7672).

2. Tour the Nelson Brewing Company and sample the local ale (250-352-3582).

3. Stroll along Baker Street and browse the craft stores, galleries, and bookstores.

4. Take a self-guided heritage tour, which includes the old Provincial Courthouse (designed by Francis Rattenbury, the British architect responsible for both the parliament buildings and the Empress Hotel in Victoria) and Cottonwood Falls (the site of the first hydroelectric generation plant in the province, opened in 1896).

5. Fish Kootenay Lake year-round; it's known worldwide for its trout.

6. Head for 257-hectare Kokanee Creek Provincial Park and one of the area's best sandy shallow beaches. (In the fall, watch salmon spawning here. And it's great for birdwatching.) For local swimming, try Lakeside Park, right beside the big orange bridge.

7. Find out about local history at the Nelson Museum (402 Anderson Street, 250-352-9813).

8. Have a picnic in Gyro Park (you can see its gazebo from Baker Street) for a great view of the town and Kootenay Lake.

9. Watch a play or concert at the restored Capitol Theatre (421 Victoria, 250-352-6363).

10. Ski Whitewater (250-354-4944; http://www.skiwhitewater.com/).

## S.S. *Nasookin*

**Paddlewheelers** of all shapes and sizes were an integral part of the transportation system in BC's early days, and the Kootenay region relied heavily on these sturdy ships. The first sternwheeler chugged up the Arrow Lakes in 1865, but when mining and settlement boomed in the 1890s, the railway companies began a fierce competition for supremacy in freight and passenger service, adding more and more vessels on the lakes and rivers. Between 1897 and 1957, a fleet of eleven of these ships plied Kootenay Lake alone.

In 1913, as part of a plan to develop the tourist trade on Kootenay Lake, the CPR launched the 1869-ton *Nasookin* on Kootenay Lake with a 15-gun salute. The ship was the largest of BC's sternwheelers and one of the most elegant, with mahogany and wicker furniture, Wilton carpets, electric lights, coloured skylights, and fine dining. All that remains of the ship today is the pilot house and observation deck. They have been restored as a private home, visible on the west side of the highway 4 km north of Nelson.

## Robert Inwood

**Heritage Revitalization Consultant, Nelson**
I started off as a carpenter, working on renovation and restoration projects in downtown Nelson. I've always enjoyed Victorian architecture, so I tended to gravitate toward the design end of things.

The initial steps for the Nelson program came from the BC Heritage Conservation Branch, which had just done a survey of the province. Because the mall had just been put in, the merchants were looking to do something with the downtown. I ended up being in the right place at the right time.

I coordinated the program for five years, starting in 1980, working with a partner from Heritage Canada. It was a long process. There were some people who were gung-ho right from day one, and others that dragged along. But one of the reasons Nelson is

such a success story is that we had amazing participation—90 percent in the first five years. Since then, virtually every store in Nelson has been renovated in some fashion. That's why it looks so good.

It's a popular program. I've worked with dozens of other BC communities: Rossland, Revelstoke, Trail, Kaslo, New Denver,

Hazelton, Keremeos, Port Hardy, Port Alberni, McBride, and Fort St. John.

I enjoy the work. Heritage revitalization gets people's mindsets turned around so they see the history of the community from a positive vantage point, rather than a bit of the past that needs to get shoved out of the way to make way for the future. The town takes pride in itself, people appreciate the historic fabric of their community more, they learn about it and talk to their friends about it. There seems to be a general deepening of their awareness of the whole history of the area.

I don't see the interest in heritage revitalization slowing down. People's appreciation of historic buildings seems to be on the upswing. And I'm already working on renovations of my renovations. Time marches on; it's a fact of life.

*Kokanee Creek drains 1981-metre-elevation Kokanee Lake.*
*Its glacial waters flow into Kootenay Lake at Kokanee Creek Provincial Park.*

## West Side of Kootenay Lake

Nelson is a good base camp for side trips and recreational activities on 120-km-long Kootenay Lake. The water is a little cold for swimming, but there are a few sandy beaches that prove the exception. Kaslo and area are best for boat rentals and charters. Besides fishing, water skiing, and paddling, visitors can look for the several rock faces on the lake that display Native rock paintings.

Just north of Nelson you can't help but notice the impressive neo-Tudor mansion on the west side of the highway. Built by Cominco president Selwyn G. Blaylock in 1934, it was designed by the same Montreal architectural firm that built the Banff Springs Hotel. One feature was the botanical gardens, which originally featured one specimen of every tree indigenous to Canada at the time. Mr. Blaylock's private home for many years, the mansion has recently been turned into a resort and health spa (1-888-788-3613).

Access to Kokanee Glacier Provincial Park is found 19 km north of Nelson. The 32,035 hectare-park features several glaciers and high-altitude lakes. Gibson Lake is a good day-hike accessible from this point. Popular with local hikers and anglers, the park is a wilderness area and visitors should be properly equipped. Other access points are found near Ainsworth, Kaslo, Slocan City and Lemon Creek.

Balfour is the ferry terminal for the trip across the lake. It's also popular with anglers.

Further north on Hwy. 31 at the tiny town of Ainsworth, it is easy to imagine yourself back in a simpler time, when mining was king and a fortune was over the next rise. The first settlement here in 1882 was overshadowed by developments elsewhere, and the

### Top Five West Kootenay Hot Springs

1.  Halcyon—developed resort. Hwy. 23 north of Nakusp.
2.  Halfway River—undeveloped. Hwy. 23 north of Nakusp. Ask locally.
3.  St Leon—undeveloped, but with concrete pool. Hwy. 23 north of Nakusp. Ask locally.
4.  Nakusp—developed, but low key. Fifteen minutes from Nakusp. Follow signs just north of town.
5.  Ainsworth—developed resort, 115km north of Nelson.

*Ainsworth once had five hotels. But the Silver Ledge, built in 1896, is the only one still standing.*

town was destroyed by fire in 1896. However, silver mines like the Pearl Lulu, Skyline, Highland, Jeff Davis, and Mile Point contributed to its recovery, and Ainsworth boomed until the turn of the century. The Silver Ledge Hotel, built in 1896, still stands, open periodically as a museum.

Nowadays people flock here for the 40°C to 43°C pools and the eerie caves at Ainsworth Hot Springs Resort (250-229-4212). The hot springs are just off the highway, beside Kootenay Lake. You can stay at the resort or other local accommodation if you can't imagine moving another inch once you've had your soak.

If you enjoy dark subterranean places, turn off Highway 31 five km north of Ainsworth. Cody Caves Provincial Park—and 800 metres of explorable passage—is 16 km along a seasonal gravel road. The impressive underground display includes stalactites, stalagmites, soda straws, tunnels, and galleries formed millions of years ago. Access to the caves is only by guided tour (one hour). Reservations are not necessary during the summer months, but reservations are required during the off-season or for advanced groups. Equipment is included in the tour fee. Wear warm clothing (250-353-7425).

## Kaslo

32 km (20 mi.) north of Balfour. Population: 1063. Info Centre: On the S.S. *Moyie.* 324 Front Street, Box 537, V0G 1M0. Phone and fax: 250-353-2525. Seasonal. Email: ssmoyie@klhs.bc.ca.

Dubbed "the quintessential Rocky Mountain town" by *National Geographic* (and it's not even in the Rockies), this is another Kootenay town that has survived the ups and downs of mining, lumbering, and orcharding. Galena ore was discovered in 1892; Kaslo was incorporated in 1893; and for a while it was a hive of activity with paddlewheelers coming and going, 20 hotels, 14 barbershops, a sawmill, and banks. It even had its own railroad, the indomitable narrow-gauge Kaslo and Slocan line. A fire and a flood in 1894 slowed the town down, but it gave the people a legacy of survival that carries through to this day.

Several heritage buildings are still in use, and some traditions like the annual May Day celebrations have been kept alive for over a century. Held every year since 1893, on the May long weekend, activities include the traditional maypole dance and logging sports. A word of warning: this little town is captivating. You wouldn't be the first person who was "just passing through" and never left.

*The restored SS Moyie, now a Kaslo museum, was the last commercial sternwheeler to operate in BC. The vessel's shallow draft allowed it to dock on beaches, making it an important means of early transportation in the Interior.*

# Side trip:
# Lardeau Valley

North of Kaslo, partly paved Hwy. 31 gives access to Meadow Creek, the Duncan Dam, and the Lardeau Valley. Southeast of Meadow Creek, the road travels to the Quaker community of Argenta and the trailhead for the Purcell Wilderness Conservancy and the Fry Creek Canyon Recreation Area, popular with hikers.

Highway 31 travels up the Lardeau River, by Trout Lake, past the sites of old mining towns like Poplar, Ferguson, and Trout Lake City. There are few amenities, but the scenery is unbeatable. The Lardeau River is the spawning place for Gerrard trout (world's largest race of rainbow trout)—a wildlife management success story. During the 1950s there were only about fifty rainbow spawning here each year, but now the annual run numbers a thousand. To protect the fish, the river is permanently closed to angling.

At Galena Bay a ferry travels across the Upper Arrow lake to Shelter Bay, where Hwy. 23 connects to Revelstoke and the Trans-Canada Highway. Self-guided tours are offered at Hill Creek Spawning Channel and Hatchery (8 km

## While You're In Kaslo ... Top Five

1. Tour the S.S. Moyie, the oldest of five remaining historic sternwheelers in Canada. Built in 1898, the boat logged over two million miles in her lifetime, carrying miners, settlers, tourists, and business people up and down the lake (www.klhs.bc.ca/htmlfiles/visitor.html).

2. Pick up a brochure on the self-guided heritage walking tour at the *Moyie* or at Kaslo City Hall—in use continuously since 1898, and a designated national historic site (250-353-2311). Also included is the Langham Centre, once a rough-and-ready hotel, then a bank, an internment centre during World War II, and now restored as an arts centre with a small theatre and gallery (250-353-2661).

3. Rent a boat and go fishing for the prized kokanee trout.

4. Drive up to Buchanan Lookout (9 km west on Hwy. 31A) to enjoy the view, hike the short interpretive trail, or watch the hang-gliders.

5. Enjoy the annual Kaslo Jazz Etc Festival, held the first week in August.

east of Galena Bay on Hwy. 31; 250-369-2234). During spawning season it's a great place to view black bear, osprey, eagles, mink, and otter. South of Galena Bay, Hwy. 23 leads to Nakusp.

## Ghost Town Highway

Highway 31A west of Kaslo continues to the "Silvery Slocan" Valley. This area was a frenzy of mining activity in the 1890s—"silver, lead, and hell" were raised in the Slocan, the saying goes.

Although towns like Nelson and Kaslo survived the boom-bust cycle, many didn't, and along this road the former towns of Retallack, Zincton, and Three Forks stand as skeletons today. Retallack (sometimes called Whitewater), at an elevation of 1085 metres, yielded over a million dollars in rich galena ore.

### Ghost Towns

**Ainsworth**—North of Nelson on Kootenay Lake, Ainsworth was one of many West Kootenay mining towns that boomed during the 1890s but battled with fires and bad luck. Now the site of a hot-springs resort; a few original buildings remain.
**Poplar**—In the Lardeau Valley, 144 km north of Nelson. At the turn of the century it was a gold prospecting town with a population of 3000, reduced to four by 1947.
**Sandon**—Between New Denver and Kaslo, Sandon was the heart of the Silvery Slocan mining boom of the 1890s. During World War II the town housed 1000 Japanese-Canadians.

*An old building in Sandon displays embellishments of the past.*

### Sandon

**One of the most famous** ghost towns is Sandon. (The turnoff is at Three Forks junction, 34 km west of Kaslo.) In 1891 prospectors discovered a rich outcropping of ore here that led to the establishment of claims like the Noble Five, the Slocan Star, and the Payne Boy. Sandon boomed, and the Silvery Slocan became one of the richest silver regions on the continent.

By 1898 Sandon had 5000 residents, 29 hotels, 28 saloons, several banks, two newspapers, an opera house, three breweries, a hydroelectric plant, two railroads and even a cigar factory. The town was rebuilt after a fire in 1900, but declining markets put it on a downhill course. Two original buildings house the Sandon Museum (250-358-7920; http://server.slocanlake.com/sandon/) and the Tin Cup Café, open during the summer. The hydroelectric plant, which won the Attractions Canada Award for 1999, is still operating (http://www.sandonbc.com/index.htm; tours available in summer), and mining continues to this day.

## Ada Robichaud

**Former Manager, Tin Cup Café, Sandon**

I think of the buildings as dream homes because somebody's dreams are locked up in them. People keep coming back—the Japanese who were here, and the miners.

A Japanese woman came through once and I was showing her around this house. She looked at the wooden bathtub in the back room and said she remembered taking baths in that. Her uncle had built it. She'd lived in the house next door during the internment.

I think ghost towns attract eccentrics. It's not your waterslide crowd. Many people have the

sense that they've been here before or they'd like to stay.

People ask if I've seen ghosts. That doesn't happen to me. I'm not afraid of dark places. I feel comfortable with ghosts. But people want there to be ghosts here.

I lived for a long time in Ferguson in the Lardeau—same time, same era. It went until the First World War and then never recovered. There were 3000 people there and now you can't tell where any of them lived. It just looks like a meadow.

## Mattie Gunterman

**Born Ida Madelaine** Werner in La Crosse, Wisconsin, in 1872, Mattie Gunterman is well-known among Canadian photographers for her images of pioneer life in the Interior.

Gunterman moved to Seattle as a teenager; an uncle there taught her to use a camera during the

early Kodak craze. Diagnosed with tuberculosis and told by doctors she didn't have long to live, in 1897 she left Seattle, and along with her husband Will, their five-year-old son Henry, dog Nero, and horse Nellie, walked 800 km to Beaton on the Arrow Lakes in the Kootenays. (The photo above, taken by Gunterman, shows the family, possibly on the Dewdney Trail in 1898.)

In 1898, the Lardeau was a vital mining area, part of the West

Kootenay mining boom. Will worked as a logger and miner in the camps around Beaton, and Mattie worked as a cook. Her photographs show ordinary activities of the community and display a sense of humour and spontaneity that contrast with the more formal portraiture popular at the time.

Hard times hit the mining communities in the Lardeau during the early 1900s and the Gunterman family suffered as well.

While working in Alberta in 1927, a fire destroyed the Gunterman home, all her original prints, and much of her equipment. She continued to live in the Lardeau area, and died of a heart attack in 1945 at age 73.

In 1961, when Ron D'Altroy of the Vancouver Public Library was travelling through Beaton, he met an old trapper who told him about some photographic plates that he had stored in a shed. The trapper was Henry Gunterman, Mattie's son. The 300 glass negatives were all that remained of Mattie Gunterman's photographs. Carefully restored, they are now part of the photographic archives of the Vancouver Public Library, and a remarkable record of pioneer days in the West Kootenay.

## New Denver

47 km (28 mi.) west of Kaslo. Population: 571. Info Centre: 513-6th Street, Box 448, V0G 1S0. 250-358-2719; Fax: 250-358-7989. (Seasonal.) Email: valhallainn@netidea.com. Web: server.slocanlake.com/¶newdenver/

Descending into New Denver along Hwy. 31, travellers see the sparkle of Slocan Lake and look right across to New Denver Glacier in Valhalla Provincial Park. Early explorers called this town Lucerne, for its similarity to the Swiss landscape, and later a romantic with big expectations named it Eldorado. As mining in the area boomed, and the mother lode turned out to be silver, not gold, the town named itself yet again. New Denver carved out a niche for itself as a supply and service centre, assuring its survival, but a walk down its main street clearly speaks to its mining past.

To the south of Carpenter Creek is the Nikkei Internment Memorial Centre, one of several sites in the Slocan Valley where hundreds of Japanese-Canadians were interned during World War II.

## Japanese-Canadian Internment

**In December 1941**, Japan attacked Pearl Harbor. Eight weeks later, in February 1942, the federal government of Canada invoked the War Measures Act and ordered the removal of all Japanese and Japanese-Canadians living on BC's coast. Most were given only 24-hours notice.

Many of the 22,000 men, women, and children labelled as "enemy aliens" had been born in Canada and spoke no Japanese. About 13,000 were "relocated" to internment and work camps in BC's Interior; others were sent east of the Rockies.

While many of the men were sent to work camps, women, children, and the elderly were often settled in the almost-ghost towns of Greenwood, Sandon, Kaslo, Slocan, and New Denver. A special camp was built at Tashme, in the mountains west of Hope. The largest number of internees (4800) were housed in the Slocan Valley south of New Denver at Lemon Creek, Passmore, and Crescent Valley.

In some places, people were housed in old buildings such as the Langham Hotel in Kaslo, the hockey rink in Slocan, or even tents. But most common as housing were the rows of uninsulated one-room shacks that accommodated two or more families.

Writer Joy Kogawa and environmentalist David Suzuki are two prominent Canadians who spent part of their childhoods in the camps.

In 1986, the federal government formally apologized and offered financial compensation to surviving internees.

Like Kaslo, this is a little town in a stunningly beautiful location that may grab your heart if you're not careful. Perhaps it's best to come here on a Sunday when the real estate office is closed.

## Side trip: Nakusp

52 km (32 mi.) north of New Denver. Population: 1813. Info Centre: 92 West 6th Avenue, Box 387, V0G

1R0. 250-265-4234, 1-800-909-8819. Fax: 250-265-3808. Email: nakcom@columbiacable.net. Web: www.nakusphotsprings.com/ The town of Nakusp sits on Upper Arrow Lake, a continuation of the Columbia River. Here the mountains—the Monashees on the west side of the lake, the Selkirks behind— are a little gentler and less imposing than those to the east.

As part of the Slocan mining boom, entrepreneurs were planning to build a smelter in Nakusp, and the Nakusp-Slocan Railway was built in 1893. But when Trail's smelter operation expanded, the plan was dropped. Agriculture, logging, and transportation became the economic mainstays.

Nakusp was an important stopover on the busy sternwheeler route up and down the lakes until the 1950s. In the 1960s, much of the surrounding land was flooded as part of the Columbia River Treaty, a controversial development that wiped out entire towns and destroyed much of the farmland.

Highway 23 runs north from Nakusp and connects with the Trans-Canada Highway at Revelstoke. Along the way you might want to stop at Halcyon Hot Springs Resort. The springs were popular with early First Nations people, and then developed as a resort and healing centre from the 1890s to 1955, when it was destroyed by fire. It has recently reopened, with accommodation, campsites, horseback riding, hiking trails, a restaurant, and other facilities. (250-265-3554; 1-888-689-4699; www. halcyon-hotsprings.com/).

The highway crosses the lake via a free (at time of publication) ferry from Galena Bay to Shelter Bay—check the schedule before you leave Nakusp. The ferry does not operate between 12:30 A.M. and 5:30 A.M.

Highway 6 continues south of town, crosses the Lower 7Arrow Lake on the free ferry from Fauquier to Needles

## While You're In New Denver ... Top Five

1. Visit the Nikkei Internment Memorial Centre, where restored buildings, interpretive signs, and gardens reflect the lives of the Japanese Canadians who were forced to live here during WW II. The only museum of its kind in the country.
2. Stroll along main street with its unassuming heritage buildings, including the Silvery Slocan Museum (250-358-2201) and its local history displays.
3. Boat across the lake to Valhalla Provincial Park, a wilderness area with several trails for day hikes or longer. Local citizens lobbied long and hard for the establishment of the park.
4. Hike or bike the Nakusp-Slocan rail line north of town, or the 13-km Galena Trail between Roseberry and Three Forks (accessible at New Denver). It includes a self-propelled cable car across Carpenter Creek, and goes right through a historic mining area (www.slocanlake.com/areainfo/recreation/galena/index.html).
5. Drive up to Idaho Lookout for a panoramic view from the fire lookout (elevation 2280 m) and glorious alpine meadows. The 12-km gravel road can be a bit tricky, so ask locally about conditions.

## While You're In Nakusp ... Top Five

1. Soak out those traveller's kinks at Nakusp Hot Springs (250-265-4528; 1-800-909-8819). Depending on the season it can top off a day of hiking, cross-country skiing, or horseback riding in Nakusp Hot Springs Provincial Park.
2. Walk along the lakefront by the Leland Hotel (250-265-4221 or 250-265-3314), one of the province's oldest operating hotels.
3. Fish for Dolly Varden and kokanee salmon on the Arrow or Summit lakes .
4. Attend a free music concert at the gazebo across from the beach every Wednesday evening during the summer, or mix with the locals at the annual fall fair in September.
5. Find out about local history at the Nakusp Museum, built as a school in 1912 (250-265-0015).

*Once a raucous mining town with a population of 6000, Slocan City is now a milltown of a few hundred.*

(a five-minute ride), and then heads west to the Okanagan. The Needles-Fauquier ferry runs every half-hour and is available on a shuttle basis from 10 P.M. to 5 A.M.

## Silverton

5 km (2 mi.) south of New Denver. Population: 246. Web: server. slocanlake.com/silverton/

From New Denver, Hwy. 6 heads south along Slocan Lake through the picturesque mining town of Silverton. The town's pebble beach is a good place to watch the clouds go by. The lake is deep, the water is cold, and hordes of tourists are unheard of. The town council operates a 15-site campground on the lake next to the boat launch.

The Silverton Gallery and Mining Museum (250-358-7788 ) is in a restored and converted 1917 schoolhouse. An outdoor mining display features both 19th- and 20th-century mining equipment from the area. The gallery features performances and displays.

Watch carefully for wildlife. There are lots of deer along this route, and too many of them are killed by inattentive motorists. Black bear, especially around Red Mountain, are not uncommon. Be sure to pull off at the lookout south of Silverton for a truly memorable view of Slocan Lake and Valhalla Provincial Park.

## Valhalla Provincial Park

Numerous alpine lakes dot the upper reaches of this 49,600-hectare wilderness area, and a hike up one of several creeks passes through a variety of forest, subalpine, and alpine terrains. The lakes are stocked with trout, and in July and August the blueberries are sweet and juicy. Wildlife such as bear, mountain goat, deer, cougar, and mountain caribou live on the slopes, and eagles soar overhead.

## Five Good Wildlife Viewing Areas

1. Hwy 6 between New Denver and Slocan—bear, deer, birds.
2. Kokanee Creek Provincial Park—spawning salmon, deer, eagle, osprey.
3. Hill Creek (Galena Bay)—spawning salmon, birds, otter, bear.
4. Walter Clough Wildlife Management Area (Lemon Creek, Slocan Valley)—birds, small mammals.
5. Hwy 23 Nakusp to Galena Bay—birds, bear, small mammals.

*Beatrice Lake is a welcome sight after hiking through Valhalla Provincial Park's wilderness trails.*

ming, but on a hot day, it's very refreshing.

## Slocan City

19 km (11 mi.) south of New Denver. Population: 263. Info Centre: 704 Arlington Street, Box 50, V0G 2C0. 250-355-2282; Fax: 250-355-2666. Seasonal.

Slocan City is a quiet town today, with one hotel and a handful of stores, but in the 1890s it was a wide open mining town. Slocan was at the end of the rail line, and sternwheelers carried miners and supplies up and down the lake from here to Silverton and New Denver. Slippery gamblers plied their trade at the 16 hotels and saloons that lined the main street, and more than one miner lost a hard-earned fortune in a card game over a bottle of whiskey. A handful of old buildings give evidence of Slocan City's colourful past, but most visitors today are interested in the recreational opportunities—the trailhead for Valhalla Park, access to Slocan River and Lake, and access to the Slocan Rail Trail, which when complete will weave 45 km south along the river.

The park is accessible by boat or logging road from several locations, including a trail from Slocan City that winds along the shore of the lake—an easy and enjoyable day trip. The parking area for the trailhead is two blocks west of the main street at the head of the Slocan River. The trailhead is across the bridge and up the road 100 metres. The park is also accessible via Drinnon Lake in the Little Slocan Valley. The turnoff is 20 km south on Hwy. 6.

Boaters can reach the park from several places along the east shore. At Slocan City, put in at the beach beside the mill and paddle up the lake. On both sides, pictographs on the rock faces tell mysterious stories. The lake is cold for swim-

## Slocan Valley

There is evidence that people have lived in the Kootenays for 7000 years, with at least 14 Native villages on the Slocan River alone. Native groups have not lived in the valley for many years, but a plan to relocate the highway over an ancient burial ground in the late 1980s brought a renewed interest in local Native history from both Natives and others. Declared extinct by the federal government in 1956,

---

### While You're In Slocan Valley ... Top Five

1. View local history through the Slocan Mural Project in Slocan Park, Winlaw, and Slocan City.
2. Kayak, canoe, or tube portions of the Slocan River. Ask about river conditions locally. (www.gowestkootenay.com/paddleslocanr.html)
3. Picnic and swim at the Winlaw Nature Park, 1 km north of Winlaw Bridge on Slocan River Road.
4. Bike the back road from Perry's Siding to Slocan Park.
5. Explore Kokanee Glacier Provincial Park from the west side—access at Lemon Creek.

descendants of the Sinixt people have been returning to Vallican, at the confluence of the Slocan and Little Slocan Rivers, over the last few years. The modern Sinixt claim that their people were not nomadic—they lived permanently in the valley—and nor are they currently extinct.

Non-Native settlement began with the mining boom in the 1890s. Other settlers homesteaded during the early 1900s. When the Doukhobor communities near Castlegar dissolved during the 1930s, many families established farms in the Slocan Valley. In the 1960s and 1970s it became a popular back-to-the-land destination for counter culture "pioneers". As you travel the highway, you'll notice many picturesque farms and old log buildings.

The Slocan River empties into the Kootenay River just west of the junctions of Highways 3A and 6. But our route heads east, back to Nelson, for the completion of the tour.

*At Balfour, just north of Nelson, you can take "the longest free ferry ride in the world."*

## Free Ferry across Kootenay Lake

Balfour, 34 km northeast of Nelson on Hwy. 3A, used to be a stop on the paddlewheeler routes up and down Kootenay Lake. Today, the small community is a popular resort area and a terminus for the "longest free ferry ride in the world" (although news reports at the time of publication suggest it may not be free for long). The schedule depends on the time of year, so check the times locally. The crossing to Kootenay Bay takes about

## While You're In Kootenay Lake East Shore ... Top Ten

1. Stop for tea or a meal at historic Wedgewood Manor (1-800-862-0022) in Crawford Bay.
2. Look for local treats at the Crawford Bay Fall Fair, a popular event since 1910, held annually in late August or early September.
3. Watch local craftspeople at work in their studios in Crawford Bay.
4. Take a hike—to the lighthouse in Pilot Bay Marine Park at Kootenay Bay; along Pebble Beach Trail near Riondel; Lockhard Creek Valley Trail near Boswell; Plaid Lake Trail near Crawford Bay; Duck Lake Dykes Trail near Sirdar.
5. Boat or canoe along the lake—view 600-million-year-old rock formations along the shore near Pilot Bay.
6. Stop and shop at Gray Creek General Store, opened in 1913 and claimed by its owners to be "the most interesting store you've ever seen."
7. Visit a genuine ashram for a browse of the bookstore or a full-length retreat (2 km off Hwy. 3A toward Riondel; Yasodhara Ashram Yoga Retreat and Study Centre, 1-800-661-8711).
8. Golf at the championship Kokanee Springs Golf Resort (1-800-979-7999).
9. Stop at the famous Glass House in Boswell , a unique free-form structure constructed from 500,000 embalming bottles by a retired funeral home director. (Tours available in summer: 250-223-8372.)
10. Dive for buried treasure near Gray Creek.

45 minutes, and as the ferry pulls away from the dock, you may catch a glimpse of an osprey dive-bombing the water in search of breakfast, or an eagle watchfully circling overhead.

## Kootenay Lake East Shore

The east shore of the lake was also part of the 1890s mining boom in the Kootenays. The old chimney at Smelter Bay, visible as the ferry approaches Kootenay Bay, was part of a plant that employed two hundred men in the early part of the decade. The smelter processed ore from the rich Blue Bell Mine in Riondel, which supported a town of one thousand. But when the Hall Smelter opened in Nelson in 1896, the Pilot Bay Smelter was no longer economical, and it closed down.

Riondel, north of Kootenay Bay, is now a retirement community, but its Blue Bell Mine was a going concern until 1957. Robert Sproule first staked the claim in 1882, but had to travel all the way to Fort Steele to make it official. While he was away, Thomas Hamill found the claim, and because he happened to be on a hunting trip with the gold commissioner, claimed ownership. Hamill was shot on the site in 1885, and Sproule was hanged for the crime in 1886, although he steadfastly proclaimed his innocence.

The east side of the lake was the Crowsnest Highway until the construction of the Salmo-Creston Skyway in 1963. This scenic route is dotted with resorts, B&Bs, and campsites. Year-round fishing on the lake is for Dolly Varden, kokanee, rainbow, and whitefish, although some restrictions may be in effect. Check locally. Boats and guides are available.

Monitor your gold fever—rumours abound of buried treasure in the Gray Creek area. One story tells of three men who in 1892 came across a huge gold nugget in these mountains, estimated then to be worth $650,000. While attempting to lower it into their row boat near Gray Creek, the rope broke and the nugget disappeared in 60 metres of water. It has yet to be recovered.

The scenic drive continues along the lakeshore for another 50 km past Boswell through the old mining town of Sanca. At Kuskanook—a Ktunaxa word meaning "end of the lake"—the popular Metis poet Pauline Johnson enthralled audiences with her mesmerizing stories on one of her cross-country tours in the 1890s.

Just before Creston there is a viewpoint at the junction of Highways 3 and 3A, which takes in the south end of the lake, the Creston flats, and the Selkirk Range.

## Fore! SuperGuide Recommends

**Balfour**

**Balfour Golf & Country Club**. Semi-private. 18 holes. Par 72. 6420 yards. Queens Bay Road, Box 139, V0G 1C0. 866-669-4653. Email: proshop@netidea.com. Web: www.golfbalfour.com

**Crawford Bay**

**Kokanee Springs Golf Resort**. 18 holes. Par 71. 6537 yards. Design: Norman Woods. Box 96, V0B 1E0. 800-979-7999. Email: info@kokaneesprings.com. Web: www.kokaneesprings.com

**Nelson**

**Granite Pointe. Semi-private**. 18 holes. Par 72. 6209 yards. Box 141, 1123 West Richards St., V1L 5P7. 1-877-677-6077. Email: Info@granitepointe.ca. Web: http://www.mjconsulting.ca/granitepointe/

**New Denver**

**Slocan Lake Golf Course**. 9 holes. Par 70. 5387 yards. 6309 Highway 6, Box 297, V0G 1S0. 250-358-2408

All courses are public, unless indicated. Play is seasonal. For information on all courses in this region: www.bcgolfguide.com.

## Five Great Hikes

1. Fry Creek Canyon, North end of Kootenay Lake— Hwy. 31 from Kaslo. Two hours to falls.
2. Pulpit Rock, Nelson— Johnstone Road, north side of orange bridge. 1-2 hours. Great views.
3. Pilot Bay Marine Park— Kootenay Bay.
4. Slocan Lake—from Slocan City along lakeshore.
5. Galena Trail—Roseberry to Sandon.

# East Kootenay

*The fertile bottomland of the Rocky Mountain Trench is visible from space, stretching 1600 km from north to south. Its width ranges from 16 km in the south to 3 km in the north.*

A t the same time that Simon Fraser was battling the turbulent waters of the river that was eventually to bear his name, David Thompson was viewing the quiet beauty of the Kootenay Valley for the first time. "It resembles a large basin, surrounded by lofty mountains which form a

vast amphitheatre and present a picturesque sight," wrote Thompson in 1808. Although the area was inhabited by Ktunaxa (Kutenai) and Secwepemc (Shuswap) people, Thompson was the first European to map and record the Rockies and Rocky Mountain Trench area with its semi-arid grasslands and mystical hot springs.

When Thompson made his observations, he was here (as was Fraser) on behalf of the North West Company. The fur-trading company was anxious to find the mouth of Columbia and exploit the river as a supply route before the Americans could. Thompson lost the race to John Jacob Astor's Pacific Fur Company by just a few weeks. But he is responsible for charting most of the Columbia River's watershed between 1807 and 1812. He established Koote-

nae House near Invermere in 1807, and several forts in Washington and Idaho.

The discovery of gold at Wild Horse Creek near present-day Fort Steele in 1864 opened up the area to settlement. When claims were staked on the Big Bend of the Columbia River in 1866, the valley became a major transportation route, with sternwheelers bustling up and down the waterways. The construction of the CPR through Rogers Pass in the early 1880s, the discovery of rich ore deposits near Kimberley and coal in the Elk Valley in the 1890s, and the completion of the CPR's Crowsnest rail line in 1898, further stimulated development and settlement.

The East Kootenay seems a world apart from the rest of the Interior. Perhaps this is because

*Opposite: Most of Top of the World Provincial Park, in the Kootenay Range of the Rocky Mountains, is in excess of 2200 m elevation.*

**165**

With the closure of the Kimberley mine threatening its economy, Kimberley has reinvented itself as a Bavarian-style four-seasons tourist destination.

the region is so far from the provincial centres of power on the coast. Or perhaps it has to do with the towering peaks of the Purcell and Rocky mountains standing sentinel on either side of the valley. As with the Ktunaxa people who resided here before the arrival of the fur traders, today's residents enjoy an easier alliance with the area east of the Rockies and the American states to the south than with the rest of BC.

The mild temperatures and varied landscape make the East Kootenay region a popular outdoor recreation destination. Vacationers can enjoy mountain climbing, alpine fishing, whitewater rafting, canoeing, swimming, and waterskiing within hours of each other. Some of the best golf courses in the province are at Fernie, Kimberley and Invermere. Ski resorts at Invermere and Fernie are establishing international reputations, and Bugaboo heli-skiing is already world famous.

Highway 93/95 travels north from Cranbrook through the wide valley of the Rocky Mountain Trench to Radium Hot Springs. One fork, Hwy. 95, continues north beside the Columbia River to Golden on the Trans-Canada; the other, Hwy. 93, through Kootenay National Park to Alberta. The two highest mountain passes on the route are both on Hwy. 93: Sinclair Pass (1486 m) and Vermilion Pass (1639 m).

## Kimberley

32 km (20 mi.) north of Cranbrook on Hwy. 95A. Population: 6908. Info Centre: 115 Gerry Sorensen Way, V1A 3E9. 250-427-3666; Fax: 250-427-5378. Email: kimbchamber@cyberlink.bc.ca. Web: www.cyberlink.bc.ca/~kimbchamber

Historically, Kimberley has depended on the riches beneath its mountains. For many years the Sullivan Mine was the largest producer of lead and zinc ore in the world; its presence provided an eco-

### Kimberley Great Outdoors ... Top Five

1. Ski North Star Mountain at the new and improved Kimberley Alpine Ski Resort (1-250-427-4881). This is the home slope of 1982 women's world downhill champion Gerry Sorensen.
2. Hike one of the Kimberley Nature Park trails (ask at the Info Centre for maps).
3. Golf at three championship courses: Trickle Creek, St. Eugene, and Kimberley.
4. Walk along the boardwalk and gravel trail (5 min.) to the Marysville Waterfalls (south of town on Hwy. 95A).
5. Go river rafting (St. Mary's and Elk rivers).

**167**

nomic base for almost a hundred years. The Sullivan discovery was made in 1892, with the first shipment to the smelter in Trail in 1900. Cominco took over the Sullivan in 1910, and production continued until 2001. Today, the town has shifted its economic base to the riches on top of the mountains—scenery, snow, and ambience.

Kimberley is nestled between the Purcells and Rockies, overlooking the Valley of a Thousand Peaks. At 1117 m above sea level, this is one of the highest cities in Canada, so it makes sense that the town adopted a Bavarian theme in 1972. The move transformed it from a drab mining town to an attractive tourist destination. Many European visitors, impressed by the clean air and other alpine attributes, have settled in the area, with the result that what began as a marketing idea now has authentic ingredients. The Old Bauernhaus Restaurant (250-427-3632) is a prime example. Two German families dismantled this 400-year-old family home in Germany and rebuilt it here in 1989.

*The 400-year-old Bauernhaus was dismantled in Bavaria in 1987 and reconstructed in Kimberley in 1989. Today it is a restaurant offering authentic German cuisine.*

## Sullivan Mine Facts

1. The mine produced ore containing 17 million tonnes of zinc and lead metal.
2. It has produced 285 million ounces of silver.
3. Total value to the provincial economy: $20 billion.
4. The lead mined was enough to produce 500 million lead-acid car batteries.
5. The zinc mined was enough to supply the zinc content of 160 million cars.

## While You're In Kimberley ... Top Five

1. Check your watch at the world's largest freestanding cuckoo clock at Bavarian Platzl on Spokane Street. The Platzl is the centre of everything, including restaurants and delis, and in the summer, wandering minstrels.
2. Visit the Heritage Museum at the end of the Platzl (250-428-7510) where mining is king, but the archival collection of photographs and newspapers is also worth a look.
3. Smell the flowers at Cominco/Kimberley Gardens, showcasing 48 varieties of flowers and over 50,000 plants (within walking distance on Fourth Avenue).
4. Ride the Bavarian Mining Railway (250-427-3666)—a 9 km, one-hour narrated train trip with a view of the city, the Rocky Mountains, and the old Sullivan Mine.
5. Drive all the way to Kootenay Lake (Gray Creek) on seasonal Hwy. 44. Or stop off at the Purcell Wilderness Conservancy and St. Mary's Alpine Park.

## Kimberley Special Events–Best Bets

**February**–Winterfest

**June**–Marysville Daze

**July**–International Old Time Accordion Championships; Julyfest

**September**–Country Fair

**October**–Oktoberfest

**November**–Christmas Light Up

## Fort Steele Provincial Heritage Site

Workers at Fort Steele Heritage Town maintain machinery and equipment from the 1890s.

This authentic steam engine is put into duty during the summer months at Fort Steele Historic Town. The historic train takes visitors on tours several times a day.

**16 km (10 mi.)** northeast of Cranbrook on Highway 3/95. 250-426-7352/417-6000. Fax: 250-489-2624. Email: info@ fortsteele.bc.ca. Web: www. fortsteele.bc.ca

With the discovery of gold at Wild Horse Creek in 1864, miners rushed to the area from Montana, Washington, and Idaho. Some, like John Galbraith, realized there was more profit in tending to the needs of the prospectors than actually doing the backbreaking work of gold mining. For the hefty price of $10 per pack horse and $5 per person, Galbraith allowed the prospectors to cross the Coot River on his cable ferry to reach the banks of the creek. Galbraith's success encouraged brother Robert to move west, and the pair opened a store and established a pack train to Walla Walla, Washington. Soon Little Lou, Axe Handle Bertha, Wildcat Jennie, and Gunpowder Sue opened up a "finishing school" in the

settlement. A town was born.

By the 1880s the gold rush was long over, and the population of several thousand gold seekers at Galbraith's Ferry had dwindled to a few hundred. But in 1887, there was conflict between the Ktunaxa Natives and the white settlers. A detachment of 75 North West Mounted Police headed by Superintendent Sam Steele set up a post, staying long enough to settle the dispute. The citizens of Galbraith's Ferry, grateful for the peaceful handling of the matter, renamed their town Fort Steele.

With the resurgence of mining activity in the Kootenays in the 1890s, Fort Steele once again became a centre of activity. It was a bitter blow to the community when the CPR's Crowsnest line went through Cranbrook further to the south in 1898. Residents left for more prosperous ventures elsewhere, and the bustle faded to a faint rustle.

Today there are over sixty

restored and reconstructed buildings on the site. In the summer months history comes alive as costumed staff recreate life in Fort Steele as it was in the 1890s, hosting wagon rides, live stage shows in the Wild Horse Theatre, steam locomotive train trips, restaurant meals, and a variety of special events. Fort Steele is open year-round, but "living history" experience is during peak season, mid-June to Labour Day.

Ask locally for directions to the graveyard at Wild Horse townsite and "the last mile" of the Dewdney Trail. This historic route was hacked through the bush from Hope in the mid-1860s in a successful attempt to maintain British sovereignty over the area. The portion here is a two-hour hike, passing the old mining site of Fisherville, the Chinese graveyard, and Wild Horse Creek.

250-417-6000; www.fort steele.bc.ca/

*First Nations people have visited Top of the World Provincial Park for at least 9000 years, mining its prized chert.*

## The Valley of a Thousand Peaks: Three Mountain Parks

Although our route turns north at the junction of Highways 95A and 93/95, you might want to detour just south of the junction to Wasa Lake, one of the most popular recreation areas in the East Kootenay. Wasa Lake Provincial Park has several beaches, an interpretive program, and self-guiding nature trails.

The scenery continues to be spectacular as Highway 93/95 winds north through grasslands and pastures and the peaks of the Rockies loom overhead. Turn east at the pulp mill town of Skookumchuk for access to Premier Lake Provincial Park and excellent trout fishing. Wildlife includes Rocky Mountain bighorn sheep, elk, deer,

osprey and deer.

Hot springs are a major attraction in the Kootenays, with two major resorts north of here featuring the natural hot pools. But those who like to do their soaking in isolation might want to explore Ram Creek Hot Springs, located in a

### Gold Fever

**Although the creeks** in this area have been well-worked by prospectors since the 1860s, gold panning is still a possibility. Some possibilities:

Findlay Creek

Boulder Creek

Wild Horse Creek

Perry Creek

Ask locally for directions.

The area around Skookumchuk Creek is good for rockhounding.

121-hectare ecological reserve. Turn off Premier Lake Road before the park and head 11.5 km up Sheep Creek Road. (www.gorp.com/gorp/ publishers/falcon/hik_hrsc. htm)

A little further north on Highway 93/95, a sign

### Hot Springs

**Ram Creek**—via Premier Lake Road just north of Skookumchuk on Hwy. 93/95.

**Fish Lake**—hike in; continue on road past Ram Creek Hot Springs.

**Lussier Hot Springs**—in White Swan Provincial Park on Hwy. 93/95 just south of Canal Flats.

**Radium Hot Springs**—developed pools in Kootenay National Park.

**Fairmont**—popular commercial development.

indicates the access roads to Whiteswan Lake Provincial Park and Top of the World Provincial Park. Whiteswan Lake, 16 km off the highway, has good trout fishing in its two lakes and the added bonus of rustic Lussier Hot Springs' several pools.

Top of the World Park is another 38 km along the road. The dominant peak of this 8791-hectare park is Mount Morro, 2912 m in elevation. (Most of the park is above the 1800-m level.) Here, early natives used to obtain chert, a highly prized hard blue-grey rock which they traded or fashioned into tools and weapons. There is big game,

## Ghost Towns

**Baynes Lake**—42 km south of Fernie, an operating general store is all that's left of this mill town, which once had two schools and a hospital. Its heyday was from 1902 to 1925.

**Bull River**—A few false-front buildings remain of this placer gold town, 20 km south of Fort Steele. It appeared in the late 1860s but disappeared when the gold ran out around 1900.

**Fisherville**—11 km from Fort Steele, northeast of Cranbrook. It was the major gold-rush town in the 1860s. Scattered remains of a town and a graveyard still exist.

**Fort Steele**—A major tourist attraction 16 km northeast of Cranbrook on Highway 93/95. The first North West Mounted police post in BC from 1877 to 1888, the town was empty by 1910. In 1961 it became a provincial historic park.

but one of the most popular activities is the trout fishing. The park's many trails attract hikers in summer and skiers in winter.

## Canal Flats
117 km (70 mi.) north of Kimberley.
Location, location, location. The Columbia River begins its 2044-kilometre journey to the Pacific Ocean at Columbia Lake, just north of this little town. And the Kootenay River, with headwaters in Kootenay National Park, passes within a kilometre of Columbia Lake south of here. In 1882 a colourful Englishman saw these two geographic facts as a great opportunity. That was the year William Adolph Baillie-Grohman hatched a scheme to build a canal that

would connect the two bodies of water. In 1889, 200 workers dug the 2-km-long canal, 14 m wide and 3-4 m deep. But the plan fell apart and Baillie-Grohman returned to England in 1893. He spent the rest of his days writing accounts—some say embellished accounts—of his adventures in the wilds of the Kootenays.

Today Canal Flats is a centre for some great water-based recreation. The Kootenay River offers a scenic canoe/kayak trip, through novice to intermediate whitewater, from north of Canal Flats to Fort Steele. Canal Flats Provincial Park has boat-launching facilities, and there is a bighorn sheep-enhancement area nearby. And the winds on Columbia Lake make it a favourite with windsurfers.

## River Rafting Companies

**Alpine Rafting**. 1-888-599-5299. Web: Kickinghorseriver.com. Rivers: Kicking Horse.

**Columbia Rafting Adventures**. 1-877-706-7238. Rivers: Kicking Horse, Columbia and Toby Creek. www.columbiarafting.com/

**Glacier Raft Co**. 250-344-6521. Rivers: Kicking Horse and White.

**Kinbasket Adventures Wilderness Tours**. 1-866-344-6012. www.bcrockiesadventures.com

**Kootenay River Runners**. 1-800-599-4399. www.raftingtherockies.com/ Rivers: Kicking Horse, Kootenay and White.

**Mountain High River Adventures**. 1-877-423-4555. www.mountainhigh.bc.ca. Rivers: Kootenay and White.

**Purcell River Odysseys**. 250-342-3932. www.rockies.net/~pro. Rivers: Toby Creek and Columbia.

**Roam the World**. 250-354-2056. http://www.roamtheworld.ca/trips/chilko_world.Rivers: Chilko/Chilcotin, Fraser.

**Rocky Mountain Rafting**. 1-888-518-7238. rockymountainadventure.com. River: Kicking Horse.

**Wet N Wild Adventures**. 1-800-668-9119. Canadianrockies.net/wetnwild. Rivers: Blaeberry, Kicking Horse, Columbia.

*Dramatic hoodoo formations stretching several kilometres along Dutch Creek are visible from Highway 93/95 south of Fairmont Hot Springs.*

## Ski Areas—SuperGuide's Best Bets

**Fairmont Hot Springs Resort Ski Area**: 304 m vertical, 14 alpine runs, 22 km of Nordic trails, 2 lifts. Accommodations, rentals, snowboard park, heli skiing, restaurants, snowmobiling, cross country, shopping, daycare, night skiing, ski shop. (250-345-6311; 1-800-663-4979; www.fairmontresort.com)

**Panorama Mountain Village (Invermere)**: 1220 m vertical (highest in the Canadian Rockies), 10 lifts, 100 runs. Longest run 5 km. 17 km of groomed cross-country trails. Ski school ranked #1 by Ski Canada Magazine. Alpine village, rentals, snowboard park, heli-skiing, restaurants, snowmobiling, cross-country, ice rink, shopping, daycare, night skiing, ski shop. The area is open in summer for hiking, horseback riding, and rafting. 1-800-663-2929; www.panoramaresort.com/ winter/index2.html

**R.K. Heli Ski**: Various packages and terrains for intermediate to expert skiers. 250-342-3889; 1-800-661-6060; Email: info@rkheliski.com

## Fore! SuperGuide Recommends

### Cranbrook

**Cranbrook Golf Course**. Semi-private. 18 holes. Par 72. 6575 yards. Design: R. Geddes, A. Finlay & F. Fergie. 2700 2nd St. S., Box 297, V1C 4H8. 888-211-8855. Email: mjmgolf@golfcranbrook.com. Web: www.golfcranbrook.com

**St. Eugene Mission Golf Resort**. 18 holes. Par 72. 7007 yards. Design: Les Furber. SS #3 S 15 C14 Mission Rd., V1C 6H3. 877-417-3133. Email: info@GolfStEugene.com. Web: www.golfsteugene.com

### Fairmont Hot Springs

**Fairmont Hot Springs Mountainside Resort**. Public. 18 holes. Par 72. 6522 yards. Box 127, V0B 1L0. 250-345-6346. Email: info@ fairmonthotsprings.com. Web: www.fairmonthotsprings.com

**Riverside Golf Resort at Fairmont**. Semi-private. 18 holes. Par 71. 6507 yards. The Columbia River winds through the course. PO Box 993, V0B 1L0. 1-800-665-2112. Email: info@golfriverside.com. Web: www.golfriverside.com

### Invermere

**Eagle Ranch Resort**. Semi-private. 18 holes. Par 72. 6650 yards. Design: William G. Robinson. RR #3 M-2, C-11, V0B 2L0. 877-877-3889. Email: info@eagleranchresort.com. Web: www.eagleranch resort.com

**Greywolf**. Semi-private. 18 holes. Par 73. 7140 yards. Design: Doug Carrick. Golf Digest's "Best New Canadian Course of 1999" is located at Panorama Resort. 250-342-6941 ext. 3840. Email: paninfo@ intrawest.com www. Web: panoramaresort.com/

### Kimberley

**Trickle Creek Golf Resort**. 18 holes. Par 72. 6896 yards. Design: Les Furber. One of Score Magazine's top 100 Canadian courses. PO Box 190, V1A 2Y6. 1-888-874-2553. Email: trickle@rockies.net. Web: www.tricklecreek.com

### Radium Hot Springs

**Radium Hot Springs Resort**. Two 18-hole courses: Resort (Par 69) & Springs (Par 72). Design: Les Furber. One of Score Magazine's top 100 Canadian courses. Box 310, V0A 1M0. 1-800-667-6444

All courses are public, unless indicated. Play is seasonal. For information on all courses in this region: www.bcgolfguide.com.

*Built in 1887, St. Peter's "Stolen" Church in Windermere has an unusual history.*

## Fairmont Hot Springs

112 km (69 mi.) north of Cranbrook

The healing powers of Fairmont Hot Springs have been attracting people for centuries. The Ktunaxa Natives revered the springs for their mystical origins. As European settlement advanced, the springs became a rest stop for stagecoach travellers. In 1922 a resort was established, which has grown into an international tourist destination (1-800-663-4979. E-mail: info@ FairmontHotSprings.com).

The hot pools—open to everyone, not just hotel guests—are the largest natural hot pools in Canada, made doubly attractive because they are fed by a calcium spring and there is no sulphur odour. Above the hotel is the simpler "Historic Baths" (formerly called the "Indian Pool")

where a soak in one of the stone bathtubs, a paddle in one of the small pools, and the view are all free. Temperatures in the hot pools range from 43°C to 48° C.

In addition to the main resort, there are a number of motels and campgrounds nearby.

## Invermere

24 km (15 mi.) north of Fairmont Hot Springs. Population: 2952. Info Centre: 651 Highway 93/95, Crossroads, Box 1019, V0A 1K0. 250-342-2844; Fax: 250-342-3261. Email: chamber@rockies.net. Web: www.adventurevalley.com/ chamberofcommerce

This picturesque town on Lake

### While You're In Invermere ... Top Five

1. View a limited edition copy of David Thompson's journal at the historic Windermere Valley Pioneer Museum (250-342-9769). The collection also features the history of the upper Columbia Valley and Banff and Kootenay national parks. The main building is the former Athalmer train station.

2. Visit St. Peter's Stolen Church (250-342-9400; Kootenay Street and Victoria Avenue in Windermere).

3. Shop for local arts and crafts at the artisans' village in downtown Windermere (glass-blowers, potters, woodcarvers), the cooperative Village Arts in Invermere (250-342-61521) or Pynelogs Cultural Centre, next to Kinsmen Beach.

4. Stroll the Creekside Gardens in Windermere.

5. Stop for a bite at Strands Old House Restaurant, built in 1912 and once housing the area's first kindergarten.

*Kootenae House was built near present-day Invermere by fur-trader David Thompson in 1808. This replica was built in 1922.*

Windermere—a windsurfer's paradise—is only a three-hour drive from Calgary, and is popular with Albertans as a summer resort. But it attracts historical interest as the site of Kootenae House, the first fur-trading fort in eastern British Columbia.

David Thompson was the explorer who mapped the Co-lumbia River system in the early 1800s. In 1807 the North West Company learned their rivals at the Pacific Fur Company were about to establish a fort at the mouth of the Co-lumbia River. Accompanied by his young Metis wife Char-lotte, and their three children, Thompson crossed the Rock-ies and built a post between the present site of Invermere and Athalmer. For the first few months Peigan Natives, with whom he had been friendly, became angry at his foray into Ktunaxa territory and laid siege to the fort. The Peigan and Ktunaxa were sworn enemies and the Peigan were fearful that Thompson would be trading knives and guns for furs with the Ktunaxa. The Peigan eventually gave up their vigil and Thompson was able to successfully chart the

## Invermere Special Events—Best Bets

**April-May**—Wings Over the Rockies Bird Festival in Inver-mere (1-888-933-3311; www.adventurevalley.com/wings)

**June**—Bull Bustin' in the Rockies Rodeo

**August**—Beside the Lake Hang Gliding & Paragliding Competi-tion at James Chabot Provincial Park

## Invermere Great Outdoors ... Top Five

1. Ski at world-class Panorama Resort. (Keep going along the road to the northern boundary of the Purcell Wilderness Conservancy and the 61-km trail over 2256-m Earl Grey Pass.)

2. Ride horses at a guest ranch.

3. Go river rafting.

4. Play golf at the championship Grey Wolf, Windermere, or Eagle Ranch courses.

5. Windsurf on the lake (or just watch).

river, but he was beaten to the coast by rival American traders. There's no trace of the fort today, but a stone cairn marks its approximate location.

The little town of Windermere just south of Invermere is also worth a stop. One of its claims to fame is the case of the missing church. In 1897, when the CPR moved its divisional point to Revelstoke from Donald (near Golden on the Trans-Canada Highway), many of Donald's buildings were torn down and moved to Revelstoke, along with its people. However, when the townspeople were ready to move the church, they discovered it was gone. A local couple, not aware of the plans for the church, had disassembled it, barged the logs down to Windermere, and rebuilt it.

## Radium Hot Springs

16 km (10 mi.) north of Invermere. Population: 651. Visitor Info Centre: 7556 Main Street East, Box 225, V0A 1M0. Seasonal. 250-347-9331; 1-800-347-9704. Fax: 250-347-9127. Email: chamber@rhs.bc.ca. Web: www.rhs.bc.ca

Radium Hot Springs is both a town and a hot springs. The town is a small logging community at the junction of Highways 93 and 95. The hot springs is at the Aquacourt in Kootenay National Park, just east of the townsite.

Travellers here have hard decisions to make. To the northwest, Highway 95 leads through the scenic Columbia wetlands to Golden. To the east, the Kootenay Parkway (Hwy. 93) travels north through Kootenay National

## Hot Springs

**The West and East** Kootenays are among the best places in the province to find hot springs—both natural and developed. In BC, hot springs seem to follow two major paths. One stretches along the coast from the Yukon to the US border, and the other is more closely connected to the Rocky Mountain Trench, making a path from northwest to southeast.

Hot springs occur when surface water finds its way underground through rock fractures and is heated by hotter rock closer to the earth's core. (The length of time it takes for the water to reach the surface varies. Estimates have the Banff waters

taking three months; Yellowstone waters, fifty years.) The temperature of the water increases approximately 1°C for every 33 metres it descends. At 2.5 kilometres beneath the earth's surface, the temperature is hot enough to boil water. Groundwater that reaches this depth percolates back to the earth's surface via other crack systems.

On its journey, the water absorbs minerals, which some feel gives it therapeutic properties. The medicinal value is debatable, but hot springs are a wonderful way to ease weary muscles.

*Between 1886 and 1914, 15 paddlewheelers travelled the Columbia River between Columbia Lake and Golden. Today, the wetlands provide a superb wildlife habitat and gentle paddling for canoeists.*

## East Kootenay Wildlife Viewing: SuperGuide's Top Picks

**Columbia Wetlands**—birds, elk, moose, bighorn sheep, deer

**Elko**—deer, mountain goat, bighorn sheep

**Kootenay National Park**—mountain goats, bighorn sheep, elk, bear, deer, wolves, birds

**Premier Lake Provincial Park**—Rocky Mountain bighorn sheep, elk deer, birds, spawning trout

**Wasa Slough Wildlife Sanctuary** (14 km north of Fort Steele)—birds and mammals

**Canal Flats Provincial Park**—birds, Rocky Mountain bighorn sheep

Park to Alberta. There are many motels and campgrounds in this area, which makes it an excellent base for forays in either direction.

## Highway 95: The Columbia Wetlands

Radium Hot Springs is about halfway along the 180 km that make up the only remaining undeveloped portion of the Columbia River. (about 30 km north of Golden, the Columbia widens into man-made Kinbasket Lake, created when Mica Creek Dam was built at the Big Bend in 1973.) Thirteen additional hydroelectric power projects dam the water along the rest of the Columbia's 2044-km journey to the Pacific Ocean, and there are dozens more on tributaries.

The 26,000-hectare natural wetland between Canal Flats and Golden houses a variety of marsh, river, and woodland habitats, supporting several species of flora and fauna. Many wintering elk in the Columbia River basin can be found here. With the spawning of kokanee in October, eagles soar overhead. Dozens of species of waterfowl, including Canada Geese, ducks, and osprey, breed here.

Between 1866 and 1914, paddlewheelers travelled the river between Columbia Lake and Golden. Today, this portion of the Columbia River is one of the best canoe routes in the province for novices. The trip between Athalmer and Golden takes about seven days.

*A climber inspects the Vowell Glacier in Bugaboo Provincial Park, which contains the largest icefields in the Purcell Mountains.*

## Bugaboo Glacier Provincial Park and Alpine Recreation Centre

At Brisco, 27 km north of Radium, a gravel road provides seasonal access to 358-hectare Bugaboo Glacier Provincial Park and the adjoining 24,624-hectare Bugaboo Alpine Recreation Area, 45 km to the east. (Beware of logging trucks. Travel with your lights on, and pull over when necessary—they have the right of way.)

There are hundreds of thousands of mountain climbers in North America, and many of them come to this rugged wilderness area. Part of the Purcell Range, the Bugaboos contain the range's largest icefield, and its peaks, many over 3000 m, are for experienced mountaineers only.

The Purcells may be just across the valley from the Rockies, but they are much older. The sedimentary rocks of the Purcells originated 1.5 billion years ago, when algae was the dominant life form. The geological turmoil caused by the development of the Rockies about 70 million years ago allowed the intrusions of molten rock in the Purcells. Over time, uplift and the erosive forces of wind, water, and glaciation removed the weakened outer layers of the peaks, creating the dramatic granite spires seen today. A privately run lodge, which is a headquarters for heli-skiing and heli-hiking, is located just outside the park boundaries (CMH Heli-Skiing,1-800-661-0252).

## Favourite Hiking Areas in East Kootenay

1. Bugaboo Glacier Provincial Park and Alpine Recreation Area—Access from Brisco. Several trails. Wilderness area.
2. Elk Lakes Provincial Park—Access from Sparwood. Several routes round Elk Lake. Wilderness.
3. Elkford Interpretive Trail System—North of Sparwood. 40 km of trails for beginner to advanced hikers.
4. Kootenay National Park—Borders both Banff and Yoho national parks. Many trails.
5. Mt. Assiniboine Provincial Park—In the Rocky Mountains. 12 trails. Wilderness area.
6. Purcell Wilderness Conservancy—West of Invermere. Earl Grey Trail to Kootenay Lake.
7. Top of the World Provincial Park—Access from Canal Flats. Wilderness.

*Construction of the Kootenay Parkway through Sinclair Canyon took 13 years between 1911 and 1924. The brightly coloured canyon rock is part of the Redwell Fault.*

## Kootenay National Park

P.O. Box 220, Radium Hot Springs, BC V0A 1M0. 250-347-9615. Email: Kootenay_reception@pch. gc.ca. Web: www.worldweb.com/ ParksCanada-Kootenay/

The boundary of Kootenay National Park lies immediately east of the town of Radium Hot Springs. The only park in Canada with both cactus and glaciers, it encompasses 1406 square km of diverse topography, flora, and fauna. The varied habitat is home to 993 plant, 92 bird, 58 mammal, 4 amphibia, and 3 reptile species.

Originally called the Banff-Windermere Highway, the Kootenay Parkway was the first road through the Rocky Mountains. It was the brainchild of Invermere businessman Randolph Bruce, who saw a great commercial advantage in having a route connect the northern Columbia valley with Alberta. Construction began in 1911, but the highway wasn't completed until 1922, after the federal government had been given land on either side of the proposed roadway in return for financing. The park was established in 1920.

One of the highlights of this park are the hot springs, just inside the west entrance. Valued by several Native tribes for their soothing powers, the pools seem to have been an ancient meeting place for Interior and Plains Natives. Hot springs water is heated deep underground, collecting minerals on its journey to the surface, which dissolve, affecting the colour and odour. Some feel the added minerals may have therapeutic properties.

Although the amount of radium in the water here is about equal to what you'd find in the dial of a luminous wristwatch, early settlers flocked to the pools in the belief that the radium content would heal all their ills. In fact, when developer Roland Stuart was trying to find financing for his hot springs project in the early 1900s, he got backing from Perrier multimillionaire John Harmsworth. Harmsworth was completely paralyzed until he spent several weeks soaking in the pool and was finally able to wiggle his foot. Today, most people come simply to relax in the soothing waters (maximum temperature: 45.5°C).

Just past the hot springs, you'll travel through colourful Sinclair Canyon. In the fur-trading days, American- and British-backed companies were vying for control of Oregon Territory and the land north of the Columbia River. In 1841, the Hudson's Bay Company sponsored 120 settlers from Manitoba's Red River Settlement in an unsuccessful attempt to maintain control of the disputed land. Led by James Sinclair, they travelled through the Rockies using the pass in the

*Mineral springs that produce iron-rich water stain the earth at the Paint Pots and Ochre Beds. First Nations people derived a coloured pigment from the clay and used it to make decorative paint.*

spectacular red-rock canyon that now bears his name. Part of Redwall Fault, the red-coloured rock was created millions of years ago when limestone, ground into fragments by the shifting of the tectonic plates, was stained by iron oxide.

Unlike Glacier National Park to the northwest, where the steep slopes create a harsh and unsympathetic environment, less snow means wildlife viewing is excellent here. Mountain goat, deer, elk, and bighorn sheep are commonly seen. Drive with caution.

The Continental Divide runs along the border between Kootenay, Banff, and Jasper national parks. All rivers and streams along the west side of this ridge run to the Pacific Ocean, while all those to the east eventually end up in the Arctic Ocean or Hudson Bay.

## While You're In Kootenay National Park ... Top Seven

1. Soak in the pools at Radium Hot Spring Aquacourt (250 347-9485; 1-800-767-1611) . A resort (1-800-667-6444) and campgrounds are close by.
2. Hike one of the trails starting at Sinclair Canyon. (Altogether the park has 200 km of trails.)
3. In the fall, view the spectacular golden show of western larch at the Kootenay Valley Viewpoint, 17 km east of Radium Hot Springs, and an extraordinary view of the Kootenay River. The appearance of western larch in the national parks in the Rockies is relatively rare. The headwaters of the Kootenay River is just north of Kootenay Crossing, about 15 km east of the viewpoint.
4. Watch for mountain goats at the mineral lick near Mount Wardel. An estimated 300 mountain goats live in the park.
5. View Mt. Assiniboine 2.5 km south of Vermilion Crossing. The highest mountain in this part of the Rockies (3618 m), it was named after the Assiniboine, or Stoney people.
6. Take the half-hour self-guided walk to the Paint Pots and Ochre Beds (80 km east of Radium Hot Springs).
7. Walk the 1-km interpretive trail along Tokumm Creek to view Marble Canyon, where over 500 million years of geological history are revealed in the limestone and dolomite rock walls. The trail criss-crosses a 600-metre-long, 36-metre-deep chasm that took nature 8000 years to carve.

## Western or Pacific Yew

**Taxus brevifolia**

The yew tree is unusual among conifers because its seeds occur in a red, berry-like structure rather than in the typical evergreen cone. Ten species occur worldwide, all in the northern hemisphere, but only two occur in Canada. The Pacific yew, the only species in BC, is found in the coastal forests and the Columbia forests of the southeastern Interior.

Yew tends to grow singly rather than in stands, in moist areas under the canopy of trees such as western hemlock and Douglas fir. Although at lower elevations a single tree can grow up to 20 metres high, at middle elevations they often form an impenetrable, sprawling undergrowth.

The distinctive thin purple bark can be peeled off, revealing yellow sapwood and the bright-orange or rose-red heartwood that is valued for decorative woodwork. Fire-grained, strong, hard but elastic, the wood was valued by Native cultures for harpoons, bows, canoe paddles, eating utensils, and splitting wedges.

Too slow-growing to be harvested commercially, some English yew trees have reached ages of 1000 to 2000 years. The flat two-toned leaves are poisonous to horses and cattle.

In 1992, Taxol, a compound obtained from yew bark, was approved as an anti-cancer drug.

## Regeneration
## The Fireweed Trail

**In old growth forests**, mature stands of trees dominate the ecosystem. They shade the ground, leave no room for new plants to grow, and eradicate the food supply of animals. After a fire in this area, lodgepole pine—which needs the heat of the fire to pop open its seed pods—began to grow. Fireweed, young spruce, and fir also took root. Shaded by the lodgepole, the fir and spruce will grow to maturity in another hundred years or more, and the cycle will repeat itself. The Fireweed Trail is just south of the eastern entrance to Kootenay National Park, at the Continental Divide.

## Parks Permits

**As in all Canadian** national parks, if you stop in Kootenay National Park, you must obtain a permit (available locally). Through traffic does not need a permit. You can buy either a day-use or an annual pass. The seasonal park information centres in Radium and Vermilion Crossing (63 km north of Radium) have maps and brochures on a variety of park-related subjects including camping, trails, safety, and regulations. (Please note that if you plan to fish, your BC license is not valid here—you'll have to buy a national parks permit.)

## Paint Pots

**The Paint Pots** are mineral springs that produce iron-rich, slightly heated water that stains the surrounding earth. The colourful residue was collected by Ktunaxa Natives, who baked the clay in round cakes and used it as the basis of a ceremonial paint. On their way to hunt across the Rockies, the Ktunaxa would stop here to gather the ochre for barter with the Blackfoot people. In the early 1900s, local businessmen tried to export the clay to a paint-manufacturing company in Calgary, but the attempt failed. Remains of the machinery can still be seen at the site.

Before crossing the suspension bridge over the Vermilion River, look for the insectivorous butterwort plant with its violet-coloured flowers. Minute hairs on the sticky, yellow leaves trap tiny insects for sustenance.

The artificial surface on the trails in this and other national parks may seem a little disappointing, but it minimizes the effect of many sightseers in a fragile environment.

# Central Interior

*Once part of a difficult canoe and portage route from the Lower Mainland to the Cariboo, Seton Lake near Lillooet is now part of the Bridge River hydroelectric project. During construction, a 12,000-year-old bowl was found at the site.*

"No man stands beside the Fraser River without sensing the precarious hold of his species upon the earth," Bruce Hutchison writes in his book *The Fraser.* When Alexander Mackenzie began his historic journey partway down the Fraser in May 1792, his

Native interpreter "shed tears on the reflection of those dangers which we might encounter in our expedition."

For centuries the Fraser River was both a welcome lifeline and a formidable obstacle to the men and women who travelled its waters, prospected its gravel beds, and built trails, roads, and railways along its banks. Never tamed by hydroelectric dams, the mighty Fraser continues to earn the respect of those who know it. The Central Interior encompasses approximately 100,000 square km of the Fraser River drainage.

Our circle tour of the region begins at Cache Creek. Highway 97 travels north through the Cariboo-Chilcotin region to Prince George over the Interior Plateau. Throughout this area, you can see evidence of the early volcanic eruptions and subsequent glacial activity that have shaped the landscape. Huge boulders seemingly out of place in the middle of rolling grasslands can be spotted from time to time. Called erratics, they were deposited by the melting ice sheets. Lava rock, glacial eskers, and canyons provide other geological attractions.

The Cariboo-Chilcotin is cowboy country. The sparsely populated area to the west of Hwy. 97 and the Fraser River is popularly referred to

*Opposite: The diverse scenery of Tweedsmuir Provincial Park, BC's largest, attract many outdoor entusiasts to the Chilcotin.*

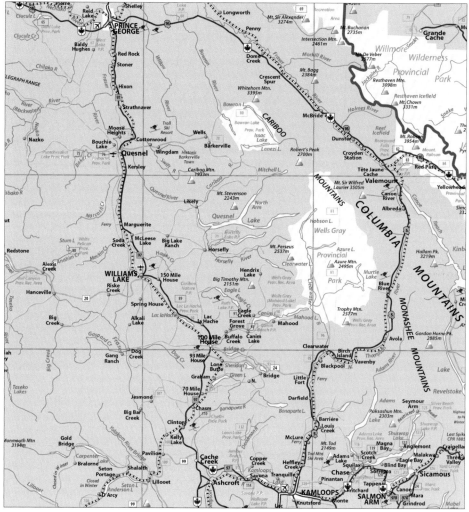

*Central Interior*

as the Chilcotin. Rolling hills, tumbling tumbleweed, and enormous cattle ranches conjure up romantic visions of the Old West in all but the most determined city slickers.

The Cariboo, the region to the east of the highway, is gold country. In the 1860s, thousands of miners rushed to the goldfields at Williams Creek, Quesnel Lake, and Keithley Creek, establishing boom towns like Barkerville and

Horsefly. Parts of Hwy. 97 follow the old Cariboo Wagon Road, one of the first highways in the province.

If you want to holiday in the Cariboo-Chilcotin, you might do just as well to get a map, close your eyes, and stick a pin in it—you can hardly go wrong. Guest ranches, rodeos, hiking, paddling, and fishing attract visitors from around the world.

At Prince George, our route

continues east along Hwy. 16 (the Yellowhead Highway), following the Fraser River almost to its headwaters near Mount Robson in the Rocky Mountains. The tour heads south from the old fur-trading centre of Tête Jaune Cache along Hwy. 5 (the Yellowhead South), accompanying the North Thompson River to Kamloops.

Less developed than the Cariboo-Chilcotin, this area is

*A blacksmith at Hat Creek Ranch shows visitors how it was done in the old days.*

popular with outdoor recreation enthusiasts who enjoy wilderness experiences. One of the major attractions on the Yellowhead South Highway is Wells Gray Provincial Park.

The main industries in the Central Interior are logging, mining, cattle ranching, tourism, and outdoor recreation. Opportunities for fishing, hiking, backpacking, canoeing, rafting, cross-country skiing, and horseback riding are plentiful.

## Hat Creek Ranch Special Events

**May**–Working Dog Demonstration

**June**–Old Fashioned Sports Day

**July**–Draft Horse Demonstration, Barn Dance & BBQ

**August**–Trapper's Races and Rendezvous; Bonaparte Pow Wow

**September**–Top Hand & Harvest Festival: BBQ & Dance

## Hat Creek Ranch

11 km north of Cache Creek, Box 8778, Cache Creek, V0K 1H0. 250-457-9722, 1-800-782-0922. Email: explore@hatcreekranch.com. Web: http://www.hatcreekranch.com/
When thousands of prospectors descended on the Cariboo in the 1860s, Governor James Douglas quickly started construction of a road to the goldfields. Construction crews completed the Cariboo Wagon Road in 1865, providing faster and cheaper access to the Interior from the coast. One of the many roadhouses along the route where stagecoach travellers and horses could rest was Hat Creek Ranch, 500 metres off Hwy. 97 on Hwy. 12.

Donald McLean, a former Hudson's Bay Company factor, began operating the roadhouse at Hat Creek in 1862. McLean was killed in the Chilcotin War in 1864, but not before he fathered three sons, the infamous McLean Gang, considered by historian T.W.

Paterson "the most notorious outlaws in provincial history." The youngest was 15 when they were hanged in 1881 for killing a police constable.

Subsequent owners enlarged and developed the Hat Creek facilities. Stephen Tingley, a legendary stagecoach whip, took over the ranch from McLean. The owner of Barnard's Express (the BX Line) between 1864 and 1897, Tingley claimed he once made the trip between Yale and Soda Creek in 30 hours. He drove a six-horse stagecoach for 28 years without a single accident.

Now preserved and managed by the BC Heritage Trust, the original Hat Creek Ranch buildings have been restored, but only structurally. The roadhouse still has the original floorboards and wallpaper. In the summer months, from among many fascinating offerings, visitors can enjoy wagon rides, trail rides, stagecoach

**185**

*Built in the 1890s, Miyazaki House is one of Lillooet's oldest structures. Dr. Masajiro Miyazaki and his family lived in the house during the internment of Japanese Canadians during WWII.*

rides, a variety of interpretive services (including a first-hand look at a working period-ranch and a newly expanded Native interpretive centre), and a walk along the original Cariboo Road.

## Side Trip: Highway 12

Although the main Cariboo Wagon road from Yale was through Lytton and Cache Creek, Mile 0 is measured from Lillooet, where one of the earliest trails to the Cariboo was established via Harrison Lake in 1858. Highway 12 north of Cache Creek off Hwy. 97 provides an interesting side trip through this historic area.

Upper Hat Creek, 22 km west of Hwy. 97, was an area of controversy in the 1980s when BC Hydro proposed hydro-electric development for the region. As part of the process,

archeologists examined the Upper Hat Creek area in the late 1970s and estimated that as many as 1350 Native sites exist in the area. At the junction with Hat Creek Road, a steep 1-km trail on the north side of Hwy. 12 leads to Native pictographs.

Marble Canyon Provincial Park is 30 km west of Hwy. 97. Limestone cliffs and dramatic rock formations tower almost a kilometre above two turquoise lakes. Pictographs, a waterfall, and good swimming and fishing make the park a popular destination. In winter, ice climbers tackle the frozen falls.

At Pavilion, Hwy. 12 heads south to Lillooet along the eroded rocks of the Fraser Canyon. To the north, the Kelly Lake road provides fair-weather access to Clinton. The community of Pavilion has

one of the oldest buildings in BC still on its original site—the still-operating Pavilion Store. Pavilion Lake has received scientific notice in recent years because of the formations of coral-like structures found in its depths. Some are up to 4 metres high, up to 11,000 years old, and covered in mysterious mats of microscopic microbes not found anywhere else in the world.

## Lillooet

65 km north of Lytton on Hwy. 12. Population: 2987. Info Centre: 790 Main Street, Box 441, V0K 1V0. 250-256-4308; Fax: 250-256-4288. Seasonal. www.teamlillooet.com/Home/home.html

Lillooet recorded one of the highest temperatures in Canadian history when the thermometer hit 44.4° C on July 16, 1941. As "gateway to the Cariboo," Lillooet was a hot spot of

In the earth beneath Lillooet's Hanging Tree lie the remains of at least two, perhaps eight, criminals sentenced by Judge Matthew Begbie.

Begbie is credited with maintaining law and order during the gold-rush years. He was knighted by Queen Victoria in 1875.

a different kind in 1860, with thirteen saloons and an itinerant population of 16,000. The town faded in importance when the main Cariboo Wagon Road bypassed it at Lytton.

One of the most colourful characters of gold rush days was Judge Matthew Begbie. Hangman's Tree Park (turn off Main Street at the United Church and head up the hill), is reputed to be one of the places where he meted out his frontier justice. A close reading of history reveals Begbie's label as the "hanging judge" to be misleading: he was regarded as strict, but fair.

The Bridge of 23 Camels south of Lillooet commemorates the beasts of burden that three entrepreneurs imported into the area during the Cariboo Gold Rush. Although the camels required less food and

## While You're In Lillooet ... Top Five

1. Browse through the Ma Murray section of the Lillooet Museum (790 Main Street, 250-256-4308). The museum also features Native and gold rush memorabilia.

2. Take the self-guided walking/biking tour of the golden mile, which includes the Bridge of 23 Camels.

3. Search for semi-precious stones with the other rockhounds. Jade and agate are the most plentiful. The largest jade boulder found here weighed more than 16 tonnes.

4. Even if you're not a golfer, play a round at farmer Dave Jones' Sheep Pasture Golf Course (8 km south on Hwy. 12; 250-256-4484). Not surprisingly, the natural obstacles include sheep.

5. Watch the annual fish-drying activities of the First Nations people on the banks of the Fraser in the fall.

## Lillooet Special Events —Best Bets

**January/February**—Ice Climbing Festival

**February**—Valentine's Pow Wow

**May**—St'át'imc Nation Gathering; May Day Celebrations

**June/July**—Strawberry Social

**July**—Gold Rush Days

**September**—First Nations Cultural Exposition; Fall Fair

water than traditional pack animals, their tender feet, bad tempers, and foul smell quickly put an end to the scheme. Some of the camels were released into the desert area between Cache Creek and Kamloops. The last one died in 1905.

Once the easy pickings were gone, most of the early gold miners looked elsewhere, but Chinese prospectors often stayed behind, carefully working the spent claims. Near Hangman's Park the Chinese Rock Pilings are a testament to the patience of these early settlers.

West of town you'll find Anderson and Seton lakes, part of one of the earliest routes to the Interior, the Harrison-Lillooet Trail. Completed in 1957, Seton Lake Dam provides hydroelectric power to the Lower Mainland. It is part of the Bridge River hydroelectric development, which includes two other dams, four powerhouses, and three reservoirs. BC Hydro's Seton Lake Recreation Area (www.bchydro.com/recreation/seton.html) has a beach, boat launching area, and interpretive trail. The steep hillsides around Seton Lake are

home to mountain goat, and salmon spawn near Seton Creek and Bridge River.

Further west, Bralorne and Gold Bridge, developed in the 1930s, turned out to be one of the richest gold-producing areas in the province. The Bralorne-Pioneer Mine produced over four million ounces of gold and 1.2 million ounces of silver before closing in 1971—more than any other mine in the province. As this is being written, plans are afoot to reopen the mine.

Highway 12 south of Lillooet to Lytton passes through a less-travelled section of the

## Ma Murray

"**Sometimes** you have to be a little raw to get the point across," Ma Murray, BC's legendary newspaperwoman, once said.

Although she only had a grade-three education, Murray's flamboyant style, down-to-earth language and outspoken opinions put her in the national spotlight.

In 1959, while editing the *Alaska Highway News* in Fort St. John, she wrote about wasteful water consumption. "We sure as hell need to use less if we are going to have this modern convenience," she wrote. "To head off this catastrophe, only flush for Number 2, curtail bathing to the Saturday night tub, go back to the old washrag which could always remove a lot of BO if applied often enough." Water consumption dropped 65,000 gallons a day, *Time* magazine ran an article about her, and she became a media celebrity.

Born in Windy Ridge, Kansas in 1888, she came to BC in 1912, marrying George Murray in 1913. They moved to Lillooet in 1933, starting the *Bridge River Lillooet News* in 1934. In 1943 they started the *Alaska Highway News* in Fort St. John.

Murray briefly toyed with politics, running provincially in 1945, but gave it up. "I didn't know what the hell they were talking about," she said.

She credited George as her mentor and teacher. "I feel very much like the man who invented the

atomic bomb," he once said. "It was a great idea at the time, but now what to do with it."

In 1970, Ma Murray was awarded an honourary doctor of laws degree from Simon Fraser University, and in 1971, the Order of Canada. She died in 1982 at the age of 95.

*The Clinton Museum was built as a schoolhouse in 1892 from locally fired brick.*

Back on Hwy. 97, 20 Mile House marks the road to Loon Lake, one of many fishing resorts in the Cariboo.

## Clinton

40 km (25 mi.) north of Cache Creek. Population: 718. Chamber of Commerce: Box 256, V0K 1K0. 250-459-2240. Village of Clinton: Email: clinton@wkpowerlink.com. Web: http://village.clinton.bc.ca/

Clinton was once an important town, sitting at the junction of the old Fraser Canyon and Lillooet gold trails. Calling itself the "Guest Ranch Capital of North America," Clinton feels like a town from the Old West. Among its restored buildings, the Clinton Museum, constructed as a schoolhouse in 1892 from handmade locally-fired brick, served as courthouse for the famous Judge Matthew Begbie. Displays feature Chinese and Native artifacts. Robertson's Store, built in 1861, was run by the Robertson family until 1978, and is still operating. Although the original Clinton Hotel burned to the ground in 1958, an impressive log lodge has replaced it, with interesting displays of archival photographs in the lobby.

## Side trip: Empire Valley

Northwest of Clinton, the 45-km drive to Big Bar Lake Provincial Park passes through the marshlands and spruce forest of the Chilcotin's Empire Valley, past several guest ranches. Eskers (long gravel ridges formed under retreating glaciers) and drumlins (tear-shaped hills created as ice walls receded), are two geological features highlighted in the

Fraser Canyon, but it has some of the most spectacular scenery in the province. South of Lillooet, the Duffey Lake Road connects the central Interior with Vancouver.

### While You're In Clinton ... Top Ten

1. Dance the night away at the Clinton May Ball. First held in 1868, it's believed to be the longest-running event in the province.
2. Sidle up to Judge Begbie's desk at the Clinton Museum (250-459-2442).
3. Feast on cougar and snake at the Outdoor Sportsman Game Dinner in April.
4. Hang-glide from Lime Mountain, reputed to be among the best in western North America. (If you don't want to jump, you can just enjoy the view.)
5. Have a family picnic in Reg Conn Centennial Park. Its five acres include a playground and picnic tables.
6. Shop for local crafts.
7. Gaze at Painted Chasm Provincial Park (15 km north, 4 km off Hwy. 97), a spectacular bedrock canyon 1.5 km long and 120 m deep, created by glacial meltwater about ten thousand years ago. A must-see.
8. Saddle up at a guest ranch.
9. Whoop and holler at the May Rodeo.
10. Cross-country ski (or hike) on the Big Bar forestry trails.

park. Ducks Unlimited has a marsh enhancement project here also, with a trail winding along the lake among lava rock, wildflowers, and glacial deposits.

Forty-six km further along this road is the 400,000-hectare Gang Ranch, at one time the largest cattle ranch in the world, and currently owned by a Saudi Arabian sheik. Jerome and Thadeus Harper drove a herd of cattle up from Oregon to Barkerville in the 1860s and bought and leased several tracts of land near Churn Creek, eventually controlling 1.6 million hectares. Some say the ranch got its name from the unique double-furrowed "gang" plough developed to work the fields.

Just a few kilometres from the Gang Ranch on the old Fraser River Trail is Dog Creek, which was once an ancient Native settlement. A huge cavern below Dog Creek Dome was part of Native rituals and contains rock paintings.

It is rumoured that in the early days, Count Versepeuch, a French nobleman and early settler, traded his satin coat and tricorne hat to Chief Alexis of the Chilcotin Band for some good horses. The Count then went on to build BC's first flour mill and a sawmill at Dog Creek in 1866.

Alkali Lake, 27 km north of the ranch, is popular with dedicated birdwatchers, who come to view rare white pelicans during spring and fall migrations.

Back on Highway 97, 70 Mile House was one of the first stopping places established on the Cariboo Wagon Road, and marks the turnoff to Green Lake Recreation Area. Fifteen-km-long Green Lake was on the Fur Brigade Trail between Fort Kamloops and Fort

## Jake Conkin–Cowboy Poet

**A cowboy poetry** roundup is a group of people who are sharing lies and stories and poetry, telling about the lifestyles of the real cowboy–the cowboy that works on the ranch with the cows and rides horses for most of his life, not the rodeo cowboy or the urban cowboy. Elko, Nevada, the "granddaddy" of them all, hosted 10,000 people at its gathering in 1991.

The poetry talks about mother nature in her glory, the bunch grass, the critters, the huge sky, and the life of the cowboy out on the range. It involves certain values that people seem to want to hang on to today, centering on honesty, integrity, good friendships in the old-fashioned way. A lot of people seem to be missing that in their lives and I think that's what attracts them to gatherings like this.

A lot of people out there involved in the ranching business

fear for their lifestyle to some extent, and I guess that's part of what the poetry is about. This lifestyle, of course, has been going on since the 1800s, and cowboys really would be considered some of the first environmentalists. They live off the land, so they really look after the land and everything else.

I've been interested in the lifestyle all my life. I've had horses. My dream has always been of going to ranches and doing the real cowboy things: getting up at three o'clock in the morning and going out and herding cows, this type of thing. I had the opportunity to do that at Douglas Lake, which is one of Canada's largest cattle ranches, at spring turnouts, cattle drives, cow camps, and so on. I had experiences that I felt I would like to share with people and decided to write some of these thoughts down on paper.

Jake Conkin's collection of cowboy poetry, *Silk and Silver and Other Things Too,* is self-published, distributed through Sand Hill Marketing of Kelowna and available at western shops throughout BC and Alberta. A former teacher, he organized BC's first cowboy poetry roundup at O'Keefe Ranch near Vernon in 1991.

*Sharp-eyed travellers will occasionally be treated to examples of whimsical folk art throughout the Interior.*

## Cariboo-Chilcotin Rodeos & Trail Rides

(In alphabetical order)
1. Anahim Lake Stampede–July
2. BCRA Rodeo, 100 Mile House–May
3. Bella Coola Rodeo–July
4. Bridge Lake Amateur Stampede–June
5. Bridge Lake Cattle Drive–July
6. Clinton Rodeo–May
7. Frontier Days Rodeo, Riske Creek–July
8. Great Cariboo Ride–July
9. Interlakes Rodeo–August
10. Nemiah Valley Rodeo–August
11. Prince George Rodeo–June
12. Quesnel Rodeo–July
13. Williams Lake Stampede–July 1

Alexandria. Now the lake is a popular recreation area. Surrounded by pine, spruce, aspen, and grassy undergrowth harbouring lupin, wild rose and Indian paintbrush, Green Lake is a beautiful spot—but buggy. Anglers fish for kokanee and trout, and birdwatchers can look for osprey and loon. In the winter months, the area is popular with snowmobilers.

## Side trip: Interlakes

Highway 24, just south of 100 Mile House, follows the Fur Brigade Trail as it passes through Bridge Lake to Little Fort. Known as the Interlakes area, this is another ancient dwelling place of Native people. Some developments on the lake have been built above ground so as not to disturb Native artifacts. Canoeing is excellent on the more than fifty lakes in the area, and locals claim the best trout fishing in the world. Guest ranches are plentiful.

Lone Butte, named for obvious reasons, was a busy centre for the ranchers who settled in the area from the early 1900s to the 1950s. The community's lone water tower, one of the last existing structures of its kind in the province, used to service the steam engines that took the cattle to market. A walk up the butte (elevation: 70 m) is actually a pleasant hike on the remains of an ancient volcano. Park at the corner of Watch Lake Road and Hwy. 24 and take the trail up the east face.

At Bridge Lake, ask for directions to the ice caves—crevasse-like openings in the side of a cliff containing huge ice stalactites, which were once popular with local ice-cream makers.

*Green Lake, now a popular resort area, was on the Fur Brigade Trail linking Fort Alexandria and Fort Kamloops between the 1820s and 1850s.*

## 100 Mile House

80 km (50 mi.) north of Clinton. Population: 2041. Info Centre: 422 Cariboo Hwy., Box 2312, V0K 2E0. 250-395-5353; Fax: 250-395-4085. Email: visitors@bcinternet.net. Web: www.princegeorge.com/tourism/100milehouse

A station on the Fur Brigade Trail from Kamloops to Fort Alexandria, 100 Mile House became an important stagecoach stop on the Cariboo Wagon Road in the 1860s. At the north end of the village, one of the original Barnard Express (BX) stagecoaches is on display. The town's first roadhouse, built in 1862, has since burned down, but 100 Mile House remains an important service centre.

To get a first-hand look at the local logging industry, a mainstay of the local economy, take a self-guided forestry tour (contact the Info Centre). An relatively new industry is log-home building. The houses are constructed locally, then disassembled and

### 100 Mile House Special Events—Best Bets

**January**—Jack Gawthorn Memorial Dogsled Race. Hills Guest Ranch (250-397-2108)

**February**—Cariboo Cross-country Ski Marathon (250-395-3487)

**May**—BCRA Rodeo, 100 Mile House (250-395-4460)

**June**—Bridge Lake Amateur Stampede (250-593-4853)

**July**—Bridge Lake Cattle Drive, 70 Mile House to Bridge Lake (250-493-4853); Great Cariboo Ride, 10-day horseback ride (250-791-5383)

**August**—Interlakes Rodeo (250-593-4956); South Cariboo Garlic Festival, Forest Grove (1-877-397-2518)

### While You're In 100 Mile House ... Top Ten

1. Walk the Nature Marsh trail by the Visitor's Centre.
2. Take a dog sled tour.
3. Stay at a guest ranch.
4. Ski Mount Timothy.
5. Attend a local rodeo.
6. Enjoy the view from Mount Begbie Lookout (accessed 16 km south of town off Hwy. 97).
7. Go fishing.
8. Cross-country ski.
9. Go on a cattle drive.
10. Canoe Moose Valley.

shipped to the United States and Japan.

This area is also important as a recreation destination for fishing, hiking, biking, and a variety of winter sports. Note the world's largest cross-country skis in front of the Visitors' Centre.

Moose Valley Provincial Park, 30 km west of 100 Mile House off Exeter Road (on the way to Dog Lake), is the site of a two-day canoe route through a chain of twelve wilderness lakes. The lakes were created at the end of the last ice age, when the glaciers retreated and the path of the Fraser River was being re-cut. In June and July, paddlers may spot moose calves and sandhill cranes. Locals claim there are very few bothersome bugs.

## Side trip: Canim Lake

Archeologists suggest that when Prairie buffalo herds diminished, Plains people came to the area around Canim Lake to fish and perhaps search for caribou. There are pictographs and remains of Native pit houses in the region. Canim Lake is one of the largest lakes in the Cariboo, and today visitors come for fishing, hiking,

## Dakelh Natives

**The Dakelh**, who used to be known as Carrier, are part of the western Dene people who have inhabited this part of the Interior Plateau for centuries. It was the custom for widowed women of the tribe to carry the ashes of their deceased husbands on their backs until a potlatch was held, thus the name "carriers". Like coastal tribes, the Dakelh relied heavily on salmon for survival, spearing and trapping the fish as they came upriver to spawn. Their diet of dried salmon was supplemented by hunting and gathering wild plants and berries.

At present there are about 7000 registered Dakelh, living in about two dozen communities. Trapper Six Mile Mary, above, was 106 years old when this photo was taken in the early 1900s.

## Birdwatching in South Cariboo

Alkali Lake—white pelicans

Canim Lake (west end)

Big Bar Lake Provincial Park, Clinton

Bridge Lake Outlet, Bridge Lake

Bull Mountain, Williams Lake

Cariboo Nature Provincial Park, Lac la Hache

Exeter Lake Wetland, 100 Mile House

Moose Valley Provincial Park, 100 Mile House

Quesnel River Hatchery, Likely

Scout Island Nature Park, Williams Lake

Sheridan Lake, 100 Mile House

Watch Creek, 100 Mile House

100 Mile Marsh Wildlife Sanctuary

130 Mile Marsh, Lac la Hache

*Log home manufacturing is a successful value-added addition to the Cariboo's forestry economy.*

spectacular scenery, and wildlife viewing.

The end of the road is Mahood Lake in Wells Gray Park—and canoeists' heaven. Mahood Falls, a 55-km drive east of the community of Canim Lake, is a magnificent cascade between Canim and Mahood lakes. Mahood Lake Campground in Wells Gray Provincial Park was once an important Native settlement and is a good place to search for pictographs. Canim Beach Provincial Park on Canim Lake makes a good base for water recreation, including great fishing and exploration of spectacular Canim Falls.

Some say the Canim River has the best fly fishing in the Cariboo, but you'll have to get there by trail. Ask locally for directions, and for how to get to Deception Falls, the Volcano Cones, and other local attractions and good fishing spots. Cross-country skiing is popular in the winter.

## 108 Mile House

Just north of 100 Mile House on Hwy. 97, 108 Mile Heritage Site (250-791-5288; www.historical.bc.ca/main.html) has a collection of seven historical buildings on three hectares of lakeside property belonging to a large resort. Visible from the highway, the old Clydesdale barn, built in 1908 and since restored, is one of the largest log barns in Canada. Originally housing over 200 Clydesdale horses, now during the summer it's the site of family-style barn dances and strawberry socials.

The resort (Hills Health Ranch) also has a world-class spa, golf and tennis, horseback riding and a variety of other recreational activities (250-791-5225).

## Lac La Hache

25 km (16 mi.) north of 100 Mile House. Population: 700.
Lac La Hache calls itself the "Longest Town in the

Cariboo" due to its location on the body of water of the same name. The lake apparently got its name when a French Canadian fur trader dropped his axe through a hole in the ice (*hache* is French for axe). As you might guess from its location, water recreation is popular here, including trout fishing (ice fishing in winter) and windsurfing. Lac La Hache Provincial Park at the head of the lake has campsites, boat launching, trails, and other amenities.

## Gold Country

At 150 Mile House, 15 km east of Williams Lake on Hwy. 97, you can follow early gold rush routes to Horsefly, Likely, Quesnel Lake, and dozens of smaller lakes. The Horsefly River winds through a beautiful valley of cottonwood and wild rose. Birdwatchers can view herons, eagles, and sandpipers.

Large spawning runs of

kokanee and sockeye occur every fall just south of the community of Horsefly (Tourist Info: 1-250-620-3440; hrealty@stardate.bc.ca), where the first Cariboo gold was discovered in 1859. Originally called Harper's Camp, after Thadeus Harper of the Gang Ranch, the town's present name is, unfortunately, descriptive and accurate. The Jack Lynn Museum (on Campbell Avenue, 250-620-3304, seasonal) displays artifacts from the early days, but the big attractions here are fishing, hiking and the great outdoors.

Originally called Quesnel Dam, the town of Likely was not renamed by an optimistic prospector, but after

successful miner "Plato" John Likely, who searched for gold and spouted philosophy in the 1860s. Appreciative followers gave Likely good tips that he followed to his advantage. Nicknamed "the nugget patch," this is one of the richest areas in the Cariboo goldfields. In 1922, one mine yielded 700 ounces in one week.

The ghost town of Quesnel Forks, once a bustling community of 5000, is 8 km past Likely. Designated as a heritage site, the town's glory days lasted for five years. The Bullion Pit, an open-pit gold mine from 1892 to 1942, is 5 km west of Likely. In order to have enough water to feed the

mine's hydraulic system, 64 km of canals were built to utilize the resources of nearby lakes and creeks. The pit is 90 m deep and 3 km long. Between 1892 and 1898, $1.25 million worth of gold was removed. As recently as 1988 a prospector found a nugget worth $10,000.

Quesnel Lake, 100 km long, is the largest in the region. Much of the early search for gold centred in this area, and early gold rush trails to the productive fields around Barkerville were via this lake. Paddling, wildlife viewing, hiking, and fishing are popular here, and there are several resorts. Anglers pull out rainbow, kokanee, lake trout, and Dolly Varden. The Quesnel River Salmon Hatchery, 2 km south of Likely, produces 2.3 million chinook fry annually. Self-guided tours are available (250-790-2442).

## SuperGuide's Top Ten Cariboo/Chilcotin Trails

(In alphabetical order)
1.  108 Mile Ranch Trails—skiing, biking, hiking, equestrian.
2.  Alexander Mackenzie Heritage Trail—This historic route begins near Quesnel.
3.  Cameron Ridge trail, in the Quesnel Highlands between Quesnel & Likely—Spectacular views of the Cariboo Mountains.
4.  Fawn Lake Recreation Trail, Interlakes—Popular destination for camping, fishing and horseback trips.
5.  Hallis Lake trails, east of Quesnel—Family skiing, hiking, biking, or walking.
6.  Jimmy's Fox Trail, Williams Lake—Easy to advanced; great viewpoints.
7.  Mt. Robson Provincial Park—In Rocky Mountains adjacent to Jasper National Park. 7. Sheridan Lake trails network, Interlakes. An extensive network of old logging roads, skid trails, fence lines, and game trails. Multi-use.
8.  South Side Trail network, Williams Lake. Maze of trails extending across the plateau above Williams Lake. For every ability.
9.  Tweedsmuir Provincial Park (North and South)—Several trails. Hunlen Falls, Turner Lake, and Rainbow Range are among the attractions. Wilderness area.
10. Wells Gray Provincial Park—Over 20 trails in a wilderness area. Wells-Barkerville area in the Cariboo Mountains—Extensive network of signed summer and winter trails. Follow the steps of the gold rush miners on a variety of historic trails and routes.

## Cariboo Ghost Towns

**Barkerville.** At the end of the old Cariboo Wagon Road east of Quesnel, in the 1860s the town was known as the "Gold Capital of the World." Restoration began in 1958 and continues today.

**Cedar Creek**, near Likely. Known for a big gold strike in 1922, it is also referred to as the Nugget Patch.

**Quesnelle Forks**. At the junction of Quesnel and Cariboo rivers, near the town of Likely. Dating back to 1859, this was the first permanent mining community in BC. It once housed the largest Chinese community north of San Francisco.

*Young calf riders at the Williams Lake Stampede in 1924, today one of the Interior's most popular annual events.*

## Williams Lake

92 km north of 100 Mile House. Population: 12,101. Info Centre: junction of Hwys. 97 and 20, 1148 Broadway South, V2G 1A2. 250-392-5025; Fax: 392-4214. Web: wlake.com/

Williams Lake is probably most famous for its annual stampede held every year on the Canada Day (July 1) long weekend. Begun in 1926 as horse races on a local farm, activities now include a parade, pancake breakfasts, and barn dancing. Canadian Professional Rodeo Association events include chuckwagon races, barrel racing, calf roping, and steer wrestling.

The community has been a focal point for ranching communities in the Cariboo since the turn of the century. The town missed its chance to cash in on the gold-rush boom of the 1860s because a local landowner refused to loan money to the road builders. Annoyed, they routed the highway through the present site of 150 Mile House instead.

The building of the Pacific Great Eastern Railway (now BC Rail) in 1920 gave Williams Lake the economic edge it needed, but the big boom came a full century after the gold rush. The population then exploded as logging and mining (copper, molybdenum, gold, and silver) became part of the economy.

### While You're In Williams Lake ... Top Eight

1. Do the stampede (1-800-71-RODEO; www.imagehouse.com/rodeo/).
2. Visit the Museum of the Cariboo Chilcotin (113 North 4th Avenue, 250-392-7404), which houses the BC Cowboys Hall of Fame and also includes Native artifacts and displays on the Cariboo Road and early mining, ranching, and logging.
3. Visit Xats'ull Heritage Village 37 km (23 mi.) north of Williams Lake near the Soda Creek Reserve. Day and weekly programs are available that explore traditions of the Shuswap people (250-297-6323; www.cariboo-net.com/xatsull.html).
4. Explore Scout Island Nature Centre (southeast of the intersection of Hwys. 97 and 20) on Williams Lake, overlooking a major staging area for migrating waterfowl. Guided tours available.
5. Go on a llama trek. Phone or fax 250-296-4745. Email: bmccleary@wlake.com
6. Hike the trail along the Williams Lake River through a scenic 12-km valley to the Fraser River.
7. Fish for kokanee, rainbow, and char at the many area lakes, including McKinley, Hen Ingram, Quesnel, Horsefly, Tyee, and Dewar.
8. Drive into the Chilcotin Country.

*The grasslands of the Interior Plateau are ideally suited to cattle ranching. Here cattle graze on rangeland in the Empire Valley.*

# Side trip: Chilcotin Highway

The 450-km Chilcotin Highway (Hwy. 20) is difficult to classify as a side trip. The route travels east from Williams Lake over the Chilcotin Plateau, the traditional home of the Chilcotin people, through Tweedsmuir Provincial Park (BC's largest), to the ancient Native village of Bella Coola on the Pacific Ocean. The only road out is back over Hwy. 20. Nearly 300 km of the highway is paved, with gravel sections west of Putzi and through Tweedsmuir Park. And there isn't one traffic light between Williams Lake and Bella Coola. The highway is well-used by logging trucks, so travel with headlights on.

The portion of the highway that travels through 981,000-hectare Tweedsmuir

Provincial Park and the Coast Range is dubbed the "Freedom Road". Locals, wanting a connection between coastal and Interior communities, built it themselves in 1953 when the government deemed it economically unfeasible. Braving "The Hill"—a 9-km series of white-knuckle gravel switchbacks (18% grade)—will reward you with spectacular scenic vistas. It descends 4000 feet in 16 km.

Alexander Mackenzie trekked through the area in 1793. Subsequently, a Hudson's Bay Company fur-trading post was established in 1828 at the confluence of the Chilko and Chilcotin rivers. And with the discovery of the rich goldfields beginning in 1858, cattle ranches were established in the 1860s to supply the hungry miners.

An attempt by Alfred

Waddington to build a gold-rush road through this area to the Interior from Bute Inlet was met with fierce resistance by the Chilcotin people in 1864. Nineteen road builders were killed, and eventually five Native men were hanged for their part in the battle. The ill-conceived road was never completed.

Richmond Hobson and Pan Philips homesteaded the area near Anahim Lake in the early 1900s. The deserted Home Ranch remains, as do Hobson's books describing the undertaking, *The Rancher Takes a Wife, Grass Beyond the Mountains,* and *Nothing Too Good for a Cowboy.* (The latter was recently made into a TV series.) The Atnarko Valley (in South Tweedsmuir Park) is where turn-of-the-century settler Ralph Edwards lived and wrote about Lonesome Lake's

**197**

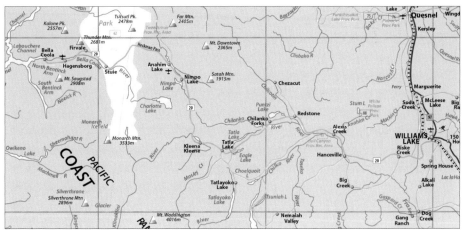

*Chilcotin Highway*

trumpeter swans. Leland Stowe's best-seller, *Crusoe of Lonesome Lake*, describes the Edwards family's homesteading triumphs.

Forestry, ranching, tourism, and outdoor recreation are now the economic lifelines, but the area has not developed like the Cariboo. Known for its rugged individuals, sparse population, and vast uninhabited areas, the Chilcotin is a land where freedom is highly valued and horses outnumber cars.

## Chilcotin Highway Highlights

Sheep Creek Bridge (about 23 km west of Williams Lake) will reward you with an excellent view of the Fraser River. With a little imagination you can almost see the Chinese farmers who grew market gardens here during the gold rush.

Across the Fraser River and atop the dry grasslands of 1200-metre-high Chilcotin Plateau, you'll see the Coast Mountains. The transmitter at the Canadian Loran C Station (north of the highway, 13 km west of the bridge) may seem oddly placed, but the facility is part of a marine navigation network that guides ships in the Pacific Ocean.

The Bighorn Sheep Reserve (13 km south of Riske Creek) is home to 500 California bighorn sheep, one-fifth of the world's population.

Farwell Canyon on the Chilcotin River has spectacular hoodoo rock formations. Native rock paintings are found on the overhang south of the bridge. The Chilcotin River is rated among the best in North America for kayaking, canoeing, and whitewater rafting. Check locally for road information.

Lee's Corner, 42 km west of Risk Creek on Hwy. 20, is named after Norman Lee, who made an ill-fated attempt to drive 500 head of cattle 2400 km through the wilderness to Dawson City during the Klondike Gold Rush. The lookout here gives a spectacular view of the Chilko Ranch; the church spire belongs to one of the many Native villages along the route.

White Pelican Provincial Park (north of Alexis Creek) is a breeding sanctuary for this species. Access to Stum Lake is restricted from March to August to protect nesting birds. But you can view feeding pelicans at remote Nazko Lake Park, also near Alexis Creek. Ask at the Info Centre in Williams Lake for specific directions, or consult the website.

## Chilcotin Special Events –Best Bets

**May**—Anahim Lake Canoe Race (250-742-3253); Alkali Lake Stampede (250-989-1300)

**July**—Bella Coola Rodeo (250-982-2208); Anahim Lake Stampede (250-742-3707); Riske Creek Frontier Days Rodeo

**August**—Discovery Coast Folk Festival (250-799-5744); Nemiah Valley Rodeo (250-392-5330)

**September**—Bella Coola Fall Fair (250-799-5554)

*Stum Lake in White Pelican Provincial Park provides the only nesting grounds in BC for the American White Pelican. Access to the park is restricted from March to September.*

Coast Mountains displays the purples, reds, and oranges of its 2500-metre peaks, providing some stunning scenery along this portion of the road. There are several places for hikers and horseback riders to get close-up views. One route is the Trail to the Rainbows. (Follow the turnoff at Heckman Pass to the trailhead.)

Within the boundaries of Tweedsmuir Provincial Park, BC's largest, the Turner Lakes chain offers wilderness camping, good trout fishing, and sandy beaches to canoeists willing to hike or fly in. Backpackers can view spectacular 259-metre Hunlen Falls at the top of Turner Lake.

Hagensborg, east of Bella Coola, was settled by Norwegians from Minnesota in 1894. This colourful village is a good spot to charter a plane for travel into the heart of the backcountry.

Bella Coola is at the highway's end on Labourchere Channel. The rock where Alexander Mackenzie noted the termination of his famous journey in 1793 is in Dean Channel to the northwest. The Bella Coola Museum (250-982-2328) has displays on the building of the Freedom Road and early history as well as information on local attractions. One of the more unusual accommodations in the area is the Tallheo Cannery Inn, a restored fish cannery from the early 1900s (250-982-2344; www.bcadventure.com/tallheo/index.html). And be sure to ask locally about the many hot springs in the area. The closest is at Thorsen Creek (undeveloped), which is also a petroglyph site.

Bull Canyon Provincial Park, located in an aspen grove on the Chilcotin River 10 km west of Alexis Creek on Hwy. 20, is near a historic battleground and cattle roundup point. It's the only provincial campsite along this route.

Chilanko Marsh, about 59 km west of Alexis Creek and on the Pacific Flyway, is great for birdwatching. To the north is Puntzi Lake, another resting place for white pelicans and previously a haven for birds of another colour, when it was a US Air Force base.

Tatla Lake, 44 km west of Chilanko Forks, offers access to Tatlayoko Lake, Homathko Icefield, and Mount Waddington, which, at 4016 metres, is the highest peak in the Coast Range. Guides are available locally for exploration of the Ice Caves in the Potato Range.

The stampede at Anahim Lake promises a real down-to-earth celebration every July. Lessard Lake Road, north of here, gives access to famous Dean River steelhead fishing, abandoned Carrier villages, and the Alexander Mackenzie Heritage Trail.

The Rainbow Range of the

## Outdoor Recreation in the Chilcotin

**For downloadable maps:** www.imagehouse.com/guidemaps/chilcotin.htm

**Alexis Creek** trail network. 2+ hours. Good variety, great viewpoints, no crowds. Biking and hiking.

**Chilko River**. Top wilderness whitewater kayaking, with extensive class 3 rapids. Great fly fishing near Chilko Lake.

**Potato Ranges** (Tatlayoko Valley Road, east of Tatla Lake). Easily accessible, top-level wilderness hiking and horseback riding.

**Dante's Inferno** (Chilcotin Plateau west of Williams Lake). Open grassland. Family day outing. Hiking, biking.

*At the confluence of the Fraser and Quesnel rivers, Quesnel was an important point on the transportation route during the Cariboo Gold Rush in the 1860s.*

## Soda Creek

Soda Creek, 33 km north of Williams Lake on Hwy. 97, was an important transportation centre during the gold-rush days. Having come this far by wagon road, bypassing the unnavigable parts of the Fraser River, travellers took paddle-wheelers upriver to Quesnel. They then followed the Cariboo road to the goldfields of Barkerville.

Xats'ull Heritage Village (250-297-6323; www.cariboonet.com/xatsull.html) near the Soda Creek Reserve operates day and weekly programs that explore traditions of the Secwepemc (Shuswap) people.

The Marguerite Ferry, 63 km north of Williams Lake, is one of the few reaction ferries left on the Fraser. The free two-vehicle vessel takes travellers across the river between April and September, when the river isn't frozen. Just north of the ferry landing,

basalt columns jut out of a field on the east side of Hwy. 97, evidence of ancient volcanic activity. Much volcanic rock is basalt; as the molten rock cools it shrinks and splits into these striking vertical columns.

About halfway between Soda Creek and Quesnel, 67 km north of Williams Lake, a cairn marks the site of the old Hudson's Bay Company post, Fort Alexandria, named after early explorer Alexander Mackenzie. This was the northern terminus of the Pacific Fur Brigade Trail and one of the last posts to be built on the Fraser. Supplies were shipped from Fort Astoria at the mouth of the Columbia, through the Okanagan to Fort Kamloops and finally here, for

### Mackenzie Grease Trail

**The Blackwater River** area west of Quesnel includes excellent fishing, canoeing, kayaking, and wildlife viewing. Natives established the "Mackenzie-Grease" Trail beside the Blackwater River centuries ago, as interior and coastal tribes traded for the oily oolichan fish. They later used the same trail to guide Alexander Mackenzie to the Pacific Ocean in 1793.

Today, experienced backpackers who trek the entire length of the 18-to-24-day Alexander Mackenzie Heritage Trail travel 420 km from the mouth of the Blackwater north of Quesnel to Sir Alexander Mackenzie Provincial Park in Dean Channel on the coast. Information is available at the Williams Lake and Quesnel Info Centres. Or write the Alexander Mackenzie Trail Association (Box 425, Stn. A, Kelowna BC V1Y 7P1; www.amvr.org/index.htm). Access is across the Moffatt Bridge in Quesnel on Nazko Road.

*Cottonwood House, a heritage site on the Gold Rush Trail to Barkerville, still offers travellers fresh baked goods and warm hospitality.*

distribution throughout New Caledonia. The importance of the fort faded once gold dominated the economy.

## Quesnel

120 km (74 mi.) north of Williams Lake. Population: 10,794. Info Centre: Le Bourdais Park, 705 Carson Avenue, V2J 2B6. 250-992-8716. 1-800-992-4922. Fax: 250-992-2181. Email: visitorinfo@city.quesnel.bc.ca.

During the 1860s many thought Quesnel was destined to become the capital of the province. It reached prominence during the Cariboo gold rush era, and has maintained its economic importance through lumber and pulp production. Today known as the "Gold Pan City," it's the gateway to historic Highway 26, Cottonwood Historic Site, Barkerville, and Bowron Lake Provincial Park.

### While You're In Quesnel ... Top Five

1. Walk through Riverfront Park and along the trail (beginning on the Fraser River across the footbridge at Front Street), past historic sites that include a restored Hudson's Bay Company post, manicured residential areas, the Quesnel River, and the rail yards.
2. Pan for gold near the confluence of the Fraser and Quesnel rivers. (Map: 250-922-4301).
3. Visit "Mandy" at the Quesnel Museum (705 Carson Avenue next to the Info Centre, 250-992-9580), which houses one of the strongest collections in the Interior, with displays on mining and ranching, Natives, and Chinese settlers.
4. Get a bird's-eye view of the forest industry at the observation tower (3 km north of town on Hwy. 97). "Three Mile Flat's" lumber, pulp and planer mills and related value-added plants are said to comprise the most concentrated area of wood products manufacturing in North America, incorporating some of the most advanced wood processing technology in the world. Ask at the Info Centre about free tours.
5. Take in the sights at Pinnacles Provincial Park (7 km from downtown), featuring hoodoo rock formations and a panoramic view.

### Quesnel Special Events –Best Bets

**January**—GRT Sled Dog Mail Run
**June**—Old Time Fiddler's Contest; Highland Games
**July**—Billy Barker Days (4 days). "BC's largest family festival"; Quesnel Rodeo
**August**—Quesnel Fall Fair (a tradition since 1912)

*Costumed interpretive staff recreate the past at Barkerville, the most famous of the Interior's gold rush towns.*

## The Gold Rush Trail: Highway 26 to Barkerville and Bowron Lake

Two of the Interior's biggest attractions lie east on Highway 26, the last leg of the old Cariboo Wagon Road. Markers along the route evoke the past, with names like Mexican Hill, Lover's Leap, Robber's Roost, Devil's Canyon, and Jaw Bone Creek.

Very few of the thousands who travelled these roads in the 1850s and 1860s found what they were looking for. Billy Barker, a typical boom-bust miner, had a town named after him and a claim valued at $600,000, but he died in Victoria in 1894, alone and broke. However, many are still searching. All along Hwy. 26, evidence of modern mines and claims abound.

Like early settlers, modern travellers can stop at Cottonwood House Provincial Historic Park, 24 km east of Quesnel (250-994-3332; www.heritage.gov.bc.ca). The old Gold Rush Trail passes right by the front door of the roadhouse, built in 1864. Besides displays of archival photos and period artifacts in the outbuildings, the interpretive staff offer baked goods fresh from Cottonwood House's wood stove along with their descriptions of early days. And you can try your hand at gold panning.

## Wells

80 km (48 mi.) east of Quesnel. Population: 265. Info Centre: 4120 Pooley Street, Box 123, V0K 2R0. Phone/fax: 250-994-2323, 1-877-451-9355. Email: info@wells bc.com. Web: www.wellsbc.com. Seasonal.

Wells is a relatively new town,

created when Fred Marshall Wells discovered gold nearby in 1932, but by 1940, 3000 people lived here. The period-style

### While You're In Wells ... Top Five

1. Take a tour of an honest-to-goodness gold mine. The Wayside Mine is reworking an old mine, and so far so good.

2. Poke around the Wells Museum in its refurbished 1930s mine building, "The Dry".

3. Search for Lady Luck at the new destination casino.

4. Enjoy the fun at the Wells Winter Carnival at the end of January.

5. Join in on Fred Wells Days during the August long weekend.

*Billy Barker, a typical boom-bust miner, had a town named after him and a claim valued at $600,000, but he died penniless in Victoria in 1894.*

false front buildings create a charming mining-town atmosphere. The townsite used to be right on Jack of Clubs Lake, but the tailings of a mining operation that closed in 1967 have adjusted the landscape. The lake offers trout fishing and the company of loons. Several tour operators offer winter or summer recreational activities, including dogsledding and hiking. If you plan to make Barkerville more than a day trip, this is a good place to stay overnight.

## Barkerville Special Events—Best Bets

**July**—Dominion (Canada) Day Celebration

**September**—Invitational Hose Carriage Races

**December**—Victorian Christmas

## Barkerville Historic Park and Gold Rush Town

82 km (51 mi.) east of Quesnel. Box 19, V0K 1B0. 250-398-4414. Email: barkerville@sbtc.gov.bc.ca. Web: www.heritage.gov.bc.ca/ark/bark.htm

Arguably BC's best-known attraction, Barkerville is an exciting "living" museum operated as a heritage site by the provincial government, and a definite must-see.

One of three "overnight" mining communities on Williams Creek, Barkerville was the hub of the Cariboo gold rush. Cornish prospector Billy Barker had dug down 12 metres and was about to give up his claim when he struck pay dirt in 1862. Some estimate over $40 million worth of gold was taken out of the area. With a population of 10,000 to

20,000 in the mid-1860s, Barkerville was a rip-roaring place—the largest town north of San Francisco and west of Chicago.

In October 1868, 116 buildings in the new town burned to the ground in one hour and fifteen minutes, at a loss of close to $700,000. However, gold seekers are a determined lot; the townspeople began rebuilding the next day.

A functioning town until the 1930s, restoration began on Barkerville in 1958. At present over 120 restored or reconstructed buildings line the streets, including several restaurants and a theatre offering live performances.

In the summer months, costumed interpretive staff greet visitors as though they had just clambered off the BX stagecoach. Playing the parts of characters from

*Sandy Lake in Bowron Lake Provincial Park is one of 10 lakes in a 116-km chain that attracts paddlers from around the world. Reservations are recommended.*

Barkerville's history, the staff offer mining demonstrations, stagecoach rides, school lessons, and guided tours. The park is open year-round, but the full interpretive program operates only in summer.

Hikers can trek to the old cemetery, "The Last Mile" of the Cariboo Wagon Road into Barkerville, and the ghost town of Richfield. Cross-country skiing is popular in winter.

Accommodation is limited, but available at two B&Bs (Kelly House: 250-994-3312. St. George Hotel: 250-994-0008).

## Bowron Lake

Canoeists from around the world come to Bowron Lake Provincial Park, 29 km east of Wells. The park's ten-lake chain takes seven to ten days and covers a 1160-km water and portage circuit through undeveloped wilderness. The best time to make the trip is between June and October. Fishing is unpredictable, but kokanee, rainbow trout, Dolly Varden, and whitefish are present. The 121,600-hectare wilderness area is also a wildlife sanctuary. In winter, the circuit can be made by snowshoe or cross-country ski. Local outfitters rent canoes and supplies. Access to the lakes is on a first-come, first-served basis. Reservations for 1 to 6 people are highly recommended. Reservations are mandatory for groups of 7 to 14. There is a fee. (1-800-HELLO-BC, 1-800-435-5622)

The park's namesake was John Bowron, an "Overlander" who came to the Cariboo in 1862. Besides being Cameron-town's first librarian, Bowron was active in Barkerville's Cariboo Amateur Dramatic Association and became the gold commissioner in 1883.

## Prince George

120 km (74 mi.) north of Quesnel. Population: 81,326. Info Centre: 1198 Victoria Street, V2L 2L2. 250-562-3700, 1-800-668-7646; Fax: 250-563-3584. Email: information @tourismpg.bc.ca. Web: www. tourismpg.bc.ca

Lheit-Lit'en (Dakelh) Natives were early residents of this region, trading with coastal people for centuries before the European explorers and fur traders arrived. Alexander Mackenzie and Simon Fraser

### SuperGuide's Cariboo-Chilcotin Paddling Picks

(In alphabetical order)
1. Blackwater River
2. Bowron Lakes
3. Cariboo River
4. Chilko River
5. Interlakes area
6. Moose Valley Provincial Park

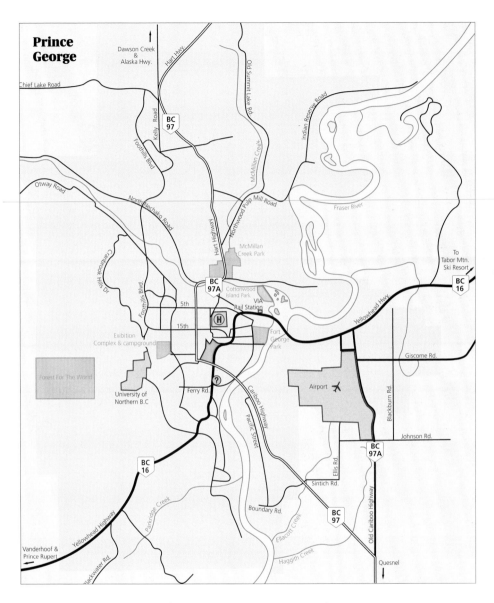

Prince George

paddled past the site on their historic journeys down the Fraser River. Simon Fraser established Fort George here in 1807, making it one of the oldest settlements in the province.

Located at the confluence of the Fraser and Nechako rivers, Prince George continues to be a transportation hub,

today sitting at the junction of two major highways—Hwy. 16 running east-west and Hwy. 97 running north-south. It is an important stop on VIA and BC Rail lines.

With the development of the railways, logging became viable. The first sawmills were established in 1906, supplying ties and materials for the

Grand Trunk Pacific Railway. Hundreds of small mills flourished until the 1950s and 1960s, when they were bought out by larger corporations. In 1964, three pulp mills opened in Prince George, triggering a population boom that has made it the second-largest city in the Interior. (Kelowna is the largest.)

## Prince George Special Events

**January**–Dog Sled Races
**February**–Mardi Gras
**May**–Canadian Northern Children's Festival and the biennial Regional Forest Exhibition
**June**–Prince George Rodeo
**August**–Simon Fraser Days; Sandblast (skiing on gravel); Prince George Exhibition
**October**–Oktoberfest

## Side trips: Living History

**The Huble Homestead**, 40 km north of Prince George off Hwy. 97. Original log home, general store, other heritage buildings, and farm animals. Seasonal. (250-564-7033)

**Fort St. James National Historic Park,** 164 km northwest of Prince George off Hwy. 16, is the site of a fur-trading post built by Simon Fraser in 1806. It operated as a Hudson's Bay Company store until the 1930s and was restored in 1971. Seasonal. (250-996-7191. Web: parkscan.harbour.com/fsj/)

*Prince George, the Interior's second-largest city, is home to BC's newest university, opened in 1994.*

## Prince George Great Outdoors–Picks

1. Teapot Mountain Hiking Trail, 50 km north on Hwy. 97, offers a short but strenuous hike with spectacular scenery and a chance to examine a large basalt flow that helped shape the land in the days before the glaciers.
2. A little less strenuous, Fort George Canyon Trail, 30 km southwest, is noted for its wildflowers and plant life.
3. Purden Ski Village, 60 km east of Prince George on Hwy. 16, has 25 runs and a shuttle service from Prince George (250-565-7777).
4. Tabor Mountain Ski Resort is 20 km east of Prince George, with 10 alpine runs and Nordic trails (250-963-7542).
5. Over 1600 lakes are within an hour of Prince George. Rainbow, brook, and lake trout, Dolly Varden, char, whitefish, and grayling are among the species here.

## While You're In Prince George ... Top Ten

1. Tour a bison farm (250-568-2285).
2. Walk around the 106-hectare Forest for the World Park and learn about reforestation as you hike the 8 km of trails.
3. Visit the University of Northern BC campus. Opened in 1994, UNBC was the first university to be built in Canada in over 25 years.
4. Learn about local history at Fraser-Fort George Regional Museum (in Fort George Park at the end of 20th Avenue, 250-562-1612), which overlooks the site of old Fort George.
5. Stop in at the Prince George Native Art Gallery (1600 Third Avenue, 250-614-7726).
6. Walk the 11-km Heritage River Trail at Cottonwood Island Park.
7. See a play at Theatre North West (250-563-6969; www.theatrenorthwest.com).
8. Attend a concert by the Prince George Symphony Orchestra (250-562-0800; www.pgso.com).
9. Explore the Prince George Railway & Forest Industry Museum (250-563-7351. Seasonal).
10. Sample the local brew at Pacific Western Brewery. (250-562-1131; www.pwbrewing.com).

*Bush planes are a lifeline for many living in the more remote areas of the Interior. Many small airlines offer charter services for recreational, business and service activities.*

## Fore! SuperGuide Recommends

**Lillooet**

**Sheep Pasture**. 9 holes. Par 35. 5464 yards. A unique course. PO Box 217, V0K 1V0. 250-256-4484.

**108 Mile House**

**108 Resort Golf Course**. 18 holes. Par 71. 6806 yards. Box 2, 4816 Telqua Drive, 100 Mile House, V0K 2Z0. 250-791-5465. www.tee-off.ca/index.html

**Prince George**

**Aberdeen Glen**. 18 holes. Par 73. 7044 yards. Design: Ted Locke. Nominated as BCPGA facility of the year, 2001. 1010 Clubhouse Drive, V2K 5R7. 250-563-8901. www.aberdeenglen.ca

**Prince George Golf Club**. Semi-private. 18 holes. Par 71. 6496 yards. Box 242, 2588 Hwy. 16 W., V2L 4S1. 250-563-4417

**Quesnel**

**Quesnel Golf Course**. Semi-private. 18 holes. Par 71. 6401 yards. 1800 Blackwater Road, V2J 4R8. 250-249-5550

**Valemount**

**Valemount Pines Golf & Country Club**. Semi-private. 18 tees, 9 greens. Par 72. 6502 yards. PO Box 167, V0E 2Z0. 250-566-4550. Email: pines@valemount.com

**Williams Lake**

**Williams Lake Golf & Tennis Club**. 18 holes. 6272 yards. 104 Fairview Dr., V2G 3T1. 250-392-6026

All courses are public, unless indicated. Play is seasonal. For information on all courses in this region: www.bcgolfguide.com.

# Highway 16: Yellowhead Highway East

The second part of our circle tour of the Central Interior heads east on the Yellowhead Highway (16) to Tête Jaune Cache, 266 km east of Prince George.

The Yellowhead gets it name from an Iroquois trapper and guide whose hair had a light tinge to it. (*Tête jaune* is French for "yellow head".) Accounts differ as to the man's identity, but most agree it was Pierre Bostonais, a former North West Company employee. In the early 1800s, Bostonais stashed his furs at a cache to the west of Mt. Robson in the Rocky Mountains, thus the name Tête Jaune Cache.

The highway was dedicated as the northern Trans-Canada route in 1990. It travels from the Pacific Ocean to Winnipeg, providing the

**207**

gentlest grades of any route through the Rockies. The elevation of Yellowhead Pass is 1066 m, compared with Rogers Pass (1327 m) and Kicking Horse Pass (1643 m). This was the route through the Rockies favoured by early CPR surveyor Walter Moberly in the 1870s.

## Mcbride

220 km (136 mi.) east of Prince George. Population: 769. Info Centre: 100-Robson Centre, Box 2, V0J 2E0. 250-569-3355. Fax: 250-569-3276.

The only service area between Prince George and Tête Jaune Cache, McBride came into being with the Grand Trunk Pacific Railway before World War I. The town was named after BC's youngest premier, Sir Richard McBride, who assumed office at age 33 and served from 1903 to 1915. Surrounded by pristine mountains, waterfalls, meadows and streams, McBride is popular with backpackers, skiers, paddlers, anglers, and cyclists.

*Fireweed is one of the first plants to grow after a forest fire. Although such fires can seem disastrous, they allow re-introduction of a variety of plant and animal life that gets excluded by mature timber stands.*

### While You're In Mcbride ... Top Seven

1. Birdwatch at Horseshoe Lake, where over 175 species of birds have been recorded.
2. Heli-ski or heli-hike.
3. Shop for local crafts.
4. Stroll through the farmer's market (summer).
5. View the scenery from McBride Peak Lookout.
6. Join in Yellowhead Loppet Ski Race in January.
7. Browse Robson Valley Fall Fair in August.

### While You're In Tête Jaune Cache ... Top Six

1. Sample fresh home baking from the Dunster Farmers Market (summer; 25 km west on the Dunster-Croydon Rd.), while you gaze at the Dunster Train Station, one of the only remaining original train stations built by the CNR in the early 1900s.
2. Watch spawning salmon at Rearguard Falls Provincial Park (5 km east on Hwy. 16), the furthest point that the fish travel up the Fraser River. The fish begin their journey at Vancouver on the Pacific Ocean some 1200 km away in July, and arrive here in August and September. The lookout provides a place to observe the salmon attempting to leap up the 10-metre-high falls. Eventually they spawn on gravel beds downstream.
3. Try heli-sightseeing, dog sledding, whitewater rafting, or horseback riding.
4. Hike the challenging 16 km trail in Mt. Terry Fox Provincial Park (south on Hwy. 5), which honours the BC athlete who died in 1981. (Or view the mountain from a lookout just beyond Rearguard Falls Park.) The one-legged runner inspired millions of people around the world with his Marathon of Hope in 1980.
5. Hike the 90-min. Lookout Trail at Kiwa Creek to a forestry lookout tower on Shere Point for a magnificent look at the Robson Valley.
6. View Mt. Robson (3954 m), the highest peak in the Canadian Rockies, or take some time and explore the 217,200-hectare provincial park, which contains the headwaters of the Fraser River, at this point only a tiny trickle. Abundant wildlife, 170 species of birds, subalpine forest vegetation, and glaciers make this a backpacker's paradise. The park office at the west gate (20 km east on Hwy. 16) has information on trails and attractions. The eastern border of the park is on the Continental Divide.

*Mt. Robson, the highest peak in the Rockies is often shrouded in clouds.*
*In 1862, the Overlander's Native guide claimed he had only seen the peak once in 29 visits.*

## Tête Jaune Cache

Once a major construction centre for the Grand Trunk Pacific Railway, and the head of navigation for Fraser River sternwheelers in the early part of the 20th century, this community marks the confluence of the Fraser and Robson rivers as well as the junction of Highways 5 (south to Kamloops) and 16 (east to Jasper). In its heyday, 5000 people lived here.

Tête Jaune Cache is surrounded by three mountain ranges—the Monashee, the Premier and the Rockies—and offers spectacular scenery and a wealth of outdoor recreation opportunities.

## The Overlanders

**In August of** 1862, the Overlanders, a group of 132 people on their way to the Cariboo goldfields, stood at Tête Jaune Cache wondering how to proceed. They had been sold "the speediest, safest and most economical route to the gold diggings" by the British Columbia Overland Transit Company, back east. The original brochure had promised stagecoaches, but by the time the travellers passed over the Great Divide they were using Native travois and mules.

The party split up at Tête Jaune Cache, most deciding to travel via the Fraser River, while a small group of about twenty chose the North Thompson. After several weeks of perilous rafting and portaging with little food, the first of the North Thompson group arrived at Fort Kamloops on October 11. Two days later, another raft arrived, carrying the expedition's only woman, Catherine Schubert. A day after that, Mrs. Schubert gave birth to a daughter, Rose, one of the first European babies born in the Interior.

*Look for evidence of ancient volcanic activity throughout the Central Interior. These basalt columns are south of Prince George.*

## Yellowhead South

South of Tête Jaune Cache, Highway 5 (the Yellowhead South Highway) follows the North Thompson River to Kamloops. The paved two-lane highway provides access to fishing, wildlife viewing, hiking, and river rafting.

## Valemount

20 km (12 mi.) south of Tête Jaune Cache. Population: 1356. Info Centre: 99 Gorse Street, Highway 5, Box 168, V0E 2Z0. 250-566-4846. Fax: 250-566-4249. Seasonal. Valemount's location on the North Thompson River and artificial Kinbasket Lake (created when the Columbia River was dammed north of Revelstoke) has made it a four-season recreation headquarters. River rafting, heli-skiing, and wildlife observation are among the options here.

## Clearwater

190 km (114 mi.) south of Valemount. 125 km (78 mi.) north of Kamloops. Population: 1666. Info Centre: 425 East Yellowhead Highway, Box 1988, RR 1, V0E 1N0. 250-674-2646. Fax: 250-674-3693. Email: clwcofc@mail.wellsgray.net. Clearwater (named for the clear waters of the nearby river) is headquarters for Wells Gray Provincial Park and offers a number of services for vacationers. The Yellowhead Museum (250-674-3660) displays pioneer and Native artifacts, as well as photographs and natural history displays. The North Thompson River from Clearwater to Kamloops is a favourite with paddlers.

### While You're In Valemount ... Top Five

1. View salmon spawning in George Hicks Regional Park (August and September).

2. Hike the hour-and-a-half trail at Robert Starratt Wildlife Sanctuary (Cranberry Marsh), 3 km south of town—a 600-acre wildlife haven.

3. Shop for unique local gifts. Don't miss Berna's Medicine (Censored) Cabinet. Ask about the store's unique name.

4. Gaze at Mt. Terry Fox from a viewpoint 8 km north of town.

5. Go river rafting in summer or heli-skiing in winter.

*Dawson Falls, one of many in Wells Gray Provincial Park, is part of the 91-metre-wide Murtle River. Located in the Cariboo Mountains, the park was created in 1939.*

## Wells Gray Provincial Park

Abandoned homesteads, mineral springs, glaciers, high mountain peaks, extinct volcanoes, waterfalls, spawning salmon, and lava beds are among the many attractions in Wells Gray Provincial Park, BC's third-largest. Helmcken Falls, at 137 m, is one of the highest waterfalls in North America. Wildlife viewing includes moose, grizzly bear, and 218 species of birds. The park's interpretive services are available only in the summer. Certified guides are available year-round.

The park is mostly wilderness, but some vehicular camping is allowed along Clearwater River. One attraction is wilderness camping and canoeing on the Clearwater-Azure lakes chain and on Murtle Lake, accessible from Blue River. From Hobson Lake in the north end of the park, a 6.5-km portage connects with Quesnel Lake in the Cariboo. Mahood Lake in the south connects with the Cariboo via a gravel road at the west end.

## North Thompson Area

South of Clearwater, Hwy. 5 continues through Little Fort, the site of an early Hudson's Bay Company post on the old Fur Brigade Trail. Highway 24 west of here connects with the Cariboo's Interlakes region and excellent fishing. Continuing south, the region around Barriere also is a favourite with anglers. South of Barriere, Hwy. 5 continues to Kamloops on the Trans-Canada Highway. Special events include the North Thompson Fall Fair in Barriere in September.

### Clearwater River Rafting Companies

**Interior Whitewater**. 1-800-661-7238. www.interiorwhitewater.bc.ca. Rivers: Chilko/Chilcotin, Thompson, Clearwater.

**Adams River Rafting**. 1-888-440-7238. Rivers: Adams, Thompson.

**Mt. Robson Adventure Holidays**. 1-800-882-9991. www.mountrobson.com. Rivers: Fraser.

**Mt. Robson Whitewater Rafting Co**. 1-888-566-7238. Rivers: Fraser.

# Reference

## Access

### Air
Vancouver International Airport is located in the suburb of Richmond, a half-hour bus ride from downtown. A hotel, banking, money exchange, restaurants, car rental, accommodation reservations, and shopping are available at the airport. Additional hotels are close at hand.

Calgary and Edmonton in Alberta also have international airports. Victoria International Airport at Sidney on Vancouver Island has commuter service to and from Seattle, Washington.

From Vancouver, connector flights are available to all major centres in the Interior via Air Canada's regional carrier, Air BC (1-800-247-2262; www.aircanada.ca). Smaller commuter and charter airlines also provide services that make most destinations in the province easily accessible.

### Ferries
The government-operated BC Ferry Corporation operates several ferries in the Interior, most of them free at the time of writing this book. But this may change in the near future. For information call 250-387-3403, visit www.gov.bc.ca/th/ or check with local tourist offices.

### Bus
Regular bus services connect BC with the rest of Canada and the United States. Greyhound Bus Lines (Vancouver, 604-482-8747) has scheduled service to many communities in BC's Interior.

Several companies offer bus tours of popular destinations in BC's Interior. Travel agents will have information.

### Rail
BC Rail, owned by the provincial government, offers regularly scheduled service to the Interior from North Vancouver to Prince George (604-984-5246; www.bcrail.com).

Rocky Mountaineer Railtours has a seasonal excursion rail service between Vancouver and Banff or Jasper with a stopover in Kamloops. All travel is during daylight hours. (1-800-665-7245. Web: www.rockymountaineer.com. Email: reservations@rockymountaineer.com)

VIA Rail, Canada's only remaining national passenger railway, accesses the province from the east through Edmonton and Jasper. From Jasper, service is offered to Prince Rupert via Prince George, or to Vancouver via Kamloops. Plan to book at least six months in advance for travel between April and October (1-800-561-8630; www.viarail.ca).

### Private Motor Vehicle
There are 17 official points of entry for vehicular traffic along the southern border between the United States and British Columbia. Those at Boundary Bay, the Blaine crossings of Douglas and Pacific Highway, Huntingdon, Osoyoos, Kingsgate, and Roosville are open 24 hours.

### Major highways accessing BC's Interior
From the south (US): Interstate 5, Highway 97, and Highway 395 from Washington state, Highway 95 from Idaho, and Highway 93 from Montana.

From Alberta: Highway 3 (the Crowsnest route), Highway 1 (the Trans-Canada) from Banff and Calgary, Highway 16 from Edmonton and Jasper, and Highways 2, 34, and 43 from Edmonton to Dawson Creek.

From the north: the Alaska Highway from Fairbanks, Alaska, and Whitehorse, Yukon Territory.

### Major highways in BC
Highway 1 (the Trans-Canada Highway). Vancouver to the Alberta border via Hope, the Fraser Canyon, Kamloops, Revelstoke, and Golden.

Highway 3 (the Crowsnest Highway). Hope to the Alberta border via Osoyoos, Castlegar, and Cranbrook.

Highway 5 (the Coquihalla Highway). Controlled-access toll route from Hope north to Kamloops.

Highway 5 (the Yellowhead South). Kamloops to Tête Jaune Cache.

Highway 16 (the Yellowhead Highway). Prince Rupert to the Alberta border via Prince George.

Highway 97. From the US

border near Osoyoos to the Yukon border. The only highway to cover the entire length of the province.

## Entering Canada
Customs and Excise officials of Revenue Canada can supply border-crossing information. (Regional Information Unit, 333 Dunsmuir Street, Vancouver BC V6B 5R4, 604-666-0545.) US citizens do not require passports, but should carry appropriate identification—proof of citizenship and proof of residence. Picture ID is always a good idea. Visitors from other countries should carry passports or other recognized travel documents. Check with the nearest Canadian consulate or embassy for current regulations.

## Tourist Information
Many Interior communities operate Visitor Info Centres, which are part of the provincially-sponsored Visitor InfoNetwork and can be identified by distinctive signs. Communities that are not part of this network often have their own, sometimes seasonal, tourism offices. Chambers of commerce may also have tourist information. All offer up-to-date information on sightseeing, recreation, accommodation, and special events.

The provincial government operates a Hello BC website (www.hellobc.com), with useful information, reservations access, and links.

You can also phone for information: In North America, including BC, call 1-800 HELLO BC. In Greater Vancouver, call 604 HELLO BC (453-5622). From overseas, call: 250-387-1642.

To write for information: Tourism BC, PO Box 9830, Stn Prov Govt, Victoria BC V8W 9W5. Tourism BC, 3 Regent Street, London, England SW1Y 4NS.

## Provincial Tourism Regions
The provincial government has divided the province into six tourist regions. Each one has a central office that provides free information about its attractions and services. The areas covered by the SuperGuide are:

Vancouver, Coast & Mountains Tourism Region, 250 - 1508 West 2nd Avenue Vancouver BC V6J 1H2, 604-739-9011, 1-800-667-3306, fax: 604-739-0153, info@coastandmountains.bc.ca, www.coastandmountains.bc.ca.

Vancouver and the Lower Mainland make up most of the region, but the zone also includes the Interior community of Hope, a portion of the Fraser Canyon, a portion of the Coquihalla Highway, and Manning Park.

Thompson Okanagan Tourism Association, 1332 Water Street, Kelowna BC V1Y 9P4, 250-860-5999, fax: 250-860-9993, info@thompsonokanagan.com, www.ThompsonOkanagan.com.

Includes the area from Princeton to Grand Forks, the Okanagan, Kamloops, and the Yellowhead route to Valemont and Mount Robson.

Tourism Rockies, Box 10, 1905 Warren Avenue, Kimberley BC V1A 2Y5, 250-427-4838, fax: 250-427-3344, info@BCRockies.com, http://BCRockies.com.

Includes the West Kootenays to the Alberta border and the US border to north of Revelstoke.

Cariboo Chilcotin Coast Tourist Association, 118a North First Avenue, Williams Lake BC V2G 1Y8, 250-392-2226, fax: 250-392-2838, cta@landwithoutlimits.com, www.landwithoutlimits.com.

Includes the areas to the west of the Fraser River (the Chilcotin), to the east of the Fraser River (the Cariboo), and Highway 97 from Cache Creek to north of Quesnel.

Northern British Columbia Tourism Association, P.O. Box 2373, Prince George BC V2N 2S6, 250-561-0432, fax: 250-561-0450, info@nbctourism.com, www.nbctourism.com.

This SuperGuide only includes a small portion of this vast area—Prince George and the Yellowhead Highway east to Valemont.

Tourism BC, Ministry of Tourism, Parliament Buildings, Victoria BC V8V 1X4, 250-387-1642, 1-800-663-6000.

## Publications
The provincial government has a number of free publications that can be very useful to travellers. They are available at Info Centres and other tourist outlets. Titles include:
*British Columbia Accommodation Guide*
*British Columbia Outdoor and Adventure Guide*
*BC Escapes*
*Freshwater Fishing Guide for BC*
*British Columbia Freshwater Fishing Regulations Synopsis*

You can also ask for road maps, camping maps, forestry maps, maps of major provincial parks. (You may be charged a fee for some maps.) And there are many privately published books with detailed information on specialized interests such as hiking trails, hot springs, canoe routes, gold panning, fishing, B&Bs, restaurants, etc.

## Suggested Further Reading

Barlee, N.L. *Gold Creeks and Ghost Towns*. Surrey, BC: Hancock House, 1984.

Barman, Jean. *The West Beyond the West*. University of Toronto Press, 1991.

Cancian, Anita. *Classic Hikes of the Lower Left-hand Corner of British Columbia*. Canmore: Altitude, 1998.

Francis, Daniel, Ed. *Encyclopedia of British Columbia*. Harbour, 2000.

Hammond, Herb. *Seeing the Forest Among the Trees*. Winlaw, BC: Polestar, 1991.

Hobson, Richmond. *The Rancher Takes a Wife. Grass Beyond the Mountains*. McClelland & Stewart, 1999.

Pole, Graeme. *Canadian Rockies SuperGuide* (1991); *Classic Hikes in the Canadian Rockies* (1994); *Walks and Easy Hikes in the Canadian Rockies* (1992). Canmore: Altitude.

Stowe, Leland. *Crusoe of Lonesome Lake*. Random House, 1957.

Turner, Nancy J. *Plants in British Columbia Indian Technology*. Royal British Columbia Museum, 1992.

Wareham, Bill. *British Columbia Wildlife Viewing Guide*. Edmonton: Lone Pine, 1991.

## Accommodation

We do not make accommodation recommendations in this guide. The British Columbia Accommodation Guide is a free publication from Tourism BC that lists all accommodations in the province. Below are other organizations that may have useful information.

Hostelling International—BC, Suite 402, 134 Abbott St. (in Gastown), Vancouver, BC V6B 2K4, (604) 684-7101, 1-800-661-0020, Email: info@hihostels.bc.ca, www.hihostels.bc.ca/.

British Columbia Automobile Association, 999 West Broadway, Vancouver BC V5Z 1K5, 604-268-5600, 1-800-663-1956, www.bcaa.bc.ca/.

BC and Yukon Hotels Association, 948 Howe Street, Vancouver BC V6Z 1N9, 604-681-7164.

BC Bed and Breakfast Association, 604-734-5486.

BC Bed and Breakfasts Only, www.pixsell.bc.ca/bcbbd.htm.

BC Motels, Campgrounds, Resorts Association, 209 - 3003 St. Johns, Port Moody BC V3H 2C4, 604-945-7676.

BC Fishing Resorts and Outfitters' Association, Box 3301, Kamloops BC V2C 6B9, 250-374-6838, Fax: 374-6640, www.bcfroa.bc.ca/, Email: bcfroa@telus.net.

## Guides and Outfitters

Association of Canadian Mountain Guides, Box 8341, Canmore AB T1W 2V1, 403-678-2885, fax: 403-609-0070, www.acmg.ca, Email: acmg@acmg.ca.

Federation of BC Naturalists, 425 – 1367 W. Broadway, Vancouver BC V6H 4A9, 604-737-3057.

Guide Outfitters' Association of BC, Box 94675, Richmond BC V6Y 4A4, 604-278-2688, fax 604-278-3440, www.goabc.org/, Email: GOABC@dowco.com.

## We Want to Hear from You!

Altitude SuperGuides are continuously revised to reflect any changes in the areas covered. Your interests, insights, and recommendations are important to us, and suggestions for improvements or additions will be gratefully received. Please feel free to contact the authors by writing to:

Altitude Publishing Ltd., 1500 Railway Ave., Canmore, Alberta T1W 1P6. orderdesk@altitudepublishing.com

# Index

Greenwood, 88-9
Grist Mill, Keremeos, 82
GST refunds, 37
guest ranches, 34
Guichon Creek Batholith, 116
guides, 214
Gunterman, Mattie, 157

**H**

Hagensborg, 199
Hammond, Herb, 18
hang-gliding, 60, 67, 144, 175
Hangman's Park, 188
Hat Creek Ranch, 185-6
Haynes Lease Ecological Reserve, 121
Haynes Point Provincial Park, 84-5
Hector, James, 68-9
Hedley, 79-80
Hell's Gate, 44-5, 47
highways, 212-3
hiking, 29, 30, 70
    in Central Interior, 195, 199, 206, 208
    along Crowsnest Hwy., 76, 77, 83, 84, 87
    in East Kootenay, 167, 178, 180
    in Okanagan, 136, 144
    along Trans-Canada Hwy., 40, 55, 65, 69
    in West Kootenay, 162, 163
historic sites, top ten, 21
history, 9-10, 19-22, 39, 42
Hobson, Richmond, 197
holidays, 37
hoodoo formations, 13, 69, 198, 201
Hope, 42, 59
Hope-Princeton Highway (Hwy.3), 74
Hope Slide, 75
horseback riding, 34, 56, 67
Horsefly, 195
hot springs
    East Kootenay, 170, 171, 174, 176, 179, 180
    West Kootenay, 153, 154, 159
houseboating, 32-3, 59
hydroelectric developments, 26

**I**

ice caves, 191, 199
ice climbing, 187
Interlakes, 191
internment camps, 89, 155, 158
Invermere, 173, 174-6
Inwood, Robert, 152

**K**

Kalamalka Lake, 138-9
Kalamalka Lake Provincial Park, 142
Kamloops, 53-6, 59, 68
Kaslo, 154, 155
kayaking, 32
    in Central Interior, 198, 199, 204
    Thompson River, 55
Keenleyside Dam, 96
Kelowna, 134-7
Kentucky-Alleyne Provincial Park, 117
Keremeos, 82, 83
Kettle Valley Railway, 30, 86, 130-1, 132, 136
Kimberley, 108, 167-8, 173
Kokanee Glacier Provincial Park, 153
Kootenay Lake, 162-3
Kootenay National Park, 178-81
Kootenay Parkway, 179
Kootenay Skyway, 97, 100
Kootenay Trout Hatchery, 105

**L**

Lac La Hache, 194
Lac Le Jeune Provincial Park, 116
Lake Koocanusa, 105-6
Lake O'Hara, 69
Lardeau Valley, 155-6
"Last Spike," 22, 61
Lee's Corner, 198
lichen, 14
Likely, 195
Lillooet, 186-9, 207
liquor laws, 36
llama trek, 196
lobster festival, 116
Logan Lake, 116
Lone Butte, 191
Lumby, 144
Lynn, Tom, 62
Lytton, 47-8

**M**

Marble Canyon, 180
Marble Canyon Provincial Park, 186
marine parks, 31, 90
Mather, Ken, 140
McBride, 208
McLean Gang, 185
Merritt, 114-6
metric conversions, 36

# Photographic Credits

All photographs by Ron Woodward except as follows (reference numbers in brackets):

**BC Parks** 76, 145, 169 left, 170, 178, 199, 204
**Environment Canada, Canadian Parks Service** 77 bottom
**Environment Canada, Canadian Parks Service/Wayne Lynch** 71 top
**Don Harmon** 209
**Stephen Hutchings** 93
**Kelowna Museum** 138 bottom
**Katie Kidwell** 140
**Myron Kozak** 206
**Eric Parmenter, courtesy of Arlene Gaal** 133
**Public Archives of BC** 19 (759), 44 (10230), 53 left (64053), 87 (2526), 91 bottom (68579), 117 left (3275), 137 (98015-1), 158 (93754), 187 (35310), 196 (94157)
**Joe Scanlon** 33 bottom
**Dennis Schmidt** 71 bottom
**Esther Schmidt** 130
**UBC Laboratory of Archaeology** 20
**UBC Library, Special Collections and University Archives Division** 21 bottom (BC188/22), 175 (BC188/25), 193 (BC928)
**Vancouver Public Library** 21 top (915), 22 (698), 46 bottom (390), 86 (1771), 117 right (1786), 128 (510), 157 bottom (2213), 188 (40325), 203 (914)
**Don Weixl** 136
**Meredith Bain Woodward** 70
**Greg Young-Ing** 129

## About the Authors

Ron Woodward has been a photographer, designer, print-production manager, and teacher for 30 years. He taught photography, graphic design, and electronic publishing for nine years at Selkirk College in Castlegar and currently teaches at Simon Fraser University in the Master of Publishing Program.

Meredith Bain Woodward was born, raised and currently lives in Vancouver. She has lived in Europe, the US, and in the West Kootenay region of BC. A former travel counselor for the BC Automobile Association, she has travelled extensively throughout the province. A professional actress, she holds a BA and an MFA from UBC, is a past editor of *Kootenay Business Journal,* has received a National Magazine award, and has written animation for children's television. She has also written two other books for Altitude: *Land of Dreams* and *Inside Passage.*